Peterhof
Tsarskoye Selo
Pavlovsk
Oranienbaum
Gatchina

Ivan Fiodorov Art Publishers
St Petersburg

$\mathcal{T}$he majestic and beautiful image of St Petersburg, the city which has been preserved by Providence during the cataclysms of the twentieth century, is inseparable from the luxurious Imperial palace-and-park residences surrounding the northern capital of Russia — Peterhof, Tsarskoye Selo, Oranienbaum and Gatchina.

All these architectural complexes taken together build up an integral historical and artistic chronicle of Russian life and culture. But each of them also bears an imprint of the activities and personal tastes, predilections and antipathies of those monarchs who gave preference to this particular place as his or her favourite country residence.

The Peterhof palaces, fountains, cascades and regular parks dating from the eighteenth century are especially evocative of the turbulent, highly creative age of Peter the Great. The palaces and parks of Tsarskoye Selo take us back to resplendent court ceremonies held during the successful reigns of Empress Elizabeth, Peter's daughter, and of Catherine the Great who ascended the throne soon after her. It is with the rule of Catherine the Great that the heyday of the residence at Oranienbaum, which incorporated the Great Palace of Prince Menshikov, Peter's outstanding companion-in-arms, is associated. Pavlovsk and Gatchina shed light on the personality of Paul, then the Heir Apparent and later the Emperor, and on the drama of his life. The architectural features of Alexandria and the Cottage Palace in Peterhof, as well as the park structures of Tsarskoye Selo, are illustrative of the reign of Nicholas I, his character and his political preferences. Gatchina was the favourite residence of Emperor Alexander III. His successor Nicholas II felt an equal attachment to Peterhof and Tsarskoye Selo and shared his time between them. His whole family permanently lived in the Alexander Palace at Tsarskoye Selo, whence the last Emperor of the ruling Romanov dynasty was forcibly deported after his abdication, together with his family, to Yekaterinburg where they met their tragic death. Therefore the royal residences in the environs of St Petersburg encompass the entire Imperial period in the history of Russia, from the inauguration of the Empire in 1721 to the end of the monarchy in 1917.

The Imperial summer residences in the environs of St Petersburg are unique assemblages of masterpieces of Baroque and Neo-Classical architecture illustrating these trends in all their variety and stylistic evolution. The regular and landscaped parks of these ensembles rival the best achievements in the art of landscape gardening.

The list of architects, sculptors and park designers engaged in their creation covers the whole history of Russian art in the eighteenth and nineteenth centuries. It is sufficient to remind that the palaces and parks were designed and decorated by such outstanding architects as Le Blond, Barolomeo Francesco Rastrelli, Charles Cameron, Vincenzo Brenna, Antonio Rinaldi, Yury Velten, Giacomo Quarenghi, Andrei Voronikhin, Jean-François Thomas de Thomon, Carlo Rossi, Vasily Stasov, Adam Menelaws and Andrei Stakenschneider.

In the changed social conditions of the twentieth century, the Imperial residences acquired the status of museums of history and art. But during the Second World War these treasure-houses of culture suffered great damage and seemed to have been lost for ever. However, Russia's indestructible creative potential has made it possible to recover the seemingly irreparable losses — thanks to the great talents and strenuous efforts of restorers the palaces have risen from the ashes and the saved authentic paintings have been gradually returned to the same display rooms.

Today, the immortal beauty of the palace-and-park ensembles which once served as Imperial residences continue to give aesthetic pleasure to people helping them overcome the tribulations of life and instilling a reverence for higher spiritual values.

Peterhof

$\mathcal{P}$eterhof, a coastal residence of the Russian Emperors which is famous the world over, has primarily become a symbol of the age of Peter the Great. The complex of palaces, fountains and decorative sculpture of the Lower Park and the Upper Gardens has epitomized the energy and creative enthusiasm of the period when Russia, led by the indomitable will of Peter the Great, received a powerful impetus for its future development.

A starting point in the chronology of Peterhof is exactly recorded in the *Travel Journal of Peter the Great*. The entry for 13 September 1705 reads that a small ship called *Munker* moored near an old farmstead which was chosen by Peter the Great as a recreation spot during sea outings and to which he gave his name. May 1714 saw the start of intense work on the construction of a state residence there. On 15 August 1723 Peter the Great marked the completion of the ambitious project by a sumptuous celebration during which the Great Cascade and sixteen fountains were inaugurated. The beauty of the newly built seaside residence amazed foreign guests, diplomats and entire St Petersburg. During the subsequent centuries the complex of Peterhof parks, palaces and fountains has been extended and enriched to become a place of fairy-tale beauty.

The palace-and-park complex of Peterhof is one of those culminating artistic accomplishments of all the times and peoples which are describable as "wonders of the world". Every year for more than two centuries the palaces, fountains and parks of Peterhof delight its visitors from the early summer to the late autumn as an unforgettable spectacle in which the fascinating examples of architecture, landscape gardening and sculpture blend into a single triumphal accord. Every detail, every part of the Peterhof ensemble, an outstanding creation by noted European and Russian masters, adds to the its powerful artistic impact.

Monument to Peter the Great. 1883–84. Sculptor Mark Antokolsky. Architect Eduard Hahn

The central ensemble of the Lower Park. The Great Cascade and the Pool (view from a helicopter)

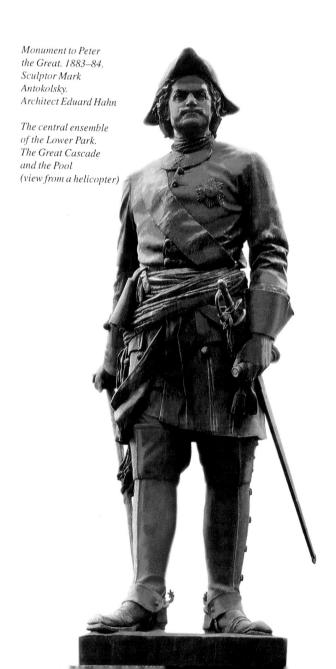

The Great Cascade is the heart of the Peterhof ensemble which conveys the idea of the celebration of Russia's victorious struggle for an exit to the sea. The Great Cascade, with its breathtaking blend of water effects and sculptural decor, was created according to the concept of Peter the Great to glorify the courage of Russian soldiers and sailors. Organically linked with the complex of the Great Cascade are the imposing palace erected above it, the Sea Canal and dozens of powerful fountains glistening with the gold of their statues, bas-reliefs and vases. The building and decoration of the Great Cascade — the dominant fountain structure of Peterhof — began in 1715 and lasted for seven years. The Tsar's ideas were creatively developed by the whole galaxy of celebrated architects including Alexander Le Blond, Johann Braunstein, Niccolo Michetti and Mikhail Zemtsov, as well as by the sculptor Carlo Bartolomeo Rastrelli and the fountain master Paul Sualem. The Great Cascade is unique for the plastic expressiveness of its architectural and sculptural forms and for a perfectly unified impression they produce which is largely due to whimsical, ever changing patterns of water jets and streams. Water is either falling down the abrupt cascade steps or gushing upwards violently, interweaving in arc-shaped curves or palpitating in iridescent designs, while its gentle murmur is filling the air.

←
*Panorama of the Great Palace,
the Great Cascade and the Alley
of Fountains*

Perspective view of the Sea Canal

Decorative statue: **Mercury**
*1800. Copy of an ancient original
from the 2nd century B.C.*

Water increases a dynamic sweep of statuary and even enhances its conceptual significance. The Great Cascade includes two seven-step cascades flanking the central three-step waterfall stairway and seventy-five water-jets. One of the most impressive among them is the Basket Fountain located in the centre of the water pageant, in front of the Large Grotto. Twenty-eight oblique jets spurting from a tufa ring are interlacing like a tracery of a flower basket. Nine stems of fantastic flowers are fluttering within its crystal frame. They are resplendent like a festive bouquet brought, as it were, to the balcony of the Great Peterhof Palace.

The flanking cascades are elaborate architectural structures, the designs and scale of which determine the diverse play of light through the water amidst the gilded statues, vases, consoles and bas-reliefs. The streams of water are falling step by step from the height of twenty metres. The curving edges of the cascade risers lend to the streams a Baroque vivacity and profusion.

*Decorative sculpture: **Perseus**. 1801*
Sculptor Feodosy Shchedrin

*Decorative statue: **Galatea**. 1801*
Sculptor Jean-Dominique Rachette

*Decorative statue: **Amazon**. Copy from an*
ancient original of the 5th–4th centuries B.C.

In sharp contrast to them are the fourteen straight water jets shooting upwards at either side of each step. Their steep edges are richly decorated with bas-reliefs and corbels.
On the parapets of the Cascade, mounted on marble pedestals are gilded bronze statues of ancient gods and heroes alternated with elaborate bronze bowls and vases . During the Petrine era the subject matter of the bas-reliefs and statues was interpreted as an allegory of glorious victories of Russia in the Northern War fought for the dominance over the Baltic shores, as well as a satire on the self-sufficient enemy — Sweden.

The decor of the Great Cascade includes 241 statues and other sculptural forms, each of which has an artistic value of its own while being an integral part of the entire composition. Linked with the Great Cascade is the Pool decorated at the sides by bronze sculptural fountain groups, *Sirens* and *Naiads*. In the middle of the Pool, on a granite rock pediment, soars the huge bronze sculptural group, *Samson Tearing Open the Jaws of the Lion* — a pathetic allegory of the victory of Russia's "Samson", Peter the Great, in the Battle of Poltava over

Charles XII of Sweden personified here by the image implying the Swedish heraldic lion. The *Samson* sculpture decorates the tallest (21 metres) and most powerful fountain of Peterhof. The first lead sculptural group was produced in 1735 by Bartolomeo Carlo Rastrelli to mark the 25th anniversary of the Poltava victory. In 1801 it was replaced by a new *Samson* cast in bronze after a model by Mikhail Kozlovsky. Carried away by the invaders in 1942–43, the statue was recreated by Vasily Simonov. The Samson Fountain is a veritable masterpiece remarkable for a harmonious combination of decorative sculpture and the dynamic water element.

Sculptural decor of the Great Cascade

The Great Cascade. Decorative statue: **Ganymede**. *Copy of an ancient original by Leochares. 1800*

The statuary decorating the Great Cascade has underwent major alterations. In the early nineteenth century lead effigies created during Peter's times were replaced by bronze casts. Seventeen of the new pieces of sculpture were modelled on ancient examples close to the originally installed statues in their plastic qualities and subject matter. Fifteen pieces were cast anew from models by the best Russian sculptors, professors of the Academy of Arts. Outstanding for their plastic perfection and emotional expressiveness are the statues of *Perseus* and *Sirens* created by Feodosy Shchedrin; *Alcides* by Ivan Prokofyev notable for its striking combination of dynamic and static qualities; *Galatea* by Jean-Dominique Rachette remarkable for its subtlest lyricism, and *Pandora* executed after a model by Fedot Shubin. All of them add to the magnificence of the Great Cascade making it a unique artistic monument of world stature.

The Great Cascade is perceived as a great musical and choreographic performance in which everything is pervaded with a pathetic exultation and joy. The singing of water jets and the splashes of streams merge into a single hymn to the glory of Russia.

The Great Cascade
The East Waterfall Stairway

The Great Cascade. The Samson Fountain

The Monplaisir complex, Peter the Great's favourite recreation place, is located in the east section of the Lower Park. Originally this name (French for "my pleasure") was applied to the "small pavilions" erected by orders of Peter the Great on the shore of the Gulf of Finland. Over the years an unusual complex of gardens, fountains and decorative sculptures emerged around them. The main fountain structure of the Monplaisir area is the Dragon Cascade (also known as the Chessboard Hill Cascade). Its slopes are faced with tufa and the stairways are decorated at the sides with marble statues of ancient deities produced by Giovanni Bonazza and Filippo Catasio. The parterre near the Chessboard Hill is adorned with the Roman Fountains designed in the early 1730s by the architects Ivan Davydov and Ivan Blank. They imitated the fountains standing in front of St Peter's in Rome, hence their names which were retained after they had been redesigned in granite and marble in 1798–1800 in the spirit of Classical architecture. Various kinds of coloured marble were used for their decoration, which was further enhanced by gilded masks, garlands and wreaths.

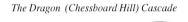

The Roman Fountains

The Dragon (Chessboard Hill) Cascade

*Sculpture: **Dragons***

The ensemble of the east section of the Lower Park is distinguished by its unusual fountains each of which is truly unique. Most of them are trick fountains intended for amusing visitors. One of them is the Sun Fountain designed by Yury Velten in the 1770s. Another popular trick fountain, the famous Chinese Umbrella, amuses both children and grown-up people already for two centuries.

The Pyramid Fountain built in the first quarter of the eighteenth century has reached us without any major alterations. It is a truly unique example of the fountain designer's art from the age of Peter the Great. The palpitating, white foamy "pyramid" which resembles a liquid monument consists of 505 water jets soaring in seven tiers. Water, falling down the marble steps fills up the pool and in smooth, mirror-like streams pours to the basin around the fountain. The composition of the Pyramid Fountain is reigned by the pattern of water jets which is emphasized by the marble of the balustrade with vases and miniature bridges spanning the surrounding basin. The fountain designed by Niccolo Michetti is a development of the concept suggested by Peter the Great himself. The work was carried out in 1721–24.

The Pyramid Fountain never fails to amaze present-day visitors to Peterhof as it astonished Friedrich Wilhelm Bergholtz, the Kammer-Junker of the Duke of Holstein, who wrote about his visit to the Lower Park in the reign of Peter the Great: "There is hardly such a large and beautiful fountain anywhere else."

The Pyramid Fountain

The Sun Fountain

The gem of Peterhof is Peter's favourite Monplaisir and its garden with fountains including two trick fountains dating back to the Petrine era. The brick masonry of the palace façade, its clear-cut and concise forms and its tent-shaped roof remind us about the Dutch tastes of Peter the Great.

The Palace of Monplaisir
The Monplaisir Garden
The Sheaf Fountain

The Cloche Fountain
Sculpture: **Psyche**. *1817*
A copy from Antonio
Canova's original

The Palace of Monplaisir was built in 1714–23 for Peter the Great after his sketches. Architecturally and artistically the palace was designed and decorated by the professional architects Braunstein, Le Blond and Michetti, the painter decorator Philippe Pillement, master craftsmen from the Moscow Armoury and icon-painters.

The State Hall, the main and largest interior of Monplaisir, as well as the galleries and rooms of the palace house Russia's first collection of Western European paintings assembled by Peter the Great. The Palace of Monplaisir is not only a very rare architectural monument, but also a witness to the age of great transformations, and this fact enables its visitors to sense a specific atmosphere of the first quarter of the eighteenth century.

The Palace of Monplaisir. The East Gallery

The State Hall. Decorative sculpture: **Spring.** *1720s. Sculptor Bartolomeo Carlo Rastrelli*

The State Hall

A remarkable feature of the east section of the Lower Park is that it is made up of small gardens, miniature ensembles with water jets as their central elements. One such ensemble is the Orangery Garden near the oval building of the Orangery. The stately edifice was erected in 1722–25 after Michetti's drawings by the architects Braunstein and Zemtsov who succeeded in endowing the utilitarian building with palatial features. In the centre of the Orangery Garden stands the fountain decorated with the sculpture *Triton Tearing Open the Jaws of a Sea Monster*. The subject is an allegory of Russia's sea victories in the Northern War. The battle scene is watched by four turtles symbolizing both the cardinal points and the states which passively participated in the coalition war against Sweden. The initially installed lead group was produced by Bartolomeo Carlo Rastrelli. 150 years later it was replaced with a new one produced after a drawing by David Jensen in Berlin. The original concept, however, was then distorted — the mythical monster was replaced by a composition with a naturalistic crocodile. This composition was plundered during the Second World War and in postwar years the original sculptural group has been recreated after eighteenth-century drawings by the sculptor Alexei Gurdzhy.

The Ramp, an entry to the Lower Park

The Orangery Fountain
The sculptural group: **Triton Tearing Open the Jaws of a Sea Monster**

The Hermitage, a small palace or pavilion, is located in the west section of the Lower Park, on the very coast of the Gulf of Finland. It was built to the design of Johann Braunstein in 1721–25. The pavilion was intended for a secluded rest of the Emperor and persons close to him. It owes its name to the French word *hermitage* meaning the habitation of a recluse. The palace's isolated position was provided by a man-made ditch around it with a drawbridge which connected the structure with the surrounding world.

The entire upper floor of the pavilion was occupied from 1759 by the Hall decorated with paintings by Flemish, Dutch, French, Italian and German artists of the seventeenth and eighteenth centuries. The history painting *The Battle of Poltava* (1727) was produced by the Russian artist Ivan Nikitin. In the middle of the Hall stands an oval table for fourteen diners. Servants and cooks who prepared meals on the ground floor used a special mechanism to lift the central section of the dining-table laid with all kinds of dishes. Any guest could order a special dish to his or her choice by ringing a hand-bell.

The Hermitage Pavilion is a very rare monument of architecture and art dating from the first quarter of the eighteenth century and recreating the atmosphere of intimate conversations characteristic of the "gallant" age. It belongs to the category of amusement pavilions popular in regular European gardens of the seventeenth and eighteenth centuries and intended for a brief pleasing relaxation in the course of promenades. The architecture of the Hermitage Pavilion is marked by a harmony of proportions. The tall windows with numerous small panes illuminate the Hall and afford a view of the sea and the park around the building both from the interior and through the pavilion.

The Hermitage Pavilion

The Hermitage Pavilion. The Hall

The spatial composition of the Lower Park is consistently based on the principle of symmetry. This principle can be traced in the placement of companion fountains, similar in their artistic features, at the intersections of the avenues and in front of the cascades. At the corners of the Great Parterre flower beds, by the foot of the Great Cascade, are the Marble Bench Fountains with the statues of *Nymph* and *Danaid* created according to a concept by Andrei Stakenschneider in 1854.

The Adam and Eve Fountains designed by Peter the Great himself can rival their most famous Peterhof counterparts. They are decorated with marble statues specially commissioned for Russia from the Venetian sculptor Giovanni Bonazza. The Adam Fountain began to operate in 1722 and the Eve Fountain was completed in 1726. Equidistant from the Great Cascade and the Sea Canal, the Adam and Eve Fountains mark the compositional pivots of the west and east sections of the Lower Park.

The artistic effect of the fountains is created by sixteen curving jets of water. They echo the octagonal pool with eight radiant avenues diverging from it and affording numerous perspective views.

The Marble Bench Fountain: **Danaid**

The Eve Fountain

View of the Marly Palace

The Golden Hill Cascade

The Marly ensemble is situated in the west section of the Lower Park. The name was borrowed by Peter the Great from the French royal residence which admired him during his visit by its system of water supply to a cascade, ponds and pavilions. However, the Marly ensemble in Peterhof, as it follows from Peter the Great's own sketches and his decrees, was not a literal copy of its French model, the Marly-le-Roi residence. It has rather become a free improvisation on the subject of its French prototype. The dominant structure of the complex — the Marly Cascade or the Golden Hill — was built in 1722–23 by Michetti, Braunstein, Zemtsov and Usov. In 1731–32 Zemtsov imparted a more up-to-date air to the Cascade — the waterfall steps (there are twenty-one of them) were covered with gilded copper plates and decorated with sculptures on the parapets and attics.

The Marly Cascade is decorated with three Medusa mascarons produced by Bartolomeo Carlo Rastrelli in 1724 and with marble statues carved in the early eighteenth century by Pietro Baratta, Giovanni Zorzoni and A. Garcia.

𝒯he Marly complex, a model
of regular planning in the French
fashion, was created in 1720–24.
The design of the two-storey Marly
Palace, a work by Johann Braunstein, was amended in the course of
the construction by Peter the Great
himself. In front of the west façade
of the palace are located four sec-
torial ponds, in front of the east one,
the large Marly Pond. Avenues
diverge from it like the points of
a trident crossing the entire Lower
Park from the west to the east.
To the north and south of the pond
are laid out gardens protected from
the seashore by an earthen rampart.
One of these gardens is dedicated
to Bacchus and adorned with the
Triton Cloche and Menazherny
(Economical) Fountains.

The Golden Hill Cascade.
Decorative sculpture: **Neptune**. *1860s*

Panorama of the Marly ensemble

The Great Palace. The Armorial Block

𝒯he large-scale Great Palace, glistening with the gilded cupolas of its wings, stands out among all other structures in the Peterhof ensemble. With its front facing the sea, it makes up, together with the Great Cascade, a single majestic monument to the eighteenth-century Russian Empire. Originally, in 1714–24, Braunstein, Le Blond and Michetti built the modest Upper Mansion. In 1745–55, Rastrelli, put in charge of its reconstruction by Empress Elizabeth Petrovna, rebuilt it into a majestic palace combining the features of the Petrine and Elizabethan Baroque. The architect extended the building adding galleries on either side and effectively completing them with two-storey wings. The final element of the west wing was the Church consecrated to the Apostles Peter and Paul and the east wing ended with the Armorial Block.

The state interiors of the Great Palace were decorated by Rastrelli with an especial luxury. The gilded wooden sculpture, high-relief decoration, ornaments, inlaid parquetry, polychrome ceiling paintings, pictorial insets, tempera decorations and damask fabrics reflected in the numerous mirrors and brightly illuminated from the wide windows, all contributed to an impression of unusual resplendence.

The great Rastrelli was at his best in the designs of the State Staircase, the Audience Room and the Ballroom (or Merchant Room). Ornamental fantasies of the architect were perfectly realized by French and Russian carvers who combined their national artistic traditions in this work.

The suite of halls and reception rooms created after drawings by Rastrelli, seems to entice the visitor to the palace into a brilliant, fascinating realm. The architect used characteristic Baroque elements in the decor of all the interiors. Nevertheless each detail was given a distinctive treatment and the decorative design of every single room and hall bears some special features of its own. The suite design of the palace corresponded to the ceremonial mode of life of the Russian Imperial court which resembled a sumptuous theatrical pageant. The splendour of the Great Palace, which witnessed the two-century history of the state, was a result of creative work by outstanding architects such as Braunstein, Le Blond, Michetti, Rastrelli, Velten and Stakenschneider.

The State Staircase of the Great Palace
Allegorical sculpture: **Summer**. *1751*
Architect Bartolomeo Francesco Rastrelli

The State Staircase of the Great Palace

The Great Palace. The Audience Hall

The Great Palace. The Throne Room

*The Throne Room. The Imperial throne
Early 18th century*

*Vigilius Erichsen. **The March of
Catherine the Great to Peterhof.** 1762*

*I*n 1763–80 the Throne Room and a number of other interiors of the Great Palace acquired a new look which suited the Classicist tastes of Empress Catherine the Great. In the Throne Room, the moulded decor was redesigned after drawings by Yury Velten and the longitudinal walls between the top-light windows were embellished with twelve painted portraits of Peter the Great's relatives. Over the four doors leading to the room were placed formal likenesses of Peter the Great, Catherine I, Anna Ioannovna and Elizabeth Petrovna, while the equestrian portrait of Catherine the Great showing her during the memorable march from St Petersburg to Peterhof in 1762 began to grace the east wall, above the throne.

𝒯he Portrait (or Picture) Room is located in the very centre of the Great Palace. During the Petrine age it was known as the Italian Salon and was thought to be the most imposing interior in the palace. In the middle of the eighteenth century the doors of the room were adorned with magnificent carved ornament after sketches by Rastrelli. In 1764 Jean-Baptiste Vallin de la Mothe redesigned the decor of the room covering its walls with paintings by Pietro Rotari. All the 368 original works have survived and after restoration of the room they have been returned to their former places.

The Great Palace. The Portrait Room

The Great (Blue) Drawing Room

The Banquet Service. 1848–52
The Imperial Porcelain Factory,
St Petersburg

The Great Palace
The West Chinese Lobby

The West Chinese Lobby
Tiled stove

The Chinese Lobbies of the Great Peterhof Palace are located at either side of the Portrait Room. They owe their names to the type of their decoration which catered the tastes of the eighteenth century with its vogue for Chinese art. The decorator of the East and West Chinese Lobbies, Vallin de la Mothe, used in the trimming of their walls the painted panels of authentic lacquered Chinese screens. He added them with lacquer insets of a Russian work stylized in the *chinoiserie* spirit. Even the ceilings of the interiors painted in lacquers are given a porcelain-like texture. Of especial value are the parquet floors inlaid of amaranth, rosewood, sandal, ebony and other precious kinds of wood. The decor of the Chinese Lobbies was recreated after the Second World War.

The Upper Gardens. The Neptune Fountain

Panoramic view of the Upper Gardens

𝒯he Upper Gardens stretch in front of the south façade of the Great Palace. They were laid out in a regular manner according to sketches by Peter the Great and drawings by Le Blond, Braunstein and the master gardener Leonard van Harnigfelt in 1724. Towards 1739 the architects Mikhail Zemtsov, Ivan Blank and Ivan Davydov as well as the sculptor Bartolomeo Carlo Rastrelli attained a perfect symmetry in the layout of this formal garden introducing five fountains with lead sculptural groups there. In the latter half of the eighteenth century the sculptural decor was altered. However, the Square Pools, the Great Pond and two round pools created in the 1730s have survived to this day. The largest fountain of the Upper Gardens is *Neptune* depicting the sea god with a fantastic retinue. The bronze group including more than thirty figures is an outstanding work produced by Nuremberg sculptors in the 1650s and 1660s. In the late eighteenth century the complex was acquired by Emperor Paul I for Gatchina, but eventually it was installed in the Upper Gardens as a befitting decoration for one of the most beautiful Peterhof fountains.

The so-called Alexandria area, the seaside residence of Nicholas I, adjoins the east border of the Lower Park. The lands of the future Alexandria were presented by Emperor Alexander I to his brother Grand Duke Nikolai Pavlovich, who in December 1825 ascended the Russian throne. On becoming the single owner of all the royal residences, Nicholas I presented this plot of land to his wife, Empress Alexandra Fiodorovna. The building of the new Imperial residence, which received the name of "Alexandria, Her Majesty's Dacha", was carried out very intensively and with a great sweep. An extensive landscaped park was being laid out, for which thousands of various trees and rare bushes were brought, roads were being built and the construction of all sorts of buildings was under way. Nicholas I entrusted Adam Menelaws, the Scottish architect, with the fulfillment of this project. His designs were used in 1826–29 to erect a palace which was named the "Cottage" or "Country House" in the English manner. Its fronts, interiors and furnishings reflect the general European romantic interest in mediaeval art, preeminently the Gothic perceived in the spirit of Walter Scott.

The Cottage Museum Palace affords a glimpse of the private life of Emperor Nicholas I, the spiritual world of his family permeated with a warmth of feeling and full of romantic comfort.

Alexandria. The Cottage Palace

The Cottage Palace. The Drawing Room of Empress Alexandra Fiodorovna

The Cathedral of the SS Apostles Peter and Paul in Peterhof. 1895–1904 Architect Nikolai Sultanov, with the participation of V. Kosiakov

Tsarskoye Selo

Tsarskoye Selo — the very name of this palace-and-park ensemble provokes a number of happy recollections. In addition to its beautiful parks and architecture, it is also associated with the great age of Russian poetry and the ceremonial glamour of the past autocratic life. In the seventeenth century, there was the Swedish farmstead Saritsa, later renamed *Saris hoff*, in this area. The Finnish name of the farmstead was *Saaris moisio* ("a farmstead on the elevation") and its Russianized form was *Sarskaya myza*. After Russia had eventually taken hold of these lands, Sarskaya myza (or Sarskoye Selo) became the property of Alexander Menshikov, and from 1708 to 1724 it was the summer residence of Peter the Great's wife, Yekaterina Alexeyevna. In 1711, after Catherine was declared "the true Sovereign", the building of a large-scale residence began on the site. Johann Braunstein and Johann Christian Förster were mainly responsible for its construction. Catherine I bequeathed Sarskoye Selo to her daughter, Tsesarevna Elizabeth Petrovna. On becoming the Empress in 1741, she, with her innate breadth of nature, did not spare funds for turning the old mansion into a luxurious palace, for building various pavilions and for laying-out gardens. In 1743–51 the Empress's projects for the extension of the suburban residence were carried out by Mikhail Zemtsov, Andrei Kvasov and Savva Chevakinsky. In 1752–56, the work on the estate, by then already renamed Tsarskoye Selo, or the Tsars' Village, was supervised by Bartolomeo Francesco Rastrelli. It was he who gave to the palace and the entire complex that luxurious Baroque appearance which was poetically compared with a "celestial constellation". During the reign of Catherine the Great Tsarskoye Selo was further enriched with the works of the architects Antonio Rinaldi, Yury Velten, Vasily Neyelov, Charles Cameron and Giacomo Quarenghi, whose tastes were formed under the influence of ancient architecture.

It is the Catherine Palace, however, the fronts of which extend for 740 metres, that dominates the entire complex of Tsarskoye Selo. Its powerful decorative forms determine the plastic expressiveness of the palace endowing it with a truly regal majesty. This impression is enhanced by the interiors of the palace the decor of which reflects the swiftly changing tastes of the crowned owners. They are recorded in the decorative styles of the rooms and halls where Baroque luxury can be met side by side with Classical elegance.

The Great Hall (or the Ballroom) is a true masterpiece of the decorative genius of Rastrelli. This is one of the largest palatial halls created by this outstanding architect in St Petersburg and its environs in the 1750s. The hall's area is 846 square metres (it is seventeen metres wide and forty-seven metres long). The impression of its great expanse is still further enhanced thanks to the illusion of space created by the two tiers of windows. The piers between the windows are covered with mirrors in gilded carved frames. A sense of lightness is increased by the mirrors imitating windows on the butt-end walls and set in the piers and on the doors. The painted ceiling and the elaborate pattern of the inlaid parquet floor also add to the striking effect of the Ballroom. Nevertheless the predominant decorative element of the interior is gilded carving. Countless figures and half-figures, ornamental interlaces, cartouches and rocailles produce an indelible impression on visitors by their fantastic ingenuity and mastery of their execution.

←←

The Great Palace. The garden front

←

*The Great Palace. The garden front
Central part*

The Great Hall (Ballroom)

The Great Hall. Overdoor decoration

The Bedroom of Maria Fiodorovna is one of the most spectacular interiors created by Cameron in the Catherine Palace. The architectural image of this room combined the intimate character of a private apartment with the luxury of a state room. Cameron used for the decor of the Bedroom moulded wall panels executed by Ivan Martos, which allegorically personified joy and happiness of family life. But the most prominent feature of the Bedroom are thin faience columns of the alcove. Lavishly ornamented and emphasized by golden strips and flutes, they seem to have come down from the murals of the Pompeiian villas. The Picture Hall, an interior the decor of which is largely devoted to painting, is characteristic of the first half of the eighteenth century. The powerful decorative effect created by tapestry-like hanging of the canvases combines here with the image of a picture gallery, an indispensable attribute in the home of an enlightened aristocrat during that period. Rastrelli completely covered the longitudinal walls with 130 paintings by Luca Giordano, Emmanuel de Witte, Adriaen van Ostade, David Teniers and other eminent Western European artists of the seventeenth and eighteenth centuries. Two paintings, *The Battle of Poltava* and *The Battle of Lesnaya*, were commissioned by Peter the Great from the French painter Pierre Denis Martin.

The Bedroom

The Picture Room

A veritable gem of the Catherine Palace was the Amber Study which is justly ranked by connoisseurs among "treasures of the world". In 1701–09 Gottfried Wolfram, Gottfried Turau and Ernst Schacht produced, after a design by Andreas Schlüter, the inlaid amber panels which in 1717 were presented by Frederick William of Prussia to Peter the Great for the decoration of the Study in his third Winter Palace at St Petersburg. In 1755 Rastrelli designed the Amber Room in the Catherine Palace enriching the famous panels with Florentine mosaics and sculpture. Plundered by the Nazi soldiers during the Second World War, the amber decoration of the Study has nowadays been completely restored.

Detail of the interior decor

The Amber Study

The Blue Drawing Room is the central apartment of the north section of the palace which was allotted by Catherine the Great to Grand Duke Pavel Petrovich, the heir to the throne, and his wife Maria Fiodorovna. Catherine the Great commissioned the designing of the heir's apartments, which included such interiors as the Green Dining Room, the Waiters' Room, the Blue Drawing Room, the Blue Chinese Drawing Room, the Bedroom and the Choir Anteroom, to the Scottish architect Charles Cameron, who brilliantly coped with the task. The Blue Drawing Room is one of the most remarkable interiors in the palace created by Cameron in the 1780s. Notable features of this interior are the silk upholstery of its walls adorned with a printed pattern, the artistic paintings of the ceilings and doors as well as the inlaid parquet floor. In all this majestic spectacle free improvisations of motifs borrowed from ancient art can be traced. Set into the moulded frieze with a gilded relief ornament are painted medallions featuring ancient images. The ceiling of the Blue Drawing Room is embellished with decorative painting based on semi-circles, rectangles and squares. Painted within the geometrical figures are mythological scenes and characters. The rich design of the inlaid parquet floor matches the elaborate compositional forms of the painted ceiling.

The decor of the Blue Drawing Room echoes the design of the Blue Chinese Drawing Room. Its walls are lined from top to bottom with blue silk which is embellished with stylized scenes of "Chinese life" painted in varicoloured inks. It is remarkable that Cameron, a convinced Classicist, combined the *chinoiserie* upholstery of the walls with ancient motifs of the ceiling painting, which lent the interior an air of artistic originality. The silk used for lining the walls in the reign of Catherine the Great was brought from China, but it was destroyed during the Second World War. The lost fabrics were recreated by restorers on the basis of a surviving sample.

The Blue Drawing Room

The Chinese Blue Drawing Room

Detail of the upholstery
of the Chinese Blue Drawing Room

The Green Dining Room, also decorated after drawings by Cameron, represents a version of the subtle interpretation of ancient motifs in the Russian interiors of the 1780s. Cameron had a profound knowledge of ancient art and in this work he freely improvised on the subject of ancient Roman decorative motifs. He attainedthe harmony of his artistic solution primarily by the use of plastic elements. The moulded details are arranged against the light green background of the walls with a thorough calculation. The main field is enlivened by a stylized representation of garden gates with medallions and moulded figures of youths and girls, seemingly supporting bas-reliefs with scenes of playing Cupids. The crowning element of the wall composition are arc-shaped twigs of vine.

The delicate tracery of details and the jeweller's modelling of sculptural forms executed by Ivan Martos after Cameron's drawings lend the Green Dining Room that sense of elegance which dominates the living apartments of the Catherine Palace.

The Green Dining Room

The State Staircase. The Upper Landing

→
Perspective view of the garden front of the Great Palace

The Grotto Pavilion (The Morning Hall)

The Hermitage Pavilion

The Upper Bath Pavilion

Sculpture: **Galatea**
Early 18th century
Sculptor Pietro Baratta

The regular garden laid out in front of the south façade of the Catherine Palace was created according to the concept of Bartolomeo Francesco Rastrelli. The architect included into his composition two garden pavilions: the Hermitage and the Grotto. Their complex plan, a play of volumes, plastic expressiveness of the silhouette and the saturated sculptural and ornamental decor emphasize the image of the pavilions which served as an "abode" for solitary repose and amusements of royal persons and their closest circle.

Rastrelli endowed the Hermitage Pavilion with such a decorative majesty that it began to resemble a miniature palace. Traditionally, the lower storey of the Hermitage Pavilion had mechanisms which were used to lift laid tables for meals held in the Central Hall of the upper floor. As a rule the procedure began in the very heat of a ball. The floors would suddenly open and exquisite dishes would appear from below to the guests' pleasant surprise.

The Grotto Pavilion built by Rastrelli on the bank of the Great Pond was used for recreation during boating parties. The pavilion's location and designation determined its fairy-tale moulded decor with sea monsters, dolphins and sea-shells. Unlike the emphatically decorative pavilions in the Baroque style, Classicist architects lent to garden structures geometrically clear-cut shapes accentuated by relief insets. Such is the Upper Bath Pavilion built in the 1770s by the architect Ilya Neyelov.

The Cameron Gallery created by Charles Cameron, an outstanding interpreter of ancient motifs, is called an architectural "poem" in the spirit of Classicism. The royal commissioner Catherine the Great formulated the idea of the project as a "Graeco-Roman rhapsody". And Cameron incarnated her dream with virtuoso mastery in 1783–87. The Cameron's Gallery, as Pushkin defined it, recalls a "huge hall" soaring towards clouds and dominating the Catherine Gardens. The stairway leading to it is striking for the rounded shape of its flights enhancing the impression that the white colonnade is hovering over the malachite of age-old tree crowns. There are fifty-four bronze busts of outstanding ancient Greeks installed in the Gallery, with the Russian scholar and poet Mikhail Lomonosov placed in the same row. In 1780–87 Cameron erected the building of the Cold Baths as a single ensemble with the Gallery. The volume and façades of the Cold Baths appear from the side of the gallery as a small pavilion, but from the side of the park it looks like a massive structure. The fronts of the Cold Baths are decorated with bronze and stone statues. The interiors of the upper floor are called the Agate Rooms. They are faced with plaques of coloured stone, mainly marble and jasper of various types and shades. The noble colours of natural stones determine the unique designs of the Amber and Agate Studies and of the Great Hall testifying to the exclusive taste of the architect, sculptors and stone carvers who created this unique ensemble.

The Cameron Gallery
Perspective view of the colonnade

The Agate Pavilion. The Great Hall

The Cameron Gallery. The State Stairway

The Ramp of the Cameron Gallery leads to the landscaped section of the Catherine Park. The architect treated it in the manner of ancient cyclopean structures like aqueducts, open waterways of Ancient Rome. The powerful, gradually descending arches divided by semicircular supports-columns bear the gently sloping descent which is linked to the Ramp Avenue. The keystones of the arches are emphasized by masks of mythological creatures carved of stone. These mascarons are unique examples of Russian decorative sculpture of the late eighteenth century. The composition of the Ramp was completed with bronze statues in 1794. Later, by order of Paul I, they were moved to Pavlovsk, and in 1828 decorative bowls reminiscent of ancient lamps were installed to replace them. The Ramp forms an effective perspective along the middle axis and produces an impression of a complex of triumphal arches from the side.

Keystone mask

Cameron's Ramp

The landscaped section of the Catherine Park is situated around the Great Pond. A number of unique park pavilions are connected with it, among which the Turkish Bath reminiscent of a miniature mosque is prominent. It was built to a design by Hypolitto Monighetti in 1850–52. The most famous monument to Catherine the Great, the Chesme Rostral Column, soars on a small island of the Great Pond. It was erected to a design by Antonio Rinaldi in 1774–76 to commemorate the victory of the Russian squadron over the Turkish fleet in Chesme Bay in the Aegean Sea in 1770. A whole complex of buildings in the Chinese fashion was put up on the orders of Catherine the Great at the border of the Catherine and Alexander Parks — the Chinese Village, the Great and Small Caprices and several bridges. One of them was built at the south corner of the Cross Canal. The Creaking Pavilion was erected nearby to the design of Yury Velten. This pavilion crowned with weather-vanes attracted visitors' attention primarily by its unusual *chinoiserie* decoration. A complex of "Chinese amusements" was increased by the construction of a group of the so-called Chinese Bridges created in the late 1770s and early 1780s. Besides the Cross Bridge, there are four of them — the Dragon Bridge, two iron Chinese bridges and the Large Stone Bridge.

The Cross Bridge

The Great Caprice

The Creaking Pavilion

The Great Pond. The Turkish Bath

The Chesme Column

A notable structure in the Catherine Park which invariably attracts visitors' attention is the bridge known under three different names — the Palladian, Marble or Siberian Bridge. The first name is connected with the Roman architect Andrea Palladio who created a prototype of the Tsarskoye Selo bridge, while the second and third ones refer to the material, Siberian marble, which Vasily Neyelov used to built this park structure.

The fountain *The Milkmaid, or Girl with a Pitcher* has been celebrated by poets. Its spring is covered by a granite boulder crowned with the bronze figure of a young girl crying over the broken pitcher.

The Palladian Bridge

The Ruin Tower. 1773. Architect Yury Velten

Fountain: **The Milkmaid, or Girl with a Pitcher**. *1817. Sculptor Pavel Sokolov*

$\mathcal{T}$he Golden Gate decorates the
main entrance to the Catherine
Palace. Behind it, in keeping with
the tradition of eighteenth-century
architecture, is the formal courtyard
arranged in front of the main north
façade of the palace. In 1745–51
Chevakinsky and Kvasov adorned
the Formal Courtyard with semicircular service wings called "circumferences". In 1752–56 Rastrelli clad
the Circumferences into sumptuous
Baroque "garments" having stylisti-
cally united the service blocks with
the courtyard. Put up in the gaps
between them were fences and gates
with pylons. The pattern of the
railings and gates brilliantly re-
vealed the architect's ingenuity and
talent. The graphic silhouette of
the forged frame is enhanced and
completed by a variety of elaborate
gilded scrolls, garlands, sea-shells,
feathers and stars. The design of the
gates and the sections of the railings
show the emphasis on symmetry,
but the openwork elegance of each
detail adds to the pierced design
a sense of ease and perfection.
The Main Gates are crowned with
the Imperial coat-of-arms, the gilded
double-headed eagle, which emphasizes the designation of Tsarskoye
Selo as a royal residence.

The Catherine Palace
The Central "Golden" Gate

The railing of the palace. The Great Gate

The Alexander Palace built by Catherine the Great as a gift to her first and favourite grandson Alexander Pavlovich (the future Alexander I) on the occasion of his wedding to Grand Duchess Elizabeth Alexeyevna, née the Baden Princess Luise-Marie-Augusta. Carrying out the Imperial commission, Giacomo Quarenghi created in 1792–96 one of the most perfect landmarks of world architecture the significance of which is not subject to the influence of time. The palace largely owes its rare magnificence to the double colonnade uniting the extending parts of the north front, with a happily found rhythm of the "movement" of slender shafts crowned by the capitals of the Corinthian order. Although Alexander I almost did not live in the palace on his accession to the throne,

The Alexander Park
The iron Chinese Bridge

The Fiodorovsky Settlement. General view

The Alexander Palace

this great creation by Cameron bears his name. During the reign of Nicholas I, however, it became the favourite residence of the Emperor's family who lived in Alexandria from the early spring till the end of May and after a short stay at Krasnoye Selo during manoeuvres returned to the Alexander Palace to spend their time there until the late autumn. Nicholas I had some rooms and the park redesigned in the then fashionable Romantic manner. Later Emperor Alexander III had his apartments in the right-hand wing of the palace.

The Alexander Palace began to play a particularly important role in the reign of Nicholas II. The Imperial family moved to the palace in 1905 and since then permanently lived there. The Alexander Palace became the official royal residence, a symbol of the last Emperor of Russia. It is with the Alexander Palace that the last days of the Romanov dynasty are connected — here in 1917 the final act of the drama connected with the crush of the Russian Empire was played. These crucial historic events gave to the masterpiece of architecture, the Alexander Palace, the status of a historical memorial.

In 1910–12 Vladimir Pokrovsky and Stepan Krichinsky erected for Nicholas II near the Alexander Palace the Cathedral of St Theodore which became the focal centre of the closed royal town. Its architecture reproduced the imagery and decorative motifs of ancient Russian Orthodox churches.

Tsarskoye Selo, which Pushkin associated in his verses with the idea of homeland, became the holy land of Russian poetry for subsequent generations. There are many buildings in Tsarskoye Selo connected with Pushkin's life — the house of Ludwig Wilhelm Tepper de Ferguson, a music teacher in the Lyceum, and the mansion of Vasily Malinovsky and Yegor Engelgardt, its first directors, the house of the writer and historian Nikolai Karamzin, and the famous Kitayeva's dacha which now houses a Pushkin museum. The poet lived at the dacha together with his young wife in 1831. But it is the Lyceum that evokes especially vivid associations connected with the poet's youth spent at Tsarskoye Selo. In 1811 the former palatial wing, linked in 1789–91 with the Great Palace by a gallery, was given to the newly founded privileged educational establishment named the Lyceum. Here Alexander Pushkin studied between 1811 and 1817. At the graduation examination the young poet recited his poem *Recollections of Tsarskoye Selo* which brought the well-known writer and statesman Gavriil Derzhavin into raptures. Pushkin devoted to the Lyceum and Tsarskoye Selo, where "the Muse appeared" to him for the first time, a number of beautiful verses. To commemorate the Lyceum years of Pushkin in honour of the centenary of the poet's birth, on 2 May 1899 a monument to the poet was laid down in the Lyceum garden. It was cast of bronze after a model by the sculptor Robert Bach and opened a year later. The inhabitants of Tsarskoye Selo collected funds for the creation of the monument which has recorded for ever their love for the poetic genius of Russia.

View of the Palace Church and the Lyceum

Monument to Alexander Pushkin in the Lyceum Garden. 1900 Sculptor Robert Bach

Domes of the Church of the Palace

Pavlovsk

avlovsk, one of the most perfect works of architecture and the art of landscape gardening, occupies a special place among royal residences in the environs of St Petersburg. Its name reminds us of a complicated and largely tragic personality of Catherine the Great's son, Emperor Paul I. The early history of Pavlovsk, which was presented by the Empress to the heir to the throne Grand Duke Pavel Petrovich and his consort Maria Fiodorovna at the end of the 1770s, turned out to be closely related to their dramatically changing destinies. The date of the foundation of "the village of Pavlovskoye" is taken to be the year 1779 when two summer houses, the *Marienthal* ("Marie's Valley" after the name of Maria Fiodorovna) and the *Paullust* (Paul's pleasure") were

built. At the same time a small park with decorative structures, cascades and bridges was laid out. In 1780–85 Charles Cameron began the formation of the heir's royal residence. He built the Palace, the Temple of Friendship, the Apollo Colonnade and the Pavilion of the Three Graces. In 1796–1801, when Pavlovsk became the Imperial summer residence, the Palace was extended and its rooms were given a new, stately appearance. In the park the Old and New Sylvia areas were laid out, the Peel Tower and the Ruin Cascade were set up. After the death of Paul I Pavlovsk turned into a summer residence of the Dowager Empress Maria Fiodorovna. In 1802–25 such outstanding architects as Voronikhin, Quarenghi and Thomas de Thomon worked there.

The Palace is the predominant structure of the Pavlovsk ensemble. It was not accidental that the site for it was chosen on the high bank of the Slavianka and the natural elevation served as a podium for the building. The ceremony of its foundation took place on 25 May 1782 and its construction was basically finished towards the summer of 1786.

←

The Pavlovsk Palace
View from the Bridge of Centaurs

The Pavlovsk Palace. Monument to Paul I
1851. Sculptor Ivan Vitali

View of the Pavlovsk Palace from a helicopter

→

The Pavlovsk Palace and the Parade Ground

Charles Cameron, the designer of the project, gave to the building classically austere proportions reducing the decor of the façades to Corinthian columns and minor relief ornaments. The central part of the palace is crowned with a drum surrounded by a ring of sixty-four columns and supporting a low dome. In the 1780s and early 1790s the interiors of the ground floor — the Ballroom, the White Dining Room, the Old Drawing Room and the Billiards Room — were decorated to designs by Cameron. The upper floor where the Halls of War and Peace, the State Bedroom, the Italian Hall and the Grecian Hall were decorated before 1793 to designs by Vincenzo Brenna. In 1803–04 Andrei Voronikhin recreated and partly refashioned the interiors of the central part of the palace destroyed by a fire. In 1822–24 Carlo Rossi arranged a Library Hall named after him on the upper floor and redesigned some rooms of the ground floor. A major contribution to the decoration of palace interiors was made by the sculptors Mikhail Kozlovsky, Ivan Prokofyev, Vasily Demuth-Malinovsky, Ivan Martos and Fiodor Gordeyev, the artists Henri-François-Gabriel Viollier and Giovanni Scotti.

The architectural and artistic overture to state rooms of the first floor are the Lower and Upper Vestibules. The Egyptian (Lower) Vestibule, designed by Cameron, is accentuated by allegorical statues of the twelve months. To match the statues, the walls are decorated with medallions showing the Zodiac signs. The Upper Vestibule on the first floor is decorated with antique military attributes and thematically matching frescoes.

The Pavlovsk Palace. The Egyptian Vestibule

The State Staircase

𝒯he Italian Hall, the compositional and artistic centre of the palace, is a model of Classicist architectural design striking for its harmony and elegance of proportions, exquisite symmetry and perfection of the decor. The two-tiered volume of the hall is crowned with a "hovering" dome. The austere centric design of the palace is enlivened by the semicircular and square niches over which are running arched apertures of the first-floor choirs accentuated by a balustrade. The piers between the choir arches are decorated with caryatids bearing the cornice of the dome and the bas-relief representations of eagles with outstretched wings. In the decor of the hall are employed authentic low-reliefs by Roman sculptors of the first and second centuries B.C.; set in niches are ancient statues. The Italian Hall — a work of art which has combined the creative efforts of Cameron, Brenna, Quarenghi and Voronikhin — is remarkable for a subtle colouring of the dome, the lilac walls of artificial marble, the ormolu mounts and rosewood panelling of the doors. In the south wing of the palace Brenna placed the Picture Gallery, semicircular in plan, with double-sided illumination. Such design of the room provides a necessary light for a display of paintings placed in the piers between window apertures and on the other walls. Put on display in this room are canvases by Italian, Flemish and Dutch artists of the seventeenth and eighteenth centuries. The Picture Gallery of the Pavlovsk Palace, which reflects the tastes of Paul I and Maria Fiodorovna, is a traditional formal interior typical of eighteenth-century royal and grand-ducal residences.

The Picture Gallery

The Italian Hall

The Boudoir of Maria Fiodorovna is remarkable in the suite of private Imperial apartments of the Pavlovsk Palace for its elegance and luxurious decor. Small in size, the interior resembles a porcelain casket in which eighteenth-century toilet items are preserved. The walls of the Boudoir are rhythmically covered with elaborate arabesques simulating Raphael's painted designs in the loggias of the Vatican Palace. The space of the walls between the pilasters is covered with ancient Roman reliefs and painted landscapes. Two large marble bas-reliefs represent Alexander the Great and his mother Olympia. This is an allusion, in an allegorical form, to the future Emperor Alexander I and his mother Maria Fiodorovna. Of spe-cial mention is a magnificent marble fireplace with columns of Roman work that is reminiscent of a triumphal arch.

The Room for the Ladies-in-Waiting
Cupid Shooting a Bow. *1761*
By Carle van Loo

The Boudoir of Maria Fiodorovna

The Large Throne Room occupying an area of 400 square metres is distinguished for the scale and luxury of its space. Brenna enhanced this effect by introducing into the decor of the interior vast arched apertures and semicircular niches in which he placed stoves with a sumptuous relief decoration. The arched window surrounds adorned with caryatids resemble triumphal arches. The bas-relief depiction of fruit, flowers and musical instruments, indispensable attributes of a royal feast, suggest that the Great Hall was originally intended for festive gatherings. After his ascension Paul I ordered that the Great Hall be used as the Throne Room. Then a special place decorated with velvet drapery trimmed with gold braids was arranged against the closed window to accommodate the Imperial throne.

Worthy of interest is the painting of the ceiling made after a sketch by Pietro Gonzago. However, the concept of the great monumental painter was not realized. It was only in 1971, during restoration, that the ceiling of the Throne Room was adorned with the author's original design. The painting not only produced an illusion of a larger interior, but also returned a triumphal character to it complementing the room's architectonics with painted representations of a classical colonnade, hanging standards of the Guards and the St Andrew flag of the Russian Navy.

Exhibited in the Large Throne Room is a unique Guryev Service produced in 1817 at the St Petersburg Imperial Porcelain Factory specially for the Pavlovsk Palace. The porcelain groups for table decoration were modelled by Stepan Pimenov. The crystal items of the service produced in England are very rare examples of artistic glasswork dating from the late eighteenth century.

The Great Throne Hall
(The State Dining Room)

The Great Throne Room. Girandole
Late 18th century. The Imperial Glass Works,
St Petersburg

The Grecian Hall is one of those works of architecture the harmony of which evokes lofty artistic associations. It might be called a hymn to the art of Ancient Greece. The inclusion into the decor of the interior of Corinthian columns, stuccowork and sculpture illustrates the designer's deep penetration into the essence of ancient artistic traditions. The hall designed by Brenna was also enriched with architectural elements added later into the decor of the interior by Voronikhin. The sixteen marine-coloured columns of artificial marble, the rich moulded decor of the ceiling, the low vault and the marble bowl lamps, all adds to the slender and festive look of the hall. The two fireplaces of white marble which had been manufac-tured for the Mikhailovsky Palace were brought to Pavlovsk in 1803 by Voronikhin who retained the stylistic integrity of the Grecian Hall.

The Third Anteroom. Clock
Second half of the 18th century
Workshop of Pierre Caron

The Grecian Hall

Clock: **Helen and Paris**
Late 18th century
Workshop of L. J. Laguesse,
Liège, France

The State Bedroom of the Empress Maria Fiodorovna designed by Vincenzo Brenna is notable for the extreme luxury of its decoration. The walls of the room are lined with silk panels painted in bright colours. Their motifs are symbols of idyllic pastoral life at one with nature. The same subject matter dominates the ceiling painting which imitates a garden trellis interwoven with flowers. The most prominent feature of the State Bedroom is the sumptuous bed lavishly decorated with gilded ornamental carving and sculptures — allegories of happiness and prosperity of the royal family. The furniture set of a canopied bed, coach and armchairs is a masterwork produced by Henri Jacob, one of the most outstanding French cabinet-makers.

The Little Lantern Study, a truly inspired work by Voronikhin, is perceived as an antithesis to the pomposity of the Bedroom. A blend of painting, sculpture, colour and light creates an impression that the Little Lantern is not only a palatial interior but a place of solitary contemplation and a "home of the Muses".

The State Bedroom

The Little Lantern Study

*T*he Pavlovsk Park is a kind of a philosophical poem about the essence of spiritual life, its secrets, joys and serene melancholy. The chapters of this poem are picturesque views of the park usually animated by a pavilion, a decorative structure or a sculpture. The Apollo Colonnade is interesting not only in terms of artistic perfection bringing forth associations with Classical Antiquity, but also for its architectural biography. In 1783 Cameron erected an open double-ring Doric colonnade at the entrance to the park and set up a statue of *Apollo Belvedere*, a copy from Leochares' original, in the centre of it. The colonnade became the emblem of Pavlovsk as an abode of poetry and art. In 1800 the Colonnade was shifted to the high bank of the Slavianka and installed along the slope of the landscaped Cascade. In 1817, during a thunderstorm, part of the Colonnade collapsed which, however, only emphasized its romantic look. The Pavilion of the Three Graces put up by Cameron in 1800–01 is also an interpretation of an ancient architectural motif. The pavilion was erected at the axis of the main avenue of Her Majesty's Own Garden laid out in the style of French regular parks. It was adorned with a marble group by the eighteenth-century Italian sculptor Paolo Triscorni. The sculptural group revealing Triscorni's consummate mastery of marble treatment is an expressive version of an ancient original with the image of the three deities personifying female beauty.

Sculpture is an almost indispensable part of the park structures. Marble and cast-iron lions embellish the Large Stone (Italian) Staircase designed by Brenna. The marble statues look particularly attractive against the greenery of the park. Especially notable among them is *Erminia* by Rinaldo Rinaldi created in the middle of the nineteenth century.

The Apollo Colonnade

Sculpture: **Erminia**. *Mid-19th century Sculptor Rinaldo Rinaldi*

The Pavilion of the Three Graces

The Large Stone (Italian) Staircase

ensemble of this kind is the Twelve Walks area, with the bronze representations of the Muses, patrons of the arts and sciences (copies from ancient originals) surrounding the statue of Apollo. A typical example is *Clio*, the Muse of History, cast by Edmonde Gastecloux at the St Petersburg Academy of Arts, where all of them were produced.

The Temple of Friendship. 1780–82

The Peel Tower. 1795–97

The Old Sylvia. The Twelve Walks area
Clio, *the Muse of History. 1794. Russia*
Cast by Edmonde Gastecloux. Copy from an ancient original of the 3rd century B.C.

$\mathcal{T}$he Temple of Friendship is the earliest pavilion structure built by Cameron in Pavlovsk. This perfect work is outstanding not only for the complex of the Pavlovsk Park, but is a masterpiece of eighteenth-century Russian Classicism as a whole. Drawing on the forms of ancient architecture, Cameron attained a striking harmony and succeeded in endowing the pavilion with a special spiritual atmosphere. In this sense Cameron could be compared with Gavriil Derzhavin who, carrying out the "most august commission", infused his verses with true inspiration.

The pavilion is dedicated by Paul and his wife Maria Fiodorovna to Empress Catherine the Great. The inscription over the doors,

"With love, reverence and gratitude devoted", alludes to this fact, as do the allegorical relief medallions Glory, Friendship, Gratitude, Justice and the traditional symbols of friendly feelings — dolphins, wreathes and vines.

The emphasized rustic simplicity of the Pavlovsk Park was enhanced by decorative pavilions. The romantic image of a peeling mill with a dilapidating tower (hence its name, the Peel Tower), built to a design by Brenna and decorated with painting by Gonzago, was a sort of theatrical mask of the palatial pavilion. Its upper floor was used as a hotel for repose and enjoyment of the scenery. The sculptural decoration of the Pavlovsk Park is thematically united. The most well-known

The Pavlovsk Park had a memorial character from the first years of its existence. In one of its quiet corners, at the wish of Paul I and Maria Fiodorovna, the Monument to the Parents of the Empress shaped as a semi-rotunda pavilion was erected. While the Monument to the Parents reflects an elegiac mood, another commemorative structure, the Mausoleum, conveys the depth of Maria Fiodorovna's suffering after the assassination of her husband, Emperor Paul I.

The inscription on the pediment reads: *To My Spouse and Benefactor*. The architect Jean-François Thomas de Thomon and the sculptor Ivan Martos, contemporaries of the palatial coup, created an image of grief at the loss — not so much of the Emperor as of the beloved man, father and the head of the family, the first owner of the Pavlovsk palace-and-park complex. These feelings of solitude and mournful sorrow are expressed in the austere architecture of the ancient temple decorated with four monolithic columns, in the emphasized monumental volume of the cella, in the monotonous rustication of the walls and especially in the frieze. The allegorical masks of tragedy with closed eyes and frozen tears symbolize eternal laments about the victim of assassination and a mute reproach to those who broke human laws.

The banks of the Slavianka River are effectively emphasized by bridges. The Visconti Bridge is especially prominent for its expressive forms, its monumental vases and the beauty of its arched span.

The Pavilion "To My Spouse and Benefactor"

The Visconti Bridge

The Palace. View from the Slavianka River

Oranienbaum

The name of Oranienbaum (German for "orange-tree"), the estate of Alexander Menshikov, Peter the Great's companion-in-arms, stresses a private rather than formal character of the summer residence of the influential courtier. The earliest mention of the site goes back to the beginning of the eighteenth century when a Finnish-Swedish farmstead on the south shore of the Gulf of Finland near the estuary of the Karost River became Menshikov's property. In 1707 a construction of his country residence began on this site. Three years later the architect Giovanni Fontana began to erect a stone palace and to lay out a regular garden. He was replaced by Johann-Gottfried Schädel who supervised all the prince's architectural projects. From January 1725 to September 1727 the Oranienbaum residence glistened almost with a royal brilliance which corresponded to the position of Russia's "half-ruling sovereign". In 1743 Oranienbaum became the summer residence of Grand Duke Piotr Fiodorovich (the future Emperor Peter III) and his wife Yekaterina Alexeyevna (the future Empress Catherine the Great). Almost for ten years the construction at Oranienbaum was supervised by Rastrelli. In 1756 the owners entrusted Antonio Rinaldi with the architectural development of the residence. To satisfy the unusual tastes of Grand Duke Piotr Fiodorovich, he created the Peterstadt Fortress. In 1762–74 the architect united the Oranienbaum structures into a single ensemble for Catherine the Great. It included the Chinese Palace, the Coasting Hill with a pavilion and a park with numerous bridges and a variety of decorative structures. Happily not occupied during the War of 1941–45, Oranienbaum, unlike the other suburban residences of St Petersburg, has retained its original artistic appearance.

The Chinese Palace created by Rinaldi in 1762–68 is distinguished for the perfect finish and refined luxury of its interior decor. The symmetrical volumes of the palace contain the state rooms and halls fanciful in composition and absolutely individual in their artistic decoration (the Great Hall, the Hall of the Muses and the Great Chinese Study), as well as the drawing

←
The Chinese Palace. View from the pond

The Great Chinese Study

The Buglework Room

rooms and living apartments of Catherine the Great and her son Paul. The three state rooms of the palace are especially remarkable because the subjects of their ceiling paintings and the motifs of their parquet designs and fabric patterns were borrowed from Chinese art (hence the present-day name of the palace). Especially resplendent is the Great Chinese Study. Its walls are faced with wooden inlaid panels which include ivory plaques representing *chinoiserie* motifs. A veritable treasure of decorative art is the Buglework Room. Its walls are adorned with twelve panels embroi-

dered in silk against a beadwork background. The panels feature fantastical landscapes of tropical woods inhabited by birds and decorated with small bridges and pavilions.

The interiors of the palace appear as an entity thanks to its inlaid floors, painted ceilings and pictures produced by such well-known Italian artists as Stefano Torelli, Francesco Zugno, Francesco Zuccarelli, Gasparo Dizziani, Giacomo Cignarolli, Giuseppe and Serafino Barozzi, Jacopo Guarano, Giovanni-Battista Pittoni and Domenico Maggiotto.

*C*oasting hills, used to slide down in sledges in winter and in special cars in summer, were a popular entertainment in the eighteenth century. Nowadays only the pavilion created by Rinaldi survives from the Oranienbaum Coasting Hill. The largest interior of the pavilion is a round hall adorned with decorative moulding and painting. The unique floor is made of artificial marble with a fanciful painted ornament. The Porcelain Study is remarkable for its moulded decor which include the figurines of monkeys and birds supporting shelves with Meissen porcelain pieces.

The Coasting Hill Pavilion

The Round Hall of the Coasting Hill Pavilion

The Porcelain Study. Porcelain composition:
The Triumph of Venus. 1772–74

𝒯he remains of Peterstadt, or Peter's city, differ from other landmarks of the Oranienbaum complex by the unusual purpose for which it was constructed. It was a small fortress built in keeping with the latest achievements of eighteenth-century fortification. The toy fortress was provided with everything necessary for real military manoeuvres and for war games which were the favourite entertainment of its owner, at that time the heir to the throne, Grand Duke Piotr Fiodorovich. Nowadays only the Honourary Gate and the Palace of Peter III have survived from the structures designed by Rinaldi. Although the toy fortress was believed to have a defensive significance and was recorded in the War Ministry, the palace of the Commander-in-Chief of Peterstadt was marked by a sumptuous, distinctly state design of its interiors.

The walls of the Large Study or Picture Gallery, the most representative interior in the palace, were covered from top to bottom with sixty-three canvases by Western European artists of the seventeenth and eighteenth centuries, while the lower portions of the walls were decorated with lacquer panels showing painted scenes on fashionable Chinese subjects (imitated by the master craftsman Fiodor Vlasov). Peter III spent his last days as the Emperor, before he was dethroned by his mutinous wife, in this palace. Surrounded by the Holstein regiments, he was waiting for the fateful news from St Petersburg without taking any resolute measures to save his position.

The Palace of Peter III

The Palace of Peter III
The Large Study (the Picture Hall)

The Honourary Gate leading to Peterstadt

Gatchina

Gatchina, the name of both the town and the palace-and-park ensemble, dates back to distant times. It probably derives from the Russian expression *gat' chinit'*, that is "to repair a road with poles" or from the German *hat schöne*, "to be beautiful". In the late fifteenth century a Russian village already existed here, which in 1712, after the eventual annexation of the Izhora lands to Russia, the area was presented by Peter the Great to his sister, Tsarevna Natalia Alexeyevna. During the subsequent years Gatchina had different owners. In 1765 Catherine the Great bought Gatchina for the state and presented it to her favourite Count Grigory Orlov, as a reward for his major role in the palatial coup of 1762. Orlov possessed Gatchina from 1766 to 1783. During this period Antonio Rinaldi put up a palace for him, laid out a park and decorated it with obelisks and monuments in honour of the Orlovs' deeds. In 1783 Catherine the Great presented Gatchina to her son, Grand Duke Pavel Petrovich and his consort. For thirty years Gatchina was the grand-ducal estate and in 1796–1801 it became the Imperial residence. During these years Vincenzo Brenna redecorated the palace and put up a number of new structures, such as the Eagle and Venus Pavilions, the portal of the Birch House and the Connetable Obelisk. In the late eighteenth and early nineteenth centuries active in Gatchina were Vasily Bazhenov, Nikolai Lvov and Andreyan Zakharov, who completed this grand ensemble of the eighteenth and nineteenth centuries.

←
The Gatchina Palace and the Parade Ground

The White Dining Room

The Anteroom

$\mathcal{T}$he Gatchina Palace originally was a hunting lodge of Grigory Orlov, a favourite of Catherine the Great. Later it became a residence of the Russian Emperors Paul I, Nicholas I, Alexander II and Alexander III. It is remarkable not only as a work of art, but also as a witness to many most important historical events, political and intimate secrets of the royal family. The palace-castle was erected on the ridge of a hill. Its north front is oriented towards the tract of greenery which skirts the mirror-like lakes and stretches to the foot of the slope. The south front is opened up to the parade ground intended for the guard mounting and exemplary military exercises. Alongside the outer border of the parade ground runs a low bastion war or parapet pierced with embrasures for cannons. The ditch around the palace emphasizes its resemblance to a castle. The volume of the palace is marked by a clear-cut silhouette and is accentuated by the pentagonal five-tiered Guard and Signal Towers. Faced with plaques and blocks of greyish-silvery and golden Pudost stone, the palace seems to be enveloped in a light haze enhancing a romantic aura of the entire edifice.

Three basic periods are clearly traced in the architectural history of the Gatchina Palace: 1765–81 — the construction and decoration of the castle for Orlov to Rinaldi's designs; the 1790s — minor alterations to Brenna's drawings in the volumes of the lateral sections and redesigning of the state interiors for Paul I and his wife; 1845–56 — the period when the architect Roman Kuzmin added the new square wings where the apartments of Nicholas I and members of his family and the premises of the court services were located.

The state apartments of the Gatchina Palace were located in the central block on the first floor. They were badly damaged during the Second World War. Some of them have been reconstructed and are open for visitors. The Marble (Dining) Hall created by Brenna attracts by its sense of space, this effect being enhanced by the white artificial marble used in the decor of the walls and the sixteen fluted marble columns.

The Anteroom (Reception Room) leads to the State Suite which is notable for a restrained plastic decor. The decoration of the Anteroom has retained some elements of the original design made by Antonio Rinaldi for Count Orlov — the painted ceiling, the moulded ornaments and the inlaid parquet floor with its pattern resembling an openwork flower.

The Throne Room of Paul I was arranged in the former study of Count Orlov. Brenna gave this small interior a grand appearance adorning it with stately details. First of all, the throne was installed on a special pediment in the pier between the windows. The walls were lined with picturesque eighteenth-century tapestries. The ceiling of the Throne Room was embellished with bands and geometric insets of classical ornamentation, their relief decoration being stressed by three-dimensional gilding. Redesigning the study into the Throne Room, Brenna paid particular attention to the ancient Roman military symbols — he added to the decor the single-headed eagle with which

The Throne Room of Paul I

*The Throne Room
of Empress Maria Fiodorovna*

The Crimson Drawing Room

The Throne of Emperor Alexander III

the standards of the Roman legions were crowned. Brenna deliberately made the doors and overdoor decorations sumptuous and imposing. Having retained Rinaldi's parquet floor, the architect perfectly solved the complex compositional problem.

In keeping with the etiquette of the royal court, Empress Maria Fiodorovna had her own Throne Room in the suite of her private apartments. Its walls were lined with crimson cloth and decorated with paintings selected so as to suit the principle of symmetry. Similarly to the other state rooms, Brenna adorned the doors, window surrounds and overdoor decorative panels of Maria Fiodorovna's Throne Room with an exquisite luxury. The major decorative feature of this Throne Room is the marble fireplace adorned with relief insets featuring ancient images. One of the most sumptuous interiors in the Gatchina Palace is the Crimson Drawing Room. Brenna embellished its walls with tapestries executed at the French Royal Manufacture in 1776–1780s. The tapestries were diplomatic presents to Grand Duke Pavel Petrovich and his consort during their visit to Paris in 1782. The tapestries show scenes illustrating episodes from the novel *Don Quixote* by Cervantes (*Ladies Attending the Knight*). The colour range and ornamental patterns of the tapestries were matched by the gilded moulding of the ceiling and especially by the decor of the door panels and painted overdoor decorations.

The last crowned owner of Gatchina was Emperor Alexander III. "The Gatchina recluse" — this is how the father of the last Russian monarch was nicknamed for his love to the romantic Gatchina scenery. Now visitors to the palace can see the gilded throne of Alexander III which reminds them about the dramatic history of the Gatchina Palace. Gatchina had not lost the significance of the main Imperial summer residence until the end of the nineteenth century.

The White Hall

The State Bedroom
Ceiling Painting: **The Wedding of Psyche**
By Gabriel François Doyen
Late 18th century

𝒯he White Hall situated in the central part of the palace charms visitors by its sense of space. Its five huge semicircular French windows lead to the balcony which affords a splendid view of the Parade Ground that served as the venue for a picturesque ceremony of guard mounting. The hall owes its name to the colour scheme of its walls. Brenna put the main plastic emphasis in his design of the hall on thirty-two Corinthian pilasters. The ceiling of the White Hall is accentuated by the painted scene produced by Gabriel-François Doyen. It matches the beautiful inlaid parquet floor executed to drawings by Rinaldi and left intact by Brenna during his redecoration of the White Hall in the late eighteenth century. Worthy of especial interest is the collection of ancient sculpture and the bas-reliefs by well-known sculptors of the seventeenth and the first half of the eighteenth centuries.

The White Hall served as a fine setting for palatial balls, festivals and the "state entries of the Imperial family", during which sumptuous garments of court ladies, gentlemen and guards officers glistened against the exquisite architecture.

The Gatchina Park has been laid out around several lakes which occupy a third part of its area. It was created in 1766–83 after Rinaldi's drawings and completed in 1783–1800 under the supervision of Brenna. The composition of the palatial park consists of a number of gardens, both regular and land-scaped ones, each of which has an artistic solution of its own. A large portion of the park is taken by the English-style garden laid out around the White and Silver Lakes. The combination of the smooth water surface, the vivid play of light and the reflections of the beautiful bank landscapes animated by the silhouettes of the palace, pavilions and smaller structures; all adds a musical quality to the atmosphere reigning the park, which has been defined as a "symphony of the North". All kinds of bridges, gates and pavilions are set into the scenery of the park, but worthy of particular note are some of them which remind of the great accomplishments of the Orlov brothers, children of an officer of Peter's army, who became famous during the reign of Catherine the Great. The Eagle (or Temple) Pavilion put up in 1792 on the bank of the so-called Long Island is one of these structures. It was surmounted with the figure of a crowned eagle. The royal bird was supposed to symbolize the Orlov family (their surname derives from the Russian word for "eagle"), an allegory of their high predestination. The Chesme Obelisk erected after drawings by Rinaldi is a memorial in honour of the victory of the Russian fleet under the command of Count Alexey Orlov-Chesmensky.

The Eagle (Temple) Pavilion

The Prior's Palace. 1799. Architect Nikolai Lvov. View from the White Lake

The Chesme Obelisk

Text by Grigory Yar
Translated from the Russian by Valery Fateyev
Designed by Yevgeny Gavrilov
Art editor Nikolai Kutovoi. Cover design by Denis Lazarev
Editor-in-Chief Sergei Vesnin. Edited by Maria Lyzhenkova
Computer layout by Yelena Morozova
Colour correction by Liubov Kornilova
Photographs by Valentin Baranovsky, Valery Barnev, Leonid Bogdanov, Vladimir Davydov, Pavel Demidov,
Vladimir Denisov, Konstantin Doka, Natalia Doka, Vladimir Dorokhov, Alexander Gronsky, Artur Kirakozov,
Boris Manushin, Vladimir Melnikov, Yury Molodkovets, Sergei Podmetin, Victor Savik, Georgy Shablovsky,
Vladimir Shlakan, Yevgeny Siniaver, Oleg Trubsky, Vladimir Vdovin, Vasily Vorontsov, Vadim Yegorovsky

ISBN 5-93893-121-5 (Softcover edition)
ISBN 5-900530-97-3 (Hardcover edition)

Ivan Fiodorov Printing Company, St Petersburg (No 1960)
Printed and bound in Russia

Safety Standards
and
Infection Control
for
Dental Assistants

Ellen Dietz, CDA, AAS, BS

DELMAR

THOMSON LEARNING™

Australia Canada Mexico Singapore Spain United Kingdom United States

Safety Standards and Infection Control for Dental Assistants
by Ellen Dietz, CDA, AAS, BS

Health Care Publishing Director:
William Brottmiller

Editorial Assistant:
Matthew Thouin

Production Editor:
Mary Colleen Liburdi

Executive Editor:
Cathy L. Esperti

Executive Marketing Manager:
Dawn F. Gerrain

Cover Design:
William Finnerty

Developmental Editor:
Marah E. Bellegarde

Channel Manager:
Jennifer McAvey

Library of Congress Cataloging-in-Publication Data

Dietz, Ellen Roberta.
    Safety standards and infection control for dental assistants / Ellen Dietz.
          p. cm
    Includes bibliographical references and index.
      ISBN 0-7668-2659-7
      1. Dental offices—Sanitation. 2. Dental assistants. 3. Dentistry—Safety measures. 4. Communicable diseases—Prevention. 5. Asepsis and antisepsis. I. Title.
      [DNLM: 1. Infection Control, Dental—methods. 2. Dental Assitants. 3. Emergencies. 4. Safety Management. WU 29 D566s 2002]
      RK52.D54 2002
      614.4'8'0246176—dc21
                                        2001053763

NOTICE TO THE READER

Publisher does not warrant or guarantee any of the products described herein or perform any independent analysis in connection with any of the product information contained herein. Publisher does not assume, and expressly dis-claims, any obligation to obtain and include information other than that provided to it by the manufacturer.

The reader is expressly warned to consider and adopt all safety precautions that might be indicated by the activities herein and to avoid all potential hazards. By following the instructions contained herein, the reader willingly assumes all risks in connection with such instructions.

The Publisher makes no representation or warranties of any kind, including but not limited to, the warranties of fitness for particular purpose or merchantability, nor are any such representations implied with respect to the material set forth herein, and the publisher takes no responsibility with respect to such material. The publisher shall not be liable for any special, consequential, or exemplary damages resulting, in whole or part, from the read-ers' use of, or reliance upon, this material.

Dedication

It is with deep appreciation that this text is dedicated to the friends and employees of Banner Health Arizona for their sustained support, encouragement, and enthusiasm—and for their periodic cheery inquiries such as, "Hey, how's the book coming?"

As a token of appreciation, a portion of the proceeds from *Safety Standards and Infection Control for Dental Assistants* will be donated to Las Fuentes Health Clinic of Guadelupe, Arizona. Las Fuentes is a nonprofit corporation that provides at cost or gratis medical and dental care to lower-income families, many of whom are members of the Yaqui Indian tribe or of Hispanic heritage.

Contents

CHAPTER 4 Legal and Ethical Considerations of Infection Control. 53

SECTION II National Guidelines, Recommendations, and Regulations Affecting Dental Practice   71

CHAPTER 5 Regulatory Government Agencies and National Associations. 73

SECTION IV   Environmental Health and Safety (Hazard Communication) in the Dental Office   183

CHAPTER 12   Hazard Communication 185

CHAPTER 13   Waterline Biofilms 211

Foreword

Infection control is a difficult discipline for the dental profession. Part of the problem centers around the fact that infection control is the newest of dental disciplines. While sterilization, a term traditionally used to describe quickly cleaning instruments and then immersing them in a cold sterilant, has been taught in dental schools and dental auxiliary schools for a number of decades, the process of protecting patients, dentists, and staff members from cross-contamination with infectious microbes has been taught seriously only in about the past 15 years. The instructors had to be taught first, and that process delayed the transfer of this vital information for several years.

Many people reading this text may rightfully question why it took so long to acknowledge that dentistry was an important link in the patient-professional-staff chain of cross-infection. The answer lies mostly in the fact that dentistry deals with hidden, quiet diseases that infect people without a traceable source of the infection. One need only study the history of the hepatitis B virus (HBV) and the number of people in the dental profession who died or were seriously compromised from the infection with HBV before healthcare professionals acknowledged that this deadly microbe could be transmitted through dental practices. Simply stated, true dental infection control was just not a great concern in most dental practices until one dramatic event demonstrated that patients, dentists, assistants, and hygienists, as well as others related to dentistry, could be targets of deadly microbes. Of course, the catalyst changing the way dentistry looked at infectious diseases challenges was the human immunodeficiency virus (HIV), the causative agent of the deadly disease known as AIDS (acquired immunodeficiency syndrome).

While we now know that HIV existed for a number of years, probably a number of decades, before its identification in the early 1980s, healthcare professionals continued to resist changing their traditional sterilization techniques until the occurrence of two significant events: (1) the Occupational Safety and Health Organization (OSHA) began examining infection control procedures and regulating the use thereof, and (2) a dentist in Florida (Dr. David Acer) was accused of infecting one of his patients (Kimberly Bergalis) with AIDS, presumably transmitted during a routine dental procedure. The result of these catalysts is well known. Dentistry began seriously changing its ways by adopting universal precautions, well-proven infection control procedures that had been developed through decades of study by a few dedicated researchers and teachers of the new discipline, dental infection control. In the short span of about one decade, dentistry seriously accepted the challenge to interrupt the chain of cross-infection through dental practice. The response was quick and effective, and dental professionals can be proud of the way they have responded to the challenge.

Infection control is now an accepted discipline in the dental office, and if the universal precautions are relatively well understood and efficiently practiced, why is another text on the discipline needed? Simply, infection control is an evolving, ever-changing discipline that must be continually reviewed and updated. The importance of infection control will not diminish in the predictable future. One need only read the headlines periodically displayed in newspapers and transmitted on television about emerging new diseases to understand that dental infection control challenges will increase and the profession must continually be alert to new discoveries and more efficient ways to refine the application of the basic universal precautions.

In all instances, the dental assistant must be a vital contributor to the success of an infection control program. Many dental assistants are currently serving as infection control coordinators or office safety supervisors, and overwhelmingly dental assistants are responsible for ensuring that infection control procedures are carefully observed. While all members of the dental team must contribute to the success of an infection control program, dental assistants are almost always universally assigned special tasks without which a comprehensive infection control program will not succeed. This additional responsibility requires dental assistants to be trained in all facets of infection control. Dental assisting should be considered a professional, specialized career, thus dental assistants must recognize the importance of their position as a valued member of a dental team delivering efficient and safe healthcare to patients.

The author of this text, Ellen Dietz, has long contributed to the refinement of infection control procedures in dentistry. Ellen is one of a select few dental auxiliaries who, early on, accepted the challenge of helping dentistry cope with the monumental challenge of changing the way infection control procedures were perceived and practiced. Ellen has been a key participant in helping dentistry accept, comprehend, and practice universal precautions. She has the education and experience to communicate this most important discipline, and she has the communication skills to transfer the information accurately.

I have followed Ellen's career for a number of years, and I have been privileged to work with her on several important infection control projects. Ellen is not a recent recruit to the war against infectious microbes. She was there through the planning and learning phases of dental infection control, and her experience is evident through the information transmitted in this text. Readers will benefit through the acceptance and application of the infection control principles defined and presented in the following pages.

R. R. Runnells, DDS
Former Director of Dental Infection Control
University of Utah Medical School

Preface

This book reflects the culmination of federally mandated sweeping changes in infection control and disease containment that have had a significant impact on dentistry during the past decade. Because the dental assistant is the team member most likely to assume responsibility for infection control measures, students enrolled in accredited dental assisting programs must receive instruction in infection control and environmental health and safety (also called hazard communication). As such, it is the goal of the dental team and a prime responsibility of the dental assistant to reduce cross-contamination—from patient to patient, from patient to dental team members, from dental team members to other patients, and from dental practice to community.

Safety Standards and Infection Control for Dental Assistants can also be used as a refresher or reference for dental assistants employed in private practice and for those sourcing a review book to prepare for the national Infection Control Exam administered by the Dental Assisting National Board (DANB).

Instructors and students are encouraged to refer to *Appendix A: DANB Infection Control Task Analysis (ICE) Requirements Cross-Referenced by Chapter* at the back of the text to find an interpretation of the DANB *Task Analysis* requirements current at the time of publication. This appendix contains two grids: (1) Correlation from our book to ICE *Task Analysis* and (2) Correlation from ICE *Task Analysis* to our book. Candidates for the national Infection Control Examination are encouraged to contact DANB periodically to inquire about updates or changes in the requirements. To obtain a copy of the current task analysis, contact DANB at 800-FOR-DANB. Appendix B contains a summary of OSHA's Bloodborne/Hazardous Materials Standard.

ORGANIZATION AND FEATURES

For ease of instruction and learning, *Safety Standards and Infection Control for Dental Assistants* is broken down into five major sections, according to their relevance to the dental assistant's role in infectious disease prevention in the dental practice. These include the following:

1. Microbiology and Disease Prevention Specific to Dentistry
2. National Guidelines, Recommendations, and Regulations Affecting Dental Practice
3. Infection Control Techniques in the Dental Office
4. Environmental Health and Safety (Hazard Communication) in the Dental Office
5. Office Communications Regarding Infection Control

Features include the following:

- *Learning Objectives* are listed at the beginning of every chapter and set the stage for what will be discussed in the chapter. We encourage the reader to go back and review the objectives after reading the chapter to ensure that the important concepts are understood.
- *Key Terms* are bolded and defined with the text. These words are all listed in the comprehensive glossary at the end of the book.
- *Skills Mastery Assessment* questions at the end of each chapter are invaluable in helping students assess their comprehension and retention of the material.
- Numerous hands-on procedures are outlined in *Procedures into Practice* boxes designed to help students put into practice the information and techniques they have learned in the chapter.
- Specific icons are also used throughout the book indicating clinical attire, protective eyewear and mask, handwashing, and protective gloves.

- To facilitate learning and putting into practice the concepts introduced herein, many useful tables, forms, and figures have been included.

The need for sound infection control practices in dentistry has never been more important. In a world in which emerging diseases are becoming commonplace, the need for continually updated information on disease prevention is essential for the new millennium.

We wish you every success in your pursuit of learning more about *Safety Standards and Infection Control for Dental Assistants* and welcome feedback from instructors and students.

Note

Completion of the content herein, including but not limited to the chapter material, *Skills Mastery Assessment, and Skill Building for Success: Student Activities,* does not imply a guarantee of successful completion or a passing score on the DANB Infection Control Exam.

INSTRUCTOR RESOURCE

Instructor's Manual to Accompany Safety Standards and Infection Control for Dental Assistants

ISBN #0766844862

The instructor's manual has been designed to assist the instructor in facilitating classroom, laboratory, and clinical exercises. It contains Skill-Building Student Exercises for every chapter. These exercises provide practical activities that involve critical thinking, research, exploratory contacts outside the classroom, and implementation of projects.

The instructor's manual also includes the answer key to the Skills Mastery Assessment exercises in the book.

About the Author

Ellen Dietz has enjoyed a successful 30-year dental career, beginning as an associate-degreed CDA (a graduate of Dutchess County Community College, Poughkeepsie, New York) and continuing in private practice. After working as a chairside assistant and office manager, she returned to college and earned her Bachelor of Science Degree in Allied Health Education in Dental Auxiliary Utilization and a Community College Teaching Certificate from the State University of New York at Buffalo.

Following a combined 7-year dental assisting teaching career at Orange County Community College, Middletown, New York; the University of North Carolina at Chapel Hill, Chapel Hill, North Carolina; Erie County BOCES, Buffalo, New York; and Niagara County Community College, Sanborn, New York, she began to pursue her true love, writing about dentistry.

Ellen initially accepted the Front Desk Column of *Dental Assisting Magazine* and one year later took over the managing editor post. In the following years, she worked in dental marketing, project management, and product development at Semantodontics (SmartPractice/SmartHealth) and as editor of *PracticeSmart Newsletter;* she also worked in legal administration for the Arizona State Board of Dental Examiners.

Ellen has published eight books in the dental assisting field, including *Delmar's Dental Office Management, Delmar's Dental Assisting Curriculum Guide,* and *Lesson Plans for the Dental Assistant,* and was a contributing author to *The Dental Assistant.* She is a member of the Organization for Safety and Asepsis Procedures (OSAP) and has been a speaker and keynote speaker at American Dental Assistants Association (ADAA) Annual Sessions.

Ellen has authored numerous accredited continuing dental education home study programs and is editor of *The Explorer,* published by the National Association of Dental Assistants in Falls Church, Virginia. Her articles have appeared in *The Dental Assistant: Journal of the American Dental Assistants Association, Dental Assisting, DENTIST, The Dental Student, Dental Economics, RDH Magazine, CONTACT,* and *Dental Teamwork Magazine.*

Ellen is also founder and executive director of Toothbrushes for Tomorrow, a nonprofit organization dedicated to the principle that no child should be without a toothbrush.

Ellen is a native of upstate New York, where her family has continuously inhabited Meadow Falls Farm for seven generations. She currently resides in Mesa, Arizona, where she runs a successful licensed business.

Acknowledgments

Many wonderful people have contributed their time and talents in making *Safety Standards and Infection Control for Dental Assistants* possible. Appreciation is extended to Dr. Robert R. Runnells, former Director of Dental Infection Control at the University of Utah Medical School, for his many years of dedication and devotion to the field of infection control and also for his patience, kindness, and willingness to share his knowledge with others through teaching and professional speaking. Heartfelt thanks deservedly go to Katherine Green of Tempe, Arizona, and to Virginia S. Helms, CDA, EFDA, of Albuquerque, New Mexico, for their support, encouragement, and many hours of proofreading and also to Ralph Richardson of Mesa, Arizona, for continued technical support, patience, and computer wisdom.

Thanks are also extended to the dedicated staff of Delmar Thomson Learning, including editors, administrative support people, sales and marketing representatives, and graphic designers.

And finally, thanks are due to the academic reviewers who have given of their experience and wisdom in reviewing chapters and providing valuable feedback.

Beatriz Blackford, RDA
RDA/Dental Instructor
American Career College
Los Angeles, CA

Lori Burch
Dental Assisting Program Chairperson
Bryman College
Reseda, CA

Robin Caplan, CDA
Dental Assistant Program Administrator
Medix School
Towson, MD

Darlene Hunziker, CDA, CDPMA
Lead Dental Assisting Instructor
Eton Technical Institute
Everett, WA

Linda Kay Hughes, RDA, NRDA
Owner/Educator
Excelle College
San Diego, CA

Betty Scott, CDA, CPMDA, AAS
Associate Professor
Dental Assisting Department
East Central College
Union, MO

Sheila Semler, RDH, MS, PhD Candidate
Director of Dental Programs
San Juan College
Farmington, NM

Kathy Tozzi, CLPN, RMA, AHI
Director of Education
Cleveland Institute for Dental-Medical Assistants
Mentor, OH

Kris Tupper, BS, CDA
Interim Program Coordinator of Dental Assisting
Lane Community College
Eugene, OR

Microbiology and Disease Prevention Specific to Dentistry

Introduction to Microbiology

LEARNING OBJECTIVES

Upon completion of this chapter, the student should be able to:

1. Describe the importance of infection control in the dental office.
2. List the routes of infection, the components in the chain of infection, and ways to prevent the spread of infection.
3. Describe how microorganisms cause disease, the types of infections, the stages of infectious disease, and the function of the immune system.
4. List and describe commonly occurring bloodborne pathogens, including hepatitis, tuberculosis, herpesvirus, HIV, and AIDS, and why they are of concern to the clinical dental assistant.

THE IMPORTANCE OF INFECTION CONTROL IN THE DENTAL OFFICE

Infection control is a primary means of disease containment in all health-care settings, including the dental office. The dental assistant who has an understanding of the disease transmission process and how to contain it can play a key role in reducing the number of potentially infectious **microorganisms** (those living things too small to be seen by the naked eye).

Microbiology is the study of microorganisms, also called microbes. Many microorganisms are useful in everyday life and are the source of medicines—penicillin is derived from mold, for example. Disease-causing microorganisms, however, may be harmful and are called **pathogens**. For a disease to be transmitted, there must be a **susceptible host**, that is, an individual who may become infected as a result of some form of transmission.

Maintaining Aseptic Technique

Crucial in infection control is maintaining **aseptic technique**, which means employing all forms of washing, sanitizing, disinfecting, and sterilizing of items that come into contact with patients to reduce the likelihood of infection with a contaminant or disease. This requires that the dental assistant use specific practices and procedures to reduce the number of viable pathogens present; it also requires firsthand knowledge of the disease transmission process and how to prevent it.

Members of the Dental Team Responsible for Infection Control

All members of the dental team, including the chairside assistant, hygienist, and dentist, are responsible for maintaining proper infection control techniques. Front desk team members, such as the receptionist, office manager, or insurance claims assistant, should also be aware of and properly trained in sound infection control and disease management principles.

It must be noted that the dentist is ultimately responsible for introducing, maintaining, updating, and managing all training and records associated with staff training; however, this duty may be delegated to another member of the dental team. Often, this person is a safety supervisor. For additional information on staff training, refer to *Chapter 6: Dental Office Safety Supervisor.*

THE SIX COMPONENTS IN THE CHAIN OF INFECTION CONTROL

Several steps are necessary for infectious diseases to spread. These required steps are known as the "chain of infection" (Figure 1–1). Each step in the infectious disease process must happen for the spread of infection to occur.

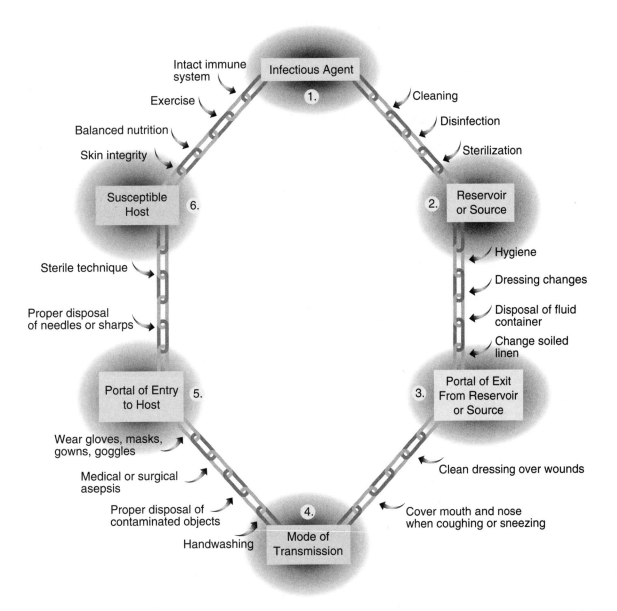

FIGURE 1–1

The chain of infection: Preventive measures follow each link of the chain. *(Adapted from* Fundamentals of Nursing: Standards and Practice, *by S. DeLaune and P. Ladner, 1998, Albany, NY: Delmar)*

Infection control is based upon the principle that transmission of infectious diseases will be prevented when any of the steps in the chain are broken or interrupted. The six components in the chain of infection include the infectious agent, a reservoir, a portal of exit, a means of transmission, a portal of entry, and a susceptible host.

Infectious Agents

The first component in the chain of infection consists of **infectious agents** (pathogenic microorganisms or pathogens), which are further broken down into five classifications: viruses, bacteria, fungi, protozoa, and rickettsia. For an infection to occur, an infectious agent must be present. Each microorganism is addressed here.

Viruses. A virus (Figure 1–2) is the smallest infectious microorganism, measuring the size of one one-hundredth of a single bacterium. Viruses can be seen only under an electron microscope. They require a living cell to reproduce and thus must live inside a host cell to multiply. Because viruses live inside cells, they are protected against many chemical disinfecting agents; however, they are susceptible to heat.

To survive, viruses have the ability to change specific characteristics to remain resistant to efforts to limit their growth. The challenge in preventing infection caused by viruses is to find a way to kill, rather than simply reduce, viral agents.

Viruses are most commonly spread from one person to another by blood and other body secretions such as mucus or saliva.

Most viruses can be killed using disinfectants or sterilization. The hepatitis B virus, however, is especially difficult to control. Diseases caused by viruses include hepatitis B, AIDS, measles, mumps, rubella, poliomyelitis, chickenpox, herpes, warts, the common cold, and influenza. While antibiotics are usually effective against bacterial infections, they have no effect upon viral infections.

Bacteria. Bacteria are single-celled microorganisms that contain no chlorophyll and live inside tissues rather than in specific cells of the body. They can be identified by characteristic shapes, and they can also be grouped according to their ability to accept staining agents in the medical laboratory. Bacteria that are gram-negative stain red under a microscope; gram-positive bacteria stain purple.

FIGURE 1–2
Viruses are so small they can be seen only under an electron microscope. *(From Delmar's Dental Assisting: A Comprehensive Approach, by D. J. Phinney and J. H. Halstead, 2000, Albany, NY: Delmar)*

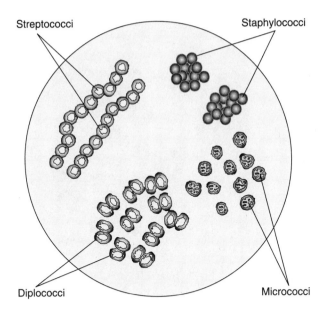

FIGURE 1–3
Cocci are round. *(From Diversified Health Occupations, by L. Simmers, 2001, Albany, NY: Delmar)*

Bacteria that do not accept stain are called **spores,** which are bacteria with an outer covering that protects them from many chemical disinfectants and higher levels of heat sterilization.

Bacteria can further be classified by their shapes. Cocci are round (Figure 1–3), bacilli are rod shaped (Figure 1–4), spirilla are spiral shaped (Figure 1–5), and vibrios are curved (Figure 1–6).

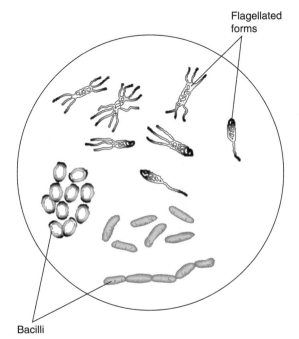

FIGURE 1–4
Bacilli are rod shaped. *(From Diversified Health Occupations, by L. Simmers, 2001, Albany, NY: Delmar)*

FIGURE 1–5

Spirilla are spiral shaped. *(From* Diversified Health Occupations, *by L. Simmers, 2001, Albany, NY: Delmar)*

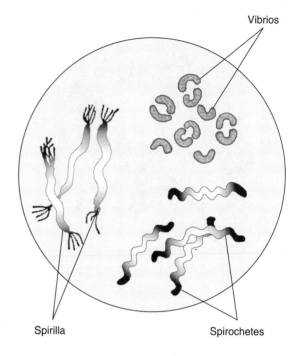

Not all bacteria are pathogenic, or disease causing. Many bacteria live on the skin and mucous membranes of the human body. Nonpathogenic bacteria use nutrients and occupy space, thus competing with pathogenic bacteria. A reduction of nonpathogenic bacteria may present an opportunity for pathogenic bacteria to grow and cause disease. One of the ways nonpathogenic microorganisms are reduced is with anti-infective drugs such as antibiotics. Pathogenic bacteria are listed in Table 1–1.

Different bacteria have different needs for oxygen to survive. *Aerobic bacteria* need oxygen to grow and live; most bacteria are aerobic. *Anaerobic bacteria* are destroyed in the presence of oxygen and live only in the absence of it. *Facultative anaerobic bacteria* grow with or without oxygen.

Bacteria reproduce in colonies, pairs, clusters, or chains (Figure 1–7). Examples of diseases caused by bacteria include tuberculosis, diphtheria, pertussis, tetanus, strep throat, and staphylococcal infections. Many infections can be safely and effectively treated with antibiotics. Overuse of antibiotics in some individuals has caused resistance to treating certain infections.

Vibrios (curved)

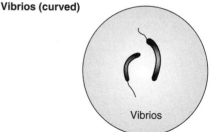

FIGURE 1–6

Vibrios are curved. *(From* Delmar's Dental Assisting: A Comprehensive Approach, *by D. J. Phinney and J. H. Halstead, 2000, Albany, NY: Delmar)*

TABLE 1-1

PATHOGENIC BACTERIAL INFECTIOUS DISEASES

Disease	Infectious Agent	Mode of Transmission
Botulism	Clostridium botulinum	Ingestion
Chlamydia	Chlamydia trachomatis	Sexual contact
Clostridial myonecrosis (Gas gangrene)	Species of gram-positive clostridia	Wound entry
Gonorrhea	Neisseria gonorrhoeae	Sexual contact
Legionnaires' disease	Legionella pneumophila	Inhalation
Meningococcal meningitis	N. Meningitidis, S. Pneumoniae, or H. Influenzae	Direct contact, inhalation
Nosocomial (hospital acquired) infection	Gram-negative bacteria	Normal flora transmitted during illness/procedures; opportunistic pathogens transmit during debilitated condition
Pulmonary tuberculosis	Mycobacterium tuberculosis	Inhalation
Salmonellosis	Salmonella	Ingestion
Shigellosis (bacillary dysentery)	Shigellae	Fecal-oral
Staphylococcal infection	Staphylococci	Direct contact, ingestion, inhalation, bloodborne, vectors (animals)
Streptococcal infection	Hemolytic streptococci (usually beta-hemolytic group A)	Inhalation
Syphilis	Treponema pallidum	Sexual contact
Tetanus (lockjaw)	Clostridium tetani	Wound entry
Typhoid fever	Salmonella typhi	Fecal-oral

From *Delmar's Clinical Medical Assisting,* by W. Q. Lindh, M. S. Pooler, C. D. Tamparo, and J. U. Cerrato, 1998, Albany, NY: Delmar. Copyright 1998 by Delmar.

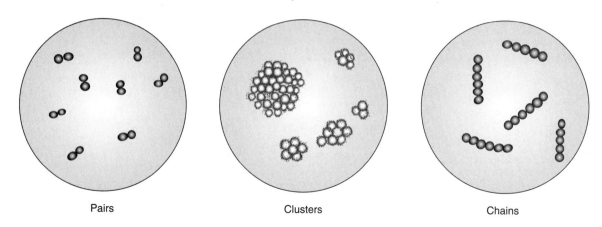

Pairs　　　　Clusters　　　　Chains

FIGURE 1–7
Bacteria reproduce in colonies, pairs, clusters, or chains. *(From* Delmar's Dental Assisting: A Comprehensive Approach, *by D. J. Phinney and J. H. Halstead, 2000, Albany, NY: Delmar)*

Fungi (Yeasts and Molds). Fungi (Figure 1–8) appear smaller than protozoa but larger than bacteria and lack chlorophyll (green pigment). These microorganisms include common yeast used in bread baking and members of the mushroom family. Blue-green mold that forms on bread or cheese is a common example of fungi. Some fungi are sporulating, meaning they reproduce by budding or forming spores, which are more difficult for heat and chemicals to penetrate. Like viruses, fungi cannot be killed by antibiotics.

Common examples of diseases caused by yeasts and molds include *candidiasis*, which is a fungal infection of the oral mucosa caused by the fungus *Candida albicans*. It may also be called thrush or moniliasis (Figure 1–9).

FIGURE 1–8
Fungi appear smaller than protozoa but larger than bacteria and lack chlorophyll. *(From* Delmar's Dental Assisting: A Comprehensive Approach, *by D. J. Phinney and J. H. Halstead, 2000, Albany, NY: Delmar)*

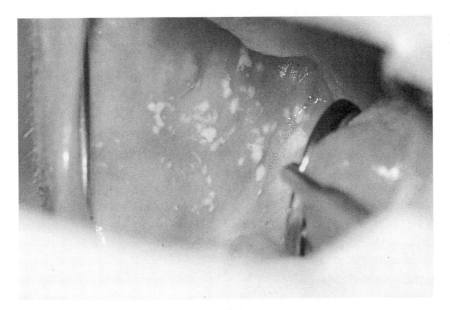

FIGURE 1–9
A patient presenting with thrush. *(Courtesy of Joseph L. Konzelman Jr., DDS)*

This infection appears as thick white or cream yellow (cottage-cheese-like) raised patches, which may become irritated and cause discomfort to the infected patient. The prescribed treatment is antifungal agents.

Tinea designates a group of common fungi that cause other infections such as athlete's foot *(tinea pedis)*, which presents as itching and cracking of the skin, especially between the toes. Ringworm *(tinea corporis)* appears circular with a raised edge in red on the body. These infections may also be treated with prescribed antifungal skin creams, lotions, ointments, or oral antifungals.

Protozoa. Protozoa are single-celled animals, often called amoeba. Protozoa reproduce by a process known as binary fission in which a transverse cell wall develops around the cell, the cell lengthens, and then it divides into two (mitosis).

Protozoa live in fluids in the bloodstream, the oral cavity, and the intestinal tract; they also live in stagnant ponds and polluted water. Some protozoa are sporulating; they engulf their food and change shape to achieve mobility (Figure 1–10). Many protozoa have flagella, which are small tail-like projections that help them move. Some protozoa contain chlorophyll; most protozoa are aerobic.

Examples of pathogenic protozoa include *amebic dysentery,* occurring most often in Third World countries where the public drinking water supply is contaminated; periodontal disease in which protozoa live in the plaque that forms inside periodontal pockets; and malaria and sleeping sickness. Malaria is transmitted by the bite of an infected mosquito; sleeping sickness is spread by bites of the tsetse fly.

Rickettsiae. Rickettsiae are similar to tiny bacteria in appearance (Figure 1–11). These pathogenic microorganisms are parasites, which means they cannot live outside a host. Lice, ticks, fleas, roaches, rats, and mites commonly act

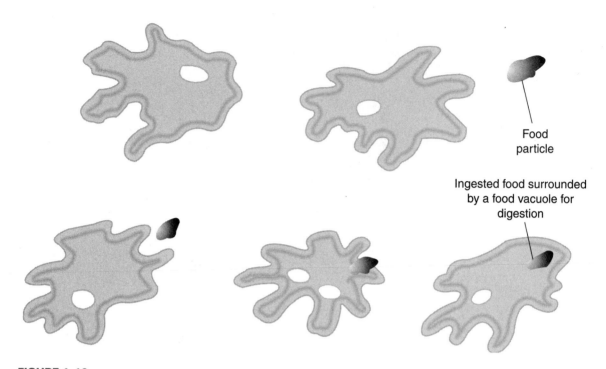

FIGURE 1–10

Protozoa engulf their food and change shape to achieve mobility. *(From Delmar's Dental Assisting: A Comprehensive Approach, by D. J. Phinney and J. H. Halstead, 2000, Albany, NY: Delmar)*

as hosts to rickettsiae. They multiply only by invading the cells of another living thing; it is the host that then transmits the disease to a human.

Diseases caused by rickettsiae include *Rocky Mountain spotted fever* and *typhus,* both of which are rare, especially in the western United States.

Reservoir

The second component in the chain of infection is the **reservoir,** which is the location of the infectious agent. A reservoir can be an individual, equipment, supplies, food, water, animals, or insects (the latter of which are

FIGURE 1–11

Rickettsiae are pathogenic microorganisms that are also parasites. *(From Delmar's Dental Assisting: A Comprehensive Approach, by D. J. Phinney and J. H. Halstead, 2000, Albany, NY: Delmar)*

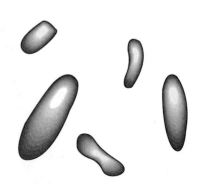

called *vectors*). Ways the dental assistant can reduce cross-contamination in the reservoir include handwashing, environmental and occupational hygiene, disinfection, sterilization, continued employee training, and keeping current with personal immunizations.

Portal of Exit

The third component in the chain of infection is the **portal** (meaning doorway) **of exit**. An infectious agent must leave the reservoir to infect another person. It does this by using a portal of exit such as through normally occurring body fluids, including excretions, secretions, skin cells, respiratory droplets, blood, and saliva.

The portal of exit may be continuous, as with respiratory droplets for example, or it may be dependent upon the body fluid exiting the body under unusual circumstances, such as when blood is drawn for diagnostic purposes or during surgical procedures.

Steps the dental assistant can take to minimize cross-infection from the portal of exit include following universal precautions and covering the mouth when coughing or sneezing.

Means of Transmission

The fourth component in the chain of infection is **means of transmission**, or how diseases are spread. Diseases are spread through a variety of means, including the following:

- Direct contact: Transmission is by touching an infected individual.
- Airborne transmission: The pathogenic microorganism is inhaled into the susceptible host's respiratory system.
- Bloodborne transmission: Infected blood enters a susceptible host.
- Ingestion: Transmission is by eating a food, drinking a beverage, or taking a medication that is contaminated.
- Indirect contact: Viable pathogenic microorganisms are left on an inanimate object such as a light switch, faucet, toilet seat, doorknob, or countertop and transmitted to a susceptible host.

The dental assistant may reduce the risk of transmission of disease by following transmission-based precautions such as universal precautions, handwashing, sanitizing, disinfecting, and sterilizing contaminated instruments and related items.

Portal of Entry

The fifth component in the chain of infection is the **portal of entry**, which allows the infectious agent to enter and potentially infect another person or a susceptible host. Common areas of the body that act as portals of entry include broken skin; mucous membranes; and systems of the body exposed to the external environment, such as the gastrointestinal, respiratory, and reproductive systems.

Inhalation of airborne microorganisms allows pathogens to spread to the lungs and, in some instances, from the lungs into the bloodstream. Ingestion of contaminated water or food is a cause of gastrointestinal infectious diseases. Sexually transmitted diseases (STDs) are spread through vaginal, oral, or anal intercourse.

Methods of protection for the dental assistant include following universal precautions and using aseptic technique.

Susceptible Host

The sixth component in the chain of infection is a susceptible host, which means the individual is able to contract the pathogenic microorganism. The susceptible host is unable to resist the pathogen. Individuals who are infected with a disease, who show no outward symptoms, and who may be unaware that they have the disease are called *carriers*.

There are a number of causes of susceptibility, including the presence of other diseases, immunosuppression (weakened immune system), surgical procedures, absence of immunity to the specific microorganism, or trauma (injury).

The susceptibility of the host depends upon several factors, which include the following:

- The number and specific type(s) of pathogen(s)
- The duration of exposure to the specific pathogen
- The general physical condition of the host
- The psychological health status of the host
- The occupation or lifestyle environment of the host
- The presence of underlying diseases or conditions of the host
- The age of the host (very young and elderly are more susceptible to infections than the rest of the population)

The dental assistant can help reduce the likelihood of cross-contamination at this final step in the chain of infection by helping to identify patients at risk for susceptibility. It is then up to the healthcare provider (physician and/or dentist) to treat those underlying conditions if possible, and finally to isolate susceptible individuals from those reservoirs that could be hazardous to them.

TYPES OF INFECTIONS

Infectious diseases may also be classified as endogenous, exogenous, nosocomial, or opportunistic.

Endogenous

Endogenous infections or diseases originate within the individual's body and are not transmitted from another infected individual. Examples of endogenous diseases include metabolic disorders, congenital abnormalities (birth defects such as cleft palate), tumors, or infections caused by micro-organisms inside the person's body.

Exogenous

Exogenous infections or diseases originate from a means outside of the individual's body. Exogenous conditions are caused by pathogenic organisms that invade the body, radiation, chemical agents, trauma (accident or injury), electric shock, or temperature extremes (frostbite or heat exhaustion).

Nosocomial

Nosocomial infections are those acquired by a patient in a hospital or long-term care facility. Common examples of nosocomial infections include *staphylococcus* and *Pseudomonas*. The most common causes of nosocomial infections include improper handwashing by patient care personnel and incomplete sterilization of instruments or breaking the chain of sterility.

Opportunistic

Opportunistic infections occur when the body's ability to resist disease is weakened. Thus, opportunistic diseases usually do not infect healthy individuals with intact immune systems. Examples of opportunistic diseases include Kaposi's sarcoma, a rare form of skin cancer often found in full-blown AIDS patients, or *Pneumocystis carinii pneumonia,* which also occurs in AIDS patients.

THE FIVE STAGES OF INFECTIOUS DISEASE

The dental assistant must be aware of the five stages of infectious disease. They are incubation, prodromal, acute, declining, and convalescent.

Incubation Stage

The **incubation stage** of infectious disease is the interval between the exposure to a pathogenic microorganism and the first appearance of signs and symptoms of the disease. Some infections have short incubation stages, while others have lengthy stages, some lasting for years.

When individuals are exposed to an infectious disease, they will become infected with disease if their immune system cannot contain the infectious agent or if medications, immunizations, or therapeutic cures are not available.

Prodromal Stage

The **prodromal stage** of infectious disease encompasses a vague or undif-ferentiated set of symptoms similar to infections of any number of other diseases; it indicates the onset of a disease. It is characterized by a number of symptoms such as headache, nausea, vomiting, diarrhea, rash, or fever.

Acute Stage

The **acute stage** of infectious disease occurs when a disease reaches its peak. The patient's symptoms are fully developed and can often be readily differentiated from other specific symptoms. The most common treatment methods include reducing the patient's discomfort, reducing the possibilities of debilitation and adverse effects, and promoting healing and recovery.

Declining Stage

The **declining stage** of infectious disease occurs when the patient's symptoms begin to subside. The infectious disease remains, although the patient demonstrates improving health.

Convalescent Stage

The **convalescent stage** (the last stage) of infectious disease is when recovery and recuperation from the effects of a specific infectious disease occur. Patients regain strength and stamina and return to their overall original state of health.

THE IMMUNE SYSTEM

The body's immune system protects against pathogens and abnormal cell growth. It is composed of numerous cells that collectively recognize, subdue, attack, and eliminate pathogens.

Immunity is the body's ability to resist an infectious disease and its toxins. There are two types of immune responses, called *cell-mediated immunity* and *humoral immunity*. Cell-mediated immunity attacks against fungi, viruses, transplanted organs, and cancer cell growth; it does not produce antibodies. Humoral immunity produces antibodies that can kill microorganisms and that will also recognize the pathogen in the future.

Host susceptibility to some infectious diseases closely parallels the individual's ability to resist the infection and its toxins.

Resistance happens after an exposure to a pathogen, which is the antigen-antibody reaction. This is the body's natural defense mechanism against disease and infection. Resistance occurs gradually as pathogens and other foreign substances such as antigens enter the body. When an antigen enters the human body, the body's immune system recognizes the antigen as a foreign body and attempts to contain and subdue it. After the completion of the stages of that infectious disease, the body retains the ability to produce antibodies in response to that specific pathogen or antigen. Immunity can last over time, sometimes providing a lifetime of protection against specific infectious diseases. There are four forms of immunity that can occur in response to specific antigens:

- *Acquired immunity,* which results from contracting the infectious disease and experiencing either an acute or subclinical infectious disease
- *Artificial active immunity,* which is achieved after administration of vaccines
- *Congenital passive immunity,* which occurs when antibodies pass to a fetus from the mother, providing short-term immunity to the newborn baby
- *Passive immunity,* which may be achieved by administration of ready-made antibodies, for example gamma globulin, used to treat or prevent infectious diseases or reduce the risk of contracting them.

Immunization

Immunization provides individuals artificial active immunity to many common diseases, including smallpox, measles, German measles (rubella), mumps, poliomyelitis, hepatitis B, diphtheria, pertussis (whooping cough), influenza, and tetanus (lockjaw).

DISEASES OF CONCERN TO THE DENTAL ASSISTANT

Dental assistants, along with other members of the clinical dental team, must be aware of and educated about specific diseases they may encounter as a result of patient contact. The dental assistant should be aware of signs and symptoms, methods of transmission, and methods of preventing the spread of these diseases. They include all strains (forms) of hepatitis, tuberculosis, HIV disease, and AIDS.

Hepatitis

Hepatitis (inflammation of the liver), in all its six strains, is more prevalent and more life threatening than human immunodeficiency virus (HIV)/AIDS. Hepatitis-infected patients, regardless of which strain of infection, present with many of the same symptoms, including fatigue, mild fever, muscle and joint aches, nausea, vomiting, diarrhea, abdominal discomfort, jaundice, and changes in urine and stool color.

While the majority of patients diagnosed with hepatitis do not require isolation, all dental healthcare workers must follow standard universal precautions when contacting or handling body fluids or treating infected patients.

To help prevent transmission of viral hepatitis, the dental assistant must be aware of its forms, methods of transmission, symptoms, and treatment available. Dental assistants must also be aware of these precautions to protect themselves, the employer, and patients from hepatitis infection from cross-contamination.

Because dental assistants are often responsible for taking the initial medical history, as well as required updates, it is their responsibility to ensure that proper infection control precautions are taken when treating known hepatitis carriers. The dental assistant must also be aware that many patients, although asymptomatic, may be carriers of the disease and thus have the potential to transmit hepatitis to others.

Hepatitis A (HAV). Also called *infectious hepatitis,* hepatitis A is transmitted through the oral-fecal route, most often through a contaminated water supply or improper handling of food, especially in restaurants. The disease is most commonly spread from droppings of infected animals, most often those of rodents or insects.

Type A hepatitis does not develop into chronic hepatitis or liver cirrhosis, and most patients recover within 6 to 10 weeks. It is estimated that upward of 50 percent of all Americans become infected with hepatitis A, most of whom have little or no symptoms. Thus, many hepatitis A victims are unaware they have been infected.

Hepatitis B (HBV). Formerly called *serum hepatitis,* hepatitis B is considered one of the most underreported diseases and presents the highest occupational risk for dental personnel; 10,000 new cases are reported each year. One of the most serious forms of hepatitis, it often progresses to cirrhosis, chronic hepatitis, or liver cancer and may be fatal. Hepatitis B is transmitted perinatally (at birth) and through needlesticks, improperly handled sharps, sexual contact, needle sharing during IV drug use, hemodialysis, and blood transfusions.

Hepatitis C (HCV). Formerly called *post-transfusion non-A, non-B hepatitis,* hepatitis C is also underreported and prevalent. It is often referred to by experts in the field of infectious disease and public health physicians as an *emerging disease;* this means it is only more recently coming to light and the disease is on the rise.

It is estimated that as many as 170,000 Americans are infected with hepatitis C annually. The public health concern is that approximately 127,500 of these individuals remain asymptomatic, while 42,500 show signs of illness, with 680 becoming fulminant (with the disease developing or progressing suddenly). Of the 85,000 patients with chronic hepatitis, an estimated 21,250 are chronic carriers.

Hepatitis C often progresses to cirrhosis, chronic hepatitis, and eventual death. Hepatitis C is transmitted through needlesticks and sharing of needles during IV drug use and tattooing. At-risk groups include homosexual males, heterosexuals with multiple partners, intravenous drug abusers, tattoo recipients, hemophiliacs, blood transfusion patients, hemodialysis patients, and healthcare personnel. In dental practices, hollow-bore needles are the most common vehicle for HCV (hepatitis C virus) transmission.

Symptoms of hepatitis C may appear 20 years or more after contracting the infection. Unfortunately, the diagnosis often comes when patients learn they have chronic liver disease, cirrhosis, or liver cancer. Of those infected with hepatitis C, 85 percent will eventually develop chronic liver infections and the potential to transmit the disease to others. Even though most patients do not die or become debilitated as a result, approximately one-fifth of those with chronic infections will develop cirrhosis within 20 to 30 years. Individuals most likely to develop severe liver disease associated with hepatitis C are those who are older when infected or those who consume alcohol.

Hepatitis D (HDV). Formerly called *delta virus,* hepatitis D causes a coinfection with hepatitis B and can progress to cirrhosis or chronic hepatitis; it has a high mortality rate.

Infection with hepatitis D occurs in individuals infected with either acute or chronic hepatitis B. It most commonly occurs in patient populations in Italy, the Middle East, Africa, and South America. Patients infected with hepatitis D experience acute hepatitis symptoms, and the disease is often fatal.

Hepatitis E (HEV). Also known as *enteric* (pertaining to the small intestine) *non-A, non-B hepatitis,* hepatitis E is transmitted through fecal contamination epidemics, usually through contaminated water supplies in underdeveloped Asian countries.

Hepatitis G (HGV). Transmitted via the blood, hepatitis G infection may persist for up to 16 years, although only a few patients develop elevated liver enzymes. Hepatitis G infection is usually benign (noncancerous). There are currently no blood-screening tests for its detection. (Note that at one time, *hepatitis F* was identified but later was found to be a variation of hepatitis B.)

Treatment of Hepatitis. Treatment of hepatitis A includes a balanced diet. Vitamins may also be prescribed, as well as a high-carbohydrate, low-fat diet. Because many hepatitis patients have little appetite, smaller but more frequent meals are indicated; infected patients should abstain from alcohol. There is no vaccination to prevent or treat hepatitis A.

Hepatitis B patients are likely to become carriers of the disease, capable of transmitting the infection via shared IV drug needles, sexual contact, or blood transfusions. Hepatitis B carriers may be asymptomatic (without symptoms) or experience ongoing signs or symptoms of infection. The asymptomatic patient is referred to as a chronic carrier. All carriers of hepatitis have the potential to transmit the disease to others.

Chronic hepatitis B carriers may undergo inoculation with *recombinant interferon,* administered over 15 weeks. As many as 40 percent of individuals who receive this therapy enter into remission, and as many as 10 percent are cured as a result.

Some patients infected with hepatitis C may receive *recombinant interferon alfa-2b* injections administered in low doses for 6 months or *Rebetron*. This therapy has been demonstrated to improve liver function in approximately one-half of chronic hepatitis C carriers.

Patients with hepatitis D may enter remission when treated with injections of *recombinant interferon;* however, they often go into remission, with relapses following the discontinuation of treatment. There is no specific treatment for hepatitis E patients. Hepatitis G is rarely fatal, and the virus has been isolated only in laboratory conditions.

Tuberculosis

Tuberculosis is caused by a bacterial infection, most often occurring in the lungs. It is not uncommon for a number of months to elapse before symptoms appear in the infected individual. Symptoms of tuberculosis may include fatigue, low-grade fever, weight loss, night sweats, and eventually a persistent cough.

Tuberculosis is spread to other susceptible individuals by airborne particles released from coughs, from contact with infected saliva, and also through dental treatment if cross-contamination is allowed to occur.

As when treating all patients, it is especially important that the dental assistant and all other members of the clinical team wear personal protective equipment, mandated by universal precautions, when treating tuberculosis-infected patients.

Tuberculosis can easily be detected using a skin prick test or by a chest radiograph. In some healthcare institutions, annual retesting of personnel is recommended. Treatment for tuberculosis is a regimen of antibiotics.

Herpesvirus

Herpesvirus, also referred to as herpes simplex, is a commonly occurring viral infection. Herpes simplex virus type 1 (HSV1) is most often associated with viral infections of the lips, mouth, face, and oral mucosa (Figure 1–12). Lesions often occur when the patient has lowered resistance to infection and may be recurrent. Persistent lesions may cause itching, burning, or tingling sensations.

Herpes simplex virus type 2 (HSV2) is sexually transmitted and most often associated with genital herpes; however, type 2 may occur in the oral mucosa. Both herpes types 1 and 2 are highly contagious and are spread by direct contact with a vesicle, which is a fluid-filled lesion, or contact with the fluid.

The majority of adults have been exposed to herpes simplex at some time in their lives. The infection may initially be associated with flulike symptoms and the appearance of a blister or fever sore in or around the oral

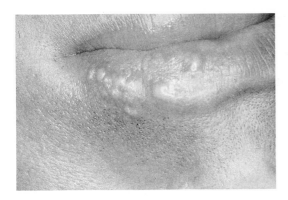

FIGURE 1-12
Herpesvirus lesions often occur when the patient has lowered resistance to infection. Persistent lesions may cause itching, burning, or tingling sensations. *(Courtesy of Joseph L. Konzelman Jr., DDS)*

cavity, which remains in the nerve cells within that area throughout the patient's life. HSV1 reactions occur when the patient's resistance is lowered, with a fever, prolonged exposure to sunlight, stress, or highly acidic foods or juices.

Herpes simplex viruses (*cold sores* and *aphthous ulcers*) recur and also tend to form in the same general areas. Herpesvirus may appear as a painful, open sore on the fingertips. On the finger, it is referred to as *herpetic whitlow;* when this infection is spread to the eyes, it may cause conjunctivitis, which means inflammation of the conjunctiva (an area of the eye), or a corneal ulcer, which may eventually result in blindness.

Patients with active herpesvirus outbreaks may require rescheduling of appointments, depending upon the site and severity of the lesion or lesions. There is no cure for herpes; however, palliative topical treatments of cream or ointment may relieve the side effects. Antiviral drugs such as acyclovir *(Zovirax)* may also be helpful.

HIV Disease

HIV disease, human immunodeficiency virus, which eventually becomes full-blown AIDS (acquired immunodeficiency syndrome), is a bloodborne pathogen. It is transmitted directly through blood or saliva-contaminated body fluids. HIV is classified as a retrovirus. HIV enters the susceptible individual's bloodstream via sexual intercourse, a transfusion of infected blood, or infected needles (such as those shared by drug addicts) or can be transmitted to the fetus from an infected mother.

Members of the dental team must be very careful to avoid and prevent accidental needlestick injuries from infected needles or sharp instruments, which may also be a source of HIV transmission.

HIV attacks T-lymphocytes (part of the body's immune system) and multiplies. In this stage of the disease, most infected patients pose no greater health risk to members of the dental team and often are unaware of their infection. Eventual symptoms include fever, unexplained weight loss, or diarrhea. Patients at this stage are referred to as having AIDS-related complex (ARC). Treatments are available to slow the symptoms of ARC; however, no reliable vaccine has been developed.

As when treating all patients, it is especially important that the dental assistant and all other members of the clinical team wear personal protective equipment, mandated by universal precautions, when treating HIV-infected patients.

AIDS

AIDS results from HIV infection. Not all patients infected with HIV eventually develop full-blown AIDS. A rare form of skin cancer, *Kaposi's sarcoma,* is associated with AIDS. The virus is spread from infected blood and/or semen from one infected individual to another susceptible individual. Casual contact does not appear to spread AIDS.

Patients with full-blown AIDS may suffer from cancer(s), bacterial and viral infections, fungal infections such as candidiasis, extreme weight loss, pneumonia, and diarrhea.

As with HIV infections, there currently is no cure or reliable vaccine to prevent AIDS. Treatment with antiviral drugs such as zidovudine (AZT) and acyclovir as well as the "AIDS cocktail" may help treat complications associated with AIDS; however, side effects may occur.

As when treating all patients, it is especially important that the dental assistant and all other members of the clinical team wear personal protective equipment, mandated by universal precautions, when treating AIDS-infected patients. In end-stage AIDS patients, most dental treatment is curtailed, except in cases of extreme emergency or to alleviate pain.

SKILLS MASTERY ASSESSMENT: POSTTEST

Directions: Select the response that best answers each of the following questions. Only one response is correct.

1. Most pathogenic viruses can be treated or contained using all of the following EXCEPT
   a. heat.
   b. disinfectants.
   c. antibiotics.
   d. electron microscopes.

2. HIV/AIDS is an example of a/an _____ infection.
   a. endogenous
   b. exogenous
   c. nosocomial
   d. opportunistic

3. A patient confined to a nursing home develops bed sores and a staph infection. These conditions are an example of _____ infections.
   a. endogenous
   b. exogenous
   c. nosocomial
   d. opportunistic

4. A newborn baby has a cleft lip and palate. This is an example of a/an
_____ condition.
a. endogenous
b. exogenous
c. nosocomial
d. opportunistic

5. The stages of an infectious disease, in sequential order, are
a. prodromal, incubation, acute, declining, convalescent.
b. incubation, prodromal, acute, declining, convalescent.
c. incubation, prodromal, declining, acute, convalescent.
d. incubation, prodromal, declining, convalescent, acute.

6. All of these statements about hepatitis B are true EXCEPT which of
the following?
a. It was formerly called serum hepatitis.
b. It is one of the most serious forms of hepatitis and often progresses
to cirrhosis, chronic hepatitis, and/or liver cancer and may be fatal.
c. It is most often carried through the oral-fecal route.
d. Ten thousand new cases are reported each year.

7. A dental assistant receives a vaccination against hepatitis B virus. This
vaccination, if effective, will provide the dental assistant with
_____ immunity.
a. acquired
b. artificial active
c. congenital passive
d. passive

8. Regardless of type (strain), hepatitis symptoms include
a. fatigue and mild fever.
b. muscle and joint aches.
c. nausea, vomiting, diarrhea, abdominal discomfort, and jaundice.
d. changes in urine and stool color.
e. Any or all of the above

9. All of these statements about hepatitis A are true EXCEPT which of
the following?
a. It is commonly called serum hepatitis.
b. It is transmitted through the oral-fecal route, most often through a
contaminated water supply or improper handling of restaurant
food.
c. It is most commonly spread from droppings of infected animals,
most often those of rodents or insects.
d. a and b only
e. b and c only

10. Hepatitis B can be transmitted through all of the following mechanisms EXCEPT
a. perinatally.
b. the oral-fecal route.
c. through needlesticks and sharing of needles for IV drug use.
d. sexual contact.
e. hemodialysis and blood transfusions.

11. Hepatitis C causes a coinfection with hepatitis B and can progress to cirrhosis or chronic hepatitis; it has a high mortality rate.
a. True   b. False

12. Hepatitis C, formerly called post-transfusion non-A, non-B hepatitis, is often referred to as an emerging disease because it is only more recently coming to light and the disease is on the rise.
a. True   b. False

13. A patient presents with symptoms that include fatigue, low-grade fever, apparent weight loss, and a persistent cough. He also complains of recurring night sweats. He may be infected with
a. candidiasis.   c. rubella.
b. tuberculosis.   d. hepatitis.

14. All of the following are methods of disease transmission for tuberculosis EXCEPT
a. airborne particles released from coughs.
b. contact with infected saliva.
c. casual contact.
d. dental treatment if contaminated instruments are used.

15. _____ can easily be detected using a skin prick test.
a. AIDS   c. Herpesvirus
b. Pneumonia   d. Tuberculosis

16. _____ is most often associated with viral infections of the lips, mouth, face, and oral mucosa.
a. Type 2 genital herpes   c. Tuberculosis
b. Type 1 herpes simplex   d. HIV

17. Both herpes types 1 and 2 are highly contagious and are spread by direct contact with a vesicle or vesicular fluid.
a. True   b. False

18. All of these statements about HIV are true EXCEPT which of the following?
a. It is transmitted directly through blood-contaminated body fluids.
b. It is classified as a retrovirus.
c. It originates as a fungal infection.
d. It may be spread from sharing infected needles.
e. It may be spread from an infected mother to the fetus.

19. As when treating all patients, it is especially important that the dental assistant and all other members of the clinical team wear personal protective equipment, mandated by universal precautions, when treating HIV-infected patients.
a. True   b. False

20. Treatment for patients suffering from full-blown AIDS includes all of the following EXCEPT
a. zidovudine (AZT).   c. acyclovir.
b. antibiotics.   d. the AIDS cocktail.

CHAPTER

2

Disease Prevention in the Dental Office

LEARNING OBJECTIVES

Upon completion of this chapter, the student should be able to:

1. Describe goals to reduce cross-contamination in the dental office through sound infection control techniques.

2. Relate the 10 basic principles of infection control to protect the practice, the patient, and members of the dental team from cross-contamination.

3. Describe and perform proper handwashing technique.

4. Relate additional techniques to reduce pathogenic microorganisms, including use of preprocedural mouthrinses, disposables, dental dam, and high-volume evacuation.

25

INFECTION CONTROL IN DENTISTRY: GOALS FOR REDUCING CROSS-CONTAMINATION

A sound infection control program in the dental office requires commitment of all members of the dental team (Figure 2–1). As such, the goal is to reduce cross-contamination—from patient to patient, from patient to dental team members, from dental team members to other patients, and from dental practice to community (Box 2–1). The dental assistant plays a significant role in preventing cross-contamination by establishing the following goals:

- Reduce the number of pathogenic microorganisms (microscopic disease-causing germs) so normal resistance can prevent infection.
- Break the cycle of infection and eliminate cross-contamination.
- Treat every patient and instrument as though potentially infectious.
- Protect patients and dental personnel from infection.

BOX 2–1

Checklist to Help Prevent Cross-Contamination in the Dental Office

There are many steps the dental assistant can employ to reduce the overall likelihood of disease transmission in the dental office. Many of these techniques employ simple common sense.

✓ Use as many disposables as possible.

✓ Handle contaminated items as little as possible—and always while wearing PPE.

✓ Dispose of all contaminated materials in sealed packaging.

✓ Minimize touching of surfaces with contaminated hands.

✓ Store all unnecessary supply items and equipment away from the treatment area. Keep as many items in a central storage or sterilization area as possible.

✓ Do not use the staff lounge/kitchen area as a combination sterilization/tray preparation area. Keep these areas separate to minimize the likelihood of disease transmission.

✓ Never store lunches, food, or beverages in the same refrigerator with dental supply items or near cleaning products or biologic specimens. Use separate storage areas or refrigerators.

✓ Avoid contamination of bulk packaged supplies and items. (Dispense individually packaged materials at the point of use and discard any leftover material at the completion of the procedure.)

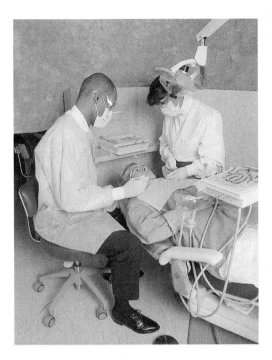

FIGURE 2–1
Sound infection control procedures require the commitment of
all members of the dental team.

TEN BASIC PRINCIPLES OF INFECTION CONTROL

The following principles are designed to minimize the risk of cross-infection and to attain the goals outlined. It is an important role of the dental assistant to ensure that these 10 principles are carried out.

Patient Screening

Screening of all patients is the first step in minimizing and reducing the risk of infectious disease transmission from patients to dental team members and to other patients. Effective patient screening requires that the dental assistant take a thorough medical/dental history on all new patients and that this medical history be updated at each subsequent visit.

Taking the original medical/dental history requires that the patient take a few extra moments prior to the initial oral exam to complete the necessary paperwork. The dental assistant may assist the patient in completing these questions and in ensuring that all questions are answered completely and honestly by the patient. This should be done in privacy, outside of the earshot of other patients. All information about patients must be kept strictly confidential.

At the subsequent visit, the dental assistant can easily make updates in the patient's medical and medication history by simply asking, "Mr. Jones, have there been any changes in your medical history or medications since your last visit with us?" The dental assistant records this information on the patient's chart, even if there has been no change. The date and dental assistant's initials should also be recorded. For further information, refer to *Chapter 3: Patient Assessment.*

Universal Precautions

Universal precautions, defined by the Centers for Disease Control and Prevention, must be used in all direct patient care and procedures performed in dentistry. Universal precautions refers to a set of precautions designed to prevent the transmission of human immunodeficiency virus (HIV), hepatitis B virus (HBV), and other bloodborne pathogens in healthcare settings, including dental offices and clinics.

Under universal precautions, blood and saliva encountered during the course of dental procedures for all patients are considered potentially infectious. Applied universal precautions means that the same infection control procedures for any given dental procedures must be employed for all patients; thus, universal precautions are procedure specific, not patient specific. For additional information on universal precautions, refer to *Chapter 12: Hazard Communication.* Universal precautions are addressed frequently throughout this book.

Training of Employees

All dental healthcare workers, including dental assistants, involved in the direct provision of patient care must undergo routine training in infection control, safety issues, and hazard communication. Training must encompass OSHA's pertinent regulations, including the Bloodborne Pathogens Standard. All new hires must receive training within 10 days of initial employment and annually thereafter. For additional information on dental staff training, refer to *Chapter 6: The Dental Office Safety Supervisor* and *Chapter 12: Hazard Communication.*

Aseptic Technique

Aseptic technique employs all forms of washing, sanitizing, disinfecting, and sterilizing of items that come into contact with patients to reduce the likelihood of infection with a contaminant or disease. Aseptic techniques also include handling of contaminated sharps and proper waste disposal, as well as placing protective barriers.

For further information, refer to *Chapter 7: Personal Safety and Barrier Protection, Chapter 8: Instrument Recirculation, Chapter 9: Environmental Surface and Equipment Asepsis, Chapter 10: Dental Laboratory Asepsis, Chapter 11: Infection Control in Dental Radiography,* and *Chapter 12: Hazard Communication.*

Personal Protection: Hepatitis B Vaccine, Barriers, and Personal Protective Equipment (PPE)

The dental assistant, along with all other clinical personnel, must employ sound principles of personal protection when working at chairside. All dental healthcare workers, including dental assistants, who have either direct or indirect contact with patients' blood and/or saliva must be immunized against hepatitis B or show serological evidence of immunity (anti-HBs) to hepatitis B virus infection.

OSHA requires that the hepatitis B vaccine and boosters be offered to employees at no charge within 10 days of employment and those who receive the vaccine series be serologically tested after the final injection to determine that they have developed immunity.

The dentist is responsible for the cost of the employee's required immunizations. If the dental assistant has already received the necessary immunization or has proof of immunity, this must be so noted in the dental assistant's medical file.

If a dental assistant chooses to decline immunizations, the assistant must sign and date a waiver to that effect. This is to protect the employer from future liability. For additional information on hepatitis B immunization procedures and guidelines, refer to *Chapter 12: Hazard Communication.*

Barriers and protective clothing, the latter called personal protective equipment (PPE), are also essential to disease prevention and risk reduction. Placing of protective barriers (Figure 2–2) on items that cannot practically be sterilized and wearing of PPE provide a barrier of protection for the dental assistant from contacting infectious agents through the skin, eyes, nose, or mouth.

For additional information on immunization protocols, barriers, and protective clothing for the dental assistant, refer to *Chapter 7: Personal Safety and Barrier Protection.*

Instrument and Handpiece Sterilization

Instrument sterilization is one of the oldest and best understood principles of infection control practiced in dentistry. All critical instruments and items that come into contact with the patient's oral tissues and that can withstand heat and/or chemical sterilization must be sterilized (Figure 2–3). If these

FIGURE 2–2
Protective barriers draped onto dental equipment reduce the likelihood of disease transmission from patient to patient. *(Courtesy of Perio Support Products, East Irvine, CA)*

FIGURE 2–3
A vital duty of the dental assistant is instrument sterilization.

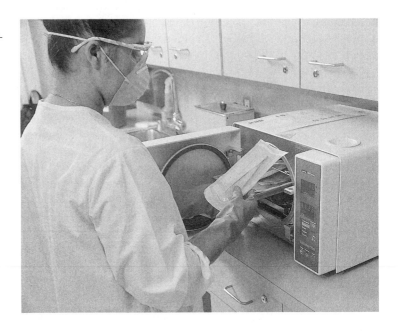

items cannot practically be sterilized, they must be disinfected according to infection control protocols.

Knowledge of instrument sterilization is especially important because this vital task most often is the responsibility of the dental assistant. For complete information and step-by-step instructions on instrument sterilization, refer to *Chapter 8: Instrument Recirculation.*

Disinfection Procedures

All semicritical and noncritical items that cannot be practically sterilized must be disinfected. This includes items that cannot withstand the heat or chemical rigors of sterilization or that are too large to fit inside a sterilizer chamber. More information and step-by-step instructions on disinfection procedures can be found in *Chapter 8: Instrument Recirculation* and *Chapter 9: Environmental Surface and Equipment Asepsis.*

Equipment Asepsis

Larger, noncritical items of dental equipment, such as the x-ray tubehead, dental chair, units, and countertops, must be cleaned and disinfected. In many cases, these items can also be covered with protective barriers, following disinfection procedures.

More information and step-by-step instructions on equipment asepsis can be found in *Chapter 9: Environmental Surface and Equipment Asepsis.*

Dental Laboratory Asepsis

In the past, the dental laboratory was often an overlooked area of the dental office with regard to infection control principles. Today, barriers are placed;

lab pumice must be discarded after use; and lab cases, both incoming and outgoing, must be disinfected prior to and after insertion into the patients' mouth.

The dental assistant has the primary role for ensuring dental laboratory aseptic conditions. For further information and step-by-step instructions, refer to *Chapter 10: Dental Laboratory Asepsis*.

Waste Management

The full cycle of infection control would not be complete without following waste management guidelines. Most often, this responsibility also falls upon the dental assistant. The dental assistant must always wear appropriate PPE when handling hazardous and nonhazardous waste products and contaminated reusable outer clinical attire to be laundered.

Hazardous waste must be properly labeled with a red or orange biohazard label or sticker and must be kept covered at all times. Disposal of all sharp items (e.g., contaminated needles) must also be handled following OSHA guidelines. For detailed, step-by-step instructions, refer to *Chapter 7: Personal Safety and Barrier Protection* and *Chapter 12: Hazard Communication*.

HANDWASHING: THE FIRST LINE OF DEFENSE IN DISEASE PREVENTION

Clean hands are the basis for preventing infectious disease in dentistry. The dental assistant must be scrupulous in handwashing procedure and technique (Figure 2–4) before and after gloving to assist with patient treatment

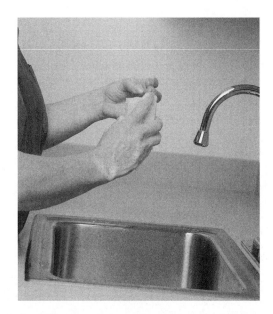

FIGURE 2–4

The dental assistant performs proper handwashing technique using an antimicrobial soap and scrub brush/sponge.

at chairside (Box 2–2). To project a professional appearance, the dental assistant should always keep fingernails short and well groomed. The nail tips should be no longer than 2 mm. Long or artificial nails should not be worn by the dental assistant because they harbor bacteria and tend to puncture gloves.

Basic handwashing is not a substitute for proper gloving, nor is it equivalent to a surgical scrub performed prior to entering a hospital operating room.

The intact skin harbors both resident flora (also referred to as colonized flora, for example, *staphylococcus epidermis*) and transient bacterial flora. These bacteria may reside permanently under several layers of the skin's surface and thus can never be removed, even with surgical scrubbing. Washing can, however, significantly reduce their numbers.

While resident dermal microflora (tiny bacterial, fungal, or viral germ growth on the skin) can cause infection when directly or indirectly spread to other people, these organisms are considered less significant in disease transmission than transient skin flora (also called contaminating flora), which contaminate the hands through contact with the environmental surfaces and contaminated instruments. These transient organisms generally do not form colonies nor survive on the hands for very long; however, they may be a potential source for disease transmission because they remain on the outer layers of the skin of the hands. With routine handwashing, dental assistants can remove or significantly reduce transient microflora on their hands.

In addition to microflora, pathogens found in blood, saliva, and dental plaque may transmit infection by entering the body through dermal (skin) defects, small cuts, or cracks in the skin. They can also be transferred to mucous membranes via the hands and subsequently enter the bloodstream.

OSHA's Handwashing Requirements

OSHA's 1991 Bloodborne Pathogens Standard requires that handwashing facilities be readily accessible to employees. The standard also requires the following:

- Employees must wash their hands immediately or as soon as is feasible after removing gloves or PPE.
- Employees must wash their hands and skin with soap and water immediately or as soon as is feasible after contact with blood or other potentially infectious materials (OPIM). Likewise, mucous membranes such as the eyes, nose, or mouth that have contacted blood, saliva, or OPIM should be flushed with water.
- If handwashing facilities are not feasible (for example, in an emergency medical situation), employers must supply antiseptic hand cleaner and towels.

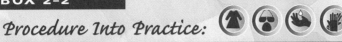

BOX 2-2

Procedure Into Practice:

Handwashing

The dental assistant should follow these steps for basic handwashing before and after gloving.

1. Approach the sink, taking care not to let any part of the uniform, scrubs, or other PPE touch the sink during the handwashing procedure.

2. Remove all jewelry from the hands and wrists. This is important because rings, watches, and bracelets harbor pathogenic microorganisms; they also cause gloves to puncture, rip, or tear.

3. Use a clean, dry paper towel (Figure 2–5A) to turn the tap water to a comfortably warm temperature. Warm water makes more productive soap suds than cold water; hot water tends to dry and chap the skin. (Pathogenic microorganisms may lodge in the roughened and broken areas of chapped hands.) Ideally, the faucet should be "no touch," that is, beam controlled or elbow controlled or have foot controls, spigot rods, electric eye sensors, or ultrasonics so touching of the faucet or handles with the hands is eliminated.

4. Wet the hands, applying about 1 teaspoon of an antimicrobial hand scrub with residual action to wash the hands. Preferred hand scrubs are *substituted phenol preparations,* such as chlorhexidine gluconscrubs or cleansers; they should be "touchless," that is, supplied in a foot-activated dispenser or by an electric motion eye beam so it is not touched during the handwashing procedure. The dental assistant should avoid using bar soap and a customary household soap dish because these harbor pathogenic microorganisms, especially when constantly bathed in a warm, moist environment; pay special attention when scrubbing the thumbs and fingertips.

5. Point the fingertips downward and use the palm of one hand to clean the back of the other hand (Figure 2–5B).

FIGURE 2–5A
The dental assistant uses a clean, dry paper towel to turn on the faucet.

FIGURE 2–5B The dental assistant points the fingertips downward and uses the palm of one hand to clean the back of the other hand.

continues

BOX 2-2 *(continued)*

6. Interlace the fingers to clean in between the fingers (Figure 2–5C).

FIGURE 2–5C The dental assistant interlaces the fingers to clean in between the fingers.

7. Carefully clean underneath the nails using an orangewood stick, rounded plastic stick, or flat toothpick (Figure 2–5D). A hand brush can also be used to clean underneath the fingernails (Figure 2–5E). (Do

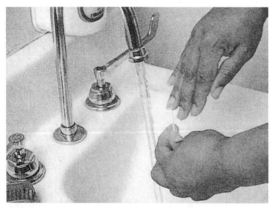

FIGURE 2–5D The dental assistant carefully cleans underneath the nails with an orangewood stick, rounded plastic stick, or flat toothpick.

this at the beginning and end of the day.) Rinse the fingers well under running water.

8. After attaining the initial lather, stop, rinse, and lather again. Using firm rubbing and

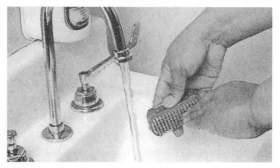

FIGURE 2–5E The dental assistant may also use a hand brush to clean underneath the fingernails.

circular motions, wash the hands (palm and back), each finger, the area between the fingers, and the knuckles.

9. Next, using firm rubbing and circular motions, wash the forearms and wrists, at least as high as contamination is likely to occur.

10. After washing both hands, with the fingertips pointing downward, rinse the hands thoroughly with cool water (Figure 2–5F). (Cool water closes the pores of the skin,

FIGURE 2–5F The dental assistant points fingertips downward to rinse hands thoroughly.

reduces the susceptibility of microorganisms to be harbored and reproduced on the skin, and minimizes the possible sensitization to latex.)

11. Dry the hands using a disposable paper towel. Dry the hands first, then the forearms.

BOX 2-2 *(continued)*

Never use cloth towels because they also harbor germs with continued use and may be a source of cross-infection.

12. After drying the hands, use the paper towel to turn off the water faucets (if the office or clinic does not have a touchless handwashing system). Once the hands have been properly washed, do not touch the faucets, trash can lids to dispose of paper towels, countertops, or anything else prior to gloving.

The dental assistant is now ready to put on gloves. (Note that use of petroleum-based hand lotions should be avoided because these products tend to weaken the integrity of some gloves.) For complete instructions on gloving, refer to *Chapter 7: Personal Safety and Barrier Protection.*

General Handwashing Guidelines

Dental assistants should use the following steps prior to donning gloves, keeping in mind to wash their hands at the beginning and end of each day, as well as between patients. They should always wash their hands in the presence of each patient, immediately after seating and draping the patient.

Professional nail brushes are commercially available from dental supply houses and should be used at the following times by the dental assistant when washing the hands:

- First thing every morning at the office
- During the final scrub of the day
- Following procedures (such as surgical cases) involving sufficient amounts of hemorrhaging
- Immediately after treating a high-risk patient

The dental assistant must be careful not to overscrub the hands with a nail brush because this may cause *dermatitis*—a general skin irritation—and may abrade the skin.

Both mechanical friction and rinsing are critical to effective handwashing. The mechanical action of handwashing suspends pathogenic microbes and dirt from the skin's surface, allowing them to be rinsed away. Plain soap and water are effective in removing dirt and some transient microbes from the hands; however, they do not inactivate any remaining pathogenic microbes. Thus, using a handwashing solution with an antimicrobial agent adds another important component to the destruction of most transient microbes and to the reduction of the number of viable resident flora.

RISK REDUCTION AT CHAIRSIDE

In addition to the 10 basic principles of infection control, there are a number of factors at chairside that can help minimize risk of infection to the dental assistant and other members of the clinical dental team (Box 2–3).

Preprocedural Antiseptic Mouthrinses

The use of an antimicrobial preprocedural mouthrinse by the patient before dental procedures is based upon the principle of reducing the number of oral microorganisms that may escape a patient's mouth during dental treatment through aerosols, spatter, or direct contact.

The mouthrinse should have *residual activity* to help maintain reduced microbial levels through the appointment. A rinse that has long-lasting antimicrobial activity (Table 2–1), such as 0.12% CHG (chlorhexidine gluconate), can suppress oral microorganisms for up to 5 hours.

Disposables

Disposable items significantly reduce the likelihood of the spread of disease because, as the name implies, they are used only once and then disposed of, thus reducing the possibility of patient-to-patient contamination.

Perhaps one of the earliest uses of disposables in dentistry was the introduction of the disposable needle and cartridge for administration of local anesthesia. (Prior to this, needles were boiled and reused!)

Other commonly used disposables include paper products such as cups, cotton rolls, 2 x 2 gauze sponges, and cotton pellets; premeasured amalgam capsules; gloves; masks; inexpensive plastic impression trays;

BOX 2-3

Checklist to Help Prevent Cross-Contamination at Chairside

In addition to the general checklist for reducing the likelihood of disease transmission throughout the office, there are steps the dental assistant can take at chairside as well.

✓ Provide all operative and surgical patients a preprocedural antimicrobial mouthrinse with residual action prior to beginning each procedure.

✓ Use dental dam (where appropriate) to prevent salivary oral microbes from splattering out of the mouth during a procedure.

✓ Employ four-handed dentistry techniques, including the use of an HVE held close to the field of operation (one-quarter inch from the edge of the proximal/distal tooth) during cavity preparation and oral debridement.

✓ Avoid touching any part of the body or clothing during an operative or surgical procedure.

✓ Wear personal protective equipment (PPE) that is as devoid of ornamentation or trim as possible.

TABLE 2-1

ANTISEPTIC PREPROCEDURAL MOUTHRINSES	
Active Ingredient	**Brand Name**
Chlorhexidine gluconate	Peridex PerioGard
Essential oils	Listerine
Phenols	Chloraseptic
Quaternary ammonium compounds	Cepacol Scope
Zinc chloride	Lavoris Listermint (alcohol free)

saliva ejectors and high-volume evacuation (HVE) tips; dental dam; wedges and matrix strips.

When considering the use of disposables, the dental assistant must weigh cost against convenience.

Dental Dam

The use of dental dam has a number of advantages, including improved visibility and access for the chairside team. Dental dam is also useful in reducing the amount of saliva, blood, spatter, or direct contact from the patient's mouth to chairside personnel.

High-Volume Evacuation

High-volume evacuation was introduced to the dental profession with the advent of four-handed, sit-down dentistry. The use of water added to the dentist's high-speed handpiece greatly reduced heat and friction, and thus reduced the amount of time the handpiece was used. The dental assistant became the dentist's other two hands, providing adequate suction with the HVE tip to remove the additional water and debris from the oral cavity.

The use of high-volume evacuation during operative procedures effectively reduces the likelihood of the dental team coming into contact with the patient's saliva, blood, or spatter. HVE is also useful in emptying the oral cavity of tooth fragments, amalgam filings, and other small or sharp items that might cause eye injuries, choking, or accidental aspiration.

SKILLS MASTERY ASSESSMENT: POSTTEST

Directions: Select the response that best answers each of the following questions. Only one response is correct.

1. The goal of a sound infection control program is to reduce cross-contamination from all of the following EXCEPT
   a. patient to patient.
   b. patient to dental team members.
   c. dental team members to other patients.
   d. the community health program to the dental practice.

2. The dental assistant plays a significant role in preventing cross-contamination by employing all of the following goals EXCEPT
   a. reducing the number of pathogenic microorganisms present so normal resistance can prevent infection.
   b. breaking the cycle of infection and eliminating cross-contamination.
   c. treating only HIV/AIDS patients as though potentially infectious.
   d. protecting high-risk patients and dental personnel from infection.

3. Which of the following is/are true regarding patient screening?
   a. Screening of all patients is the first step in minimizing and reducing the risk of infectious disease transmission from patients to dental team members and to other patients.
   b. The dental assistant must take a thorough medical/dental history on all new patients and update it at each subsequent recall visit.
   c. The dental assistant may be required to assist the patient in completing medical health history forms.
   d. a and b only
   e. All of the above are true.

4. Universal precautions are patient specific, not procedure specific.
   a. True   b. False

5. All dental assistants involved in the direct provision of patient care must undergo routine training in
   a. infection control, safety issues, and hazard communication.
   b. charting, taking patients' vital signs, and using the office intercom system.
   c. infection control, uniform sizing, and ordering of disposables.
   d. hazardous waste management, charting, and application of dental dam.

6. All dental assistants who have either direct or indirect contact with patients' blood and/or saliva must be immunized against hepatitis A or show serological evidence of immunity (anti-HBs) to hepatitis A virus infection.
   a. True   b. False

7. Placing of protective barriers on items that cannot practically be sterilized and wearing of PPE provide a barrier of protection for the dental assistant from contacting infectious agents through the skin, eyes, nose, or mouth.
   a. True   b. False

8. Instrument sterilization is especially important because this vital task most often is the responsibility of the _____.
   a. dental laboratory technician   c. dental assistant
   b. dental hygienist   d. dentist

9. Both incoming and outgoing lab cases must be disinfected before and after insertion into the patient's mouth.
   a. True   b. False

10. The dental assistant must always wear appropriate PPE when handling hazardous and nonhazardous waste products and contaminated reusable outer clinical attire to be laundered.
    a. True   b. False

11. To project a professional appearance regarding hand and nail care, the dental assistant should
    a. always keep fingernails short and well groomed.
    b. keep the nail tips no more than 2 mm long.
    c. avoid wearing long or artificial nails because they harbor bacteria and tend to puncture gloves.
    d. a and b only
    e. b and c only
    f. All of the above are true regarding the dental assistant's nails.

12. Which of the following statements is true regarding basic handwashing technique?
    a. It is a substitute for proper gloving.
    b. It is equivalent to a surgical scrub.
    c. It is the basis for preventing infectious disease transmission in the dental office.
    d. All of the above are true.

13. All of these statements regarding transient bacterial flora are true EXCEPT which of the following?
    a. These bacteria may reside permanently under several layers of the skin's surface.
    b. These bacteria can never be removed, even with surgical scrubbing.
    c. Washing can significantly reduce their numbers.
    d. These bacteria tend to survive on the hands for many days.

14. OSHA's 1991 Bloodborne Pathogens Standard requires that handwashing facilities be readily accessible to employees and additionally all of these EXCEPT which of the following?
    a. Employees must wash their hands immediately or as soon as is feasible after removing gloves or PPE.

b. Employees must wash their hands and skin with soap and water immediately or as soon as is feasible after contact with blood or OPIM.

c. If handwashing facilities are not feasible (for example, in a emergency medical situation), employers must supply antiseptic towelettes.

d. All of the above are required by OSHA.

15. The dental assistant should remove all jewelry from the hands and wrists prior to handwashing because
   a. rings, watches, and bracelets harbor pathogenic microorganisms.
   b. jewelry tends to cause gloves to puncture, rip, or tear.
   c. jewelry cannot be seen or admired underneath gloves.
   d. a and b only
   e. All of the above are valid reasons.

16. The use of an antimicrobial preprocedural mouthrinse by the patient helps reduce the number of oral microorganisms that may escape a patient's mouth during dental treatment through aerosols, spatter, or direct contact.
   a. True   b. False

17. Disposable items significantly _____ the likelihood of the spread of disease because they are used only once and then disposed of, thus _____ the possibility of patient-to-patient contamination.
   a. reduce/increasing
   b. reduce/reducing
   c. increase/increasing
   d. increase/reducing

18. When considering the use of disposables, the dental assistant must weigh cost against convenience.
   a. True   b. False

3

Patient Assessment

CHAPTER

KEY TERMS

emerging diseases

financial responsibility form

informed consent form

latex sensitivity

medical/dental history form

LEARNING OBJECTIVES

Upon completion of this chapter, the student should be able to:

1. Explain and relate the importance of taking a medical history on each patient.

2. Describe the information necessary in a patient's medical history.

3. Describe the growing concern for latex allergy, the importance of recording related information on the medical history form, and methods to reduce latex sensitivity for patients.

4. Explain the legal importance of obtaining informed consent prior to initiating dental treatment.

5. Complete a routine medical history form for each patient.

6. Relate how to interact with a patient while obtaining a medical history.

7. Relate strategies for dealing with difficult patients.

8. Relate methods of managing sensitive topics with regard to patients' health histories.

9. Demonstrate familiarity with other forms required for the first patient visit.

FUNCTION AND IMPORTANCE OF A MEDICAL/DENTAL HISTORY

Prior to examining a patient or initiating treatment, it is essential to have the patient, parent, or legal guardian complete or update a **medical/dental history form** (Figure 3–1). This form includes the patient's medical history, the reason for the initial visit, and other pertinent information required before treating the patient.

The medical/dental history form provides an excellent opportunity to note the patient's feelings and attitudes about his or her teeth, to list current dental complaints or concerns and the reason for the first appointment, and to record goals for improved oral health.

When necessary, the office manager should assist the new patient in completing the medical history forms and all other forms; no blank spaces should be left on these forms.

In addition to name, address, telephone numbers, medications, and supplements currently taken, the medical history form requires that information be completed about childhood diseases and immunizations.

The health history form should include information about the patient's family physician, the physician's office telephone number, and any recent hospitalizations or surgeries. It should contain the name and telephone number of a responsible party to contact in the event of a medical emergency.

Prior to initiating treatment on any patient, the dentist must have the opportunity to review that patient's medical history, including past diseases; major surgeries; drug interactions; sexually transmitted diseases; chronic or current medical conditions (such as a history of cardiac disease including heart valve or joint replacement, diabetes, hypertension, hepatitis, or HIV disease); and a listing of all medications, over-the-counter drugs, and supplements taken. The dentist must also be aware of *drug allergies* or known *sensitivities* prior to determining a diagnosis and treatment plan, alleviating immediate pain or infection, or writing prescriptions.

Updating the Medical History

In addition to having a completed health history on file for every patient, the dental assistant or receptionist should update this information at each subsequent recall visit. This can quickly and easily be accomplished by asking, "Mr. Harris, has there been any change in your medical treatment or medications within the past six months?" The assistant then marks, dates, and initials the chart to that effect.

Obtaining, recording, and updating of current information on all patients is also a legal obligation of the dentist. This is important because specific information may be required later in the event of a malpractice suit or complaint filed with the State Board of Dental Examiners. Having written documentation is key in defending the office (for additional information, refer to *Chapter 4: Legal and Ethical Considerations of Infection Control*).

HEALTH HISTORY & REGISTRATION

Patient Number _____   A B C

PATIENT INFORMATION

PATIENT'S NAME Last _____ First _____ Middle Initial ____ SEX: M F   BIRTHDATE _____ AGE ____

Soc. Sec. # _____ If Patient is a Minor, give Parent's or Guardian's Name _____ TODAY'S DATE _____

Who May We Thank for Referring You to our Office? _____ Reason for this Visit _____

RESPONSIBLE PARTY INFORMATION

NAME Last _____ First _____ Middle _____ MARITAL STATUS _____

RESIDENCE Street _____ Apt. # ____ City _____ State ____ Zip ____

MAILING ADDRESS Street _____ Apt. # ____ City _____ State ____ Zip ____

HOW LONG AT THIS ADDRESS _____ HOME PHONE _____ WORK PHONE _____

PREVIOUS ADDRESS (if less than 3 yrs.) Street _____ City _____ State _____ Zip _____ How Long _____

SOCIAL SECURITY # _____ BIRTHDATE _____ DRIVER'S LICENSE # _____ RELATION TO PATIENT _____

EMPLOYER _____ OCCUPATION _____ NO. YEARS EMPLOYED _____

RESPONSIBLE PARTY'S SPOUSE

NAME _____ LAST _____ FIRST _____ MIDDLE

EMPLOYER _____ NO. YEARS EMPLOYED ____

OCCUPATION _____ SOC. SEC. # _____

WORK PHONE _____ BIRTHDATE _____

EMERGENCY INFORMATION: RELATIVE NOT LIVING WITH YOU.

| RELATIONSHIP

NAME _____

ADDRESS _____

CITY, STATE _____ PHONE _____

DENTAL INSURANCE INFORMATION (Primary Carrier)

Insured's Name _____

Insurance Co. _____

Insurance Co. Address _____

Insured's Employer _____
Insured's
Soc. Sec. # _____ Group # ____ Local # ____

If you have double dental insurance coverage, complete this for the second coverage.

Insured's Name _____

Insurance Co. _____

Insurance Co. Address _____

Insured's Employer _____
Insured's
Soc. Sec. # _____ Group # ____ Local # ____

It is important that I know about your Medical and Dental History. These facts have a direct bearing on your Dental Health. This information is strictly confidential and will not be released to anyone. Thank you for taking the time to completely fill out this questionnaire.

DENTAL HISTORY	YES	NO
HOW LONG SINCE you have seen a Dentist?		
Last COMPLETE Dental Exam, Date:		
Last FULL MOUTH X-RAYS, DATE: (16 small Films or Panoramic)		
Are you having PROBLEMS now?	☐	☐
WHAT?		
Is your present dental health POOR?	☐	☐
Do you wear DENTURES? (Partials or Full)	☐	☐
Are you UNHAPPY with your dentures?	☐	☐
Would you like to know more about PERMANENT REPLACEMENTS?	☐	☐
Are you APPREHENSIVE about dental treatment?	☐	☐
Have you had any PERIODONTAL (GUM) treatments?	☐	☐
Do your gums BLEED, or feel TENDER or IRRITATED?	☐	☐
Are your teeth SENSITIVE to hot, cold, sweets, pressure? (circle)	☐	☐
Are you UNHAPPY with the APPEARANCE of your teeth?	☐	☐
Are you aware of GRINDING or CLENCHING your teeth?	☐	☐
Do you have HEADACHES, EARACHES, or NECK PAINS?	☐	☐
Have you worn BRACES on your teeth? (ORTHODONTICS)	☐	☐
Do you have DISCOLORED teeth that bother you?	☐	☐
Would you like your smile to LOOK BETTER or DIFFERENT?	☐	☐
Do you REGULARLY use DENTAL FLOSS?	☐	☐

Name of Previous Dentist: _____

City: _____ State: _____

How do you feel about your teeth? _____

Please RANK the following in the order in which they would KEEP YOU FROM having dental treatment.

FEAR of pain	#	LACK of concern	#
COST of treatment	#	MISSING work time	#

MEDICAL HISTORY	YES	NO
Do you have any CURRENT HEALTH PROBLEMS?	☐	☐
Are you under a PHYSICIAN'S CARE now?	☐	☐
For What?		
What MEDICATIONS are you currently taking?		
Are you PREGNANT?	☐	☐
Do you use cigars/cigarettes, pipe or chewing tobacco? Circle	☐	☐

CIRCLE ANY OF THE FOLLOWING WHICH YOU HAVE HAD, OR PRESENTLY HAVE:

Heart Disease or Attack	A.I.D.S./A.R.C./HIV Pos.	Bruise Easily
Angina Pectoris	Hepatitis A (infectious)	Emphysema
High Blood Pressure	Hepatitis B (serum)	Tuberculosis (TB)
Heart Murmur	Liver Disease	Asthma
Rheumatic Fever	Blood Transfusion	Hay Fever
Congenital Heart Lesions	Drug Addiction	Sinus Trouble
Mitral Valve Prolapse	Hemophilia (Bleeding Problems)	Allergies or Hives
Artificial Heart Valve	Fever Blisters	Diabetes
Heart Pacemaker	Epilepsy or Seizures	Thyroid Disease
Heart Surgery	Nervousness	Radiation Treatment
Artificial Joints (Hip, Knee)	Psychiatric Treatment	Arthritis
Anemia	Glaucoma	Cortisone Medicine
Stroke	Chemotherapy (Cancer, Leukemia)	Pain in Jaw Joints
Kidney Trouble	Venereal Disease	Alcoholism
Ulcers	(Syphilis, Gonorrhea, etc.)	Cosmetic Surgery

ARE YOU ALLERGIC TO OR HAVE YOU REACTED ADVERSELY TO ANY OF THE FOLLOWING MEDICATIONS?

Aspirin	Local Anesthetic	Erythromycin
Nitrous Oxide	Codeine	Penicillin

Are you aware of being allergic to any other medications or substances? _____

If yes, please list: _____
Is there any other Medical or Dental information that you feel I should know about? _____

FAMILY PHYSICIAN _____ PHONE NO. _____

PATIENT Signature (Parent of Child) _____ Date: _____ DENTIST Signature _____

1995© **R₁ I_C** (303) 751-3321

FIGURE 3–1

Sample medical/dental history form. *(Reprinted courtesy of ©SmartPractice, Inc., Phoenix, AZ. All rights reserved. To order call 800-522-0800.)*

Filing Lab Test Results

Another aspect of keeping medical histories is maintaining information on patients' medical laboratory reports, including results of *antibody-antigen* tests for infectious diseases. This has become especially important because of new or **emerging diseases** (those transmitted from other countries to the United States) that have recently received greater attention. Examples of emerging diseases include hepatitis C, lyme disease, and encephalitis.

While ordering and filing of lab test results has traditionally been done in medical offices, dentists sometimes request medical testing for specific diseases prior to initiating a patient's treatment.

LATEX SENSITIVITY

The growing awareness of **latex sensitivity** (having an allergic reaction or sensitivity to products containing natural rubber latex; the reaction may be immediate or delayed) has made it imperative that dental offices inquire about latex sensitivity of patients. This is because many items routinely used in the dental office are made from or contain natural rubber latex (NRL).

These items include latex examination gloves, dental dam, stoppers on medicine vials, stethoscopes, ambu/resuscitation bags, tubing, rubber prophylaxis cups, and nitrous oxide nosepieces.

Two common latex allergic reactions are *contact dermatitis* and *sensitization* to latex. Symptoms can range from itchiness and redness to respiratory distress and occasionally fatal anaphylaxis. Reactions can include the following:

- Immediate hypersensitivity (type I)
- Delayed hypersensitivity (type IV)
- Irritant dermatitis (ID)

It is currently estimated that 100,000 people in the United States are at risk for latex sensitivity, which can arise from either direct contact with latex or by indirect inhalation of particles released from latex gloves. Latex proteins are carried in the air and through the office's or clinic's ventilation system.

Methods to Combat Allergic Responses to Latex

The following strategies may be incorporated into office policies and procedures to help reduce or prevent allergic responses to latex and latex-containing devices used in the dental office:

1. Switch to nonlatex gloves. Vinyl gloves are an acceptable alternative, although they have less elasticity and offer less protection against hepatitis B virus and HIV.
2. Look for low protein content on glove boxes. The Food and Drug Administration has suggested that lowering protein levels in gloves may significantly reduce the risk and incidence of problems associated

with latex sensitivity. As a result, many glove manufacturers are improving processes to ensure lower protein content.

3. If the practice uses latex dental dam, consider switching to a nonlatex product.

4. Avoid coming into contact with other dental products containing latex, such as rubber bite blocks, banana-flavored topical anesthetic, latex prophy cups, amalgam carriers with rubber tips (use ones made of Teflon), liquid droppers or rubber stoppers on bottles, orthodontic elastics, or saliva ejectors.

5. Remember that products labeled *hypoallergenic* (meaning less likely to cause an allergic reaction in sensitive users) are not necessarily allergy free. Check FDA-required package labeling for content.

6. Be alert to the possibility of an allergic reaction whenever devices containing latex are used in the dental office, especially when the latex will contact the patient's oral mucosa.

7. Advise all patients of a possible latex sensitivity if they develop signs and symptoms following a dental appointment in which latex-containing items were used. If patients develop symptoms associated with latex allergy, they should be advised to contact their family physicians.

8. Stress to all latex-sensitive patients that they should inform all their healthcare providers about their latex sensitivity.

9. Consider posting a sign in the reception area stating that the office does everything possible to minimize patients' sensitivity to latex by using latex-free products whenever possible.

Screening Patients for Latex Allergy

Practices should have a question or space on their medical/dental health history form regarding latex allergy/sensitivity (Box 3–1).

COMPLETING MEDICAL/DENTAL HISTORY FORMS

At the new patient visit, it is the role of the dental assistant, office manager, or receptionist to complete a variety of forms for that patient, including a medical history form; a financial responsibility form, which indicates the person who is financially responsible for treatment provided; insurance information; and any related forms, such as a patient profile sheet. The latter is a relational marketing information sheet that asks questions about hobbies, social and civic organization memberships, and other interests.

Interacting with the Patient

When interacting with a patient, the dental assistant or office manager must take great care to maintain patient privacy and confidentiality (for additional information, refer to *Chapter 4: Legal and Ethical Considerations of Infection Control*) and to provide an area in which the patient or responsible

BOX 3-1

Screening Patients for Latex Sensitivity

In practices that do not have a space on their medical/dental health history form regarding possible latex sensitivity, the following questions may be helpful in screening patients who may be latex sensitive:

1. Are you allergic to latex or rubber?
2. Have you ever had surgery?
3. Have you ever experienced any complications during surgery or a medical procedure requiring resuscitation?
4. Have you ever worked in an environment that brought you into constant contact with latex products?
5. Have you ever experienced wheezing, difficulty in breathing, coughing, rashes, swelling, hives, itching or watery eyes when coming into contact with rubber items, such as balloons?
6. Are you allergic to bananas, avocados, chestnuts, kiwi, passion fruit, potatoes, or other foods?
7. Do you have a history of asthma, hay fever, eczema, or dermatitis?
8. Does maintaining your health require frequent mucous membrane exposure to products containing latex?
9. Have you ever experienced swelling of the mouth or other adverse symptoms after dental procedures or with denture wear?
10. Do you frequently wear rubber gloves at home?

If patients respond affirmatively to any of the above questions, they may have experienced an allergic reaction to NRL or may be sensitive to products containing it. If so, the dental assistant must report this to the dentist immediately and make a permanent notation on the patient's chart.

family member can complete the necessary forms in private. If additional information is needed that the dental assistant must inquire about, this must be obtained in a private office or in another area out of earshot of other patients (Box 3–2).

As the first contact with patients, the receptionist, office manager, or dental assistant must help put patients at ease (Figure 3–2). Often, patients feel nervous or anxious about seeking treatment in a new office and may be in need of reassurance.

When helping the patient complete medical history forms, the dental assistant should maintain eye contact and speak in a professional (not shrill) voice. The dental assistant should avoid talking too fast and should also avoid using medical or dental jargon and terminology that may put the patient at a distance.

During the completion of forms, the dental assistant should also keep focused, not allowing the conversation to diverge from the topic. Ask-

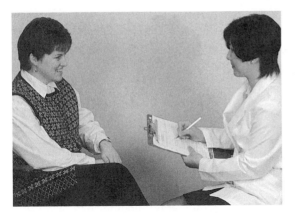

FIGURE 3–2
The dental assistant maintains professional focus and ensures patient confidentiality when taking a medical/dental history on a new patient.

ing questions in a methodical, logical order and allowing the patient time to respond without feeling rushed can also help enhance communication and help make the patient feel at ease and welcomed in a new place.

The assistant should avoid asking more sensitive questions, for example, about lifestyle or sexually transmitted diseases, possible pregnancy, or history of substance abuse until a rapport has been built with the patient. The assistant must also refrain from showing embarrassment or surprise at responses made by the patient. These questions, however, must be asked if the dentist requires them to be answered.

Managing Difficult Patients

Occasionally, everyone experiences a bad day. Patients may arrive at the office in some degree of stress, fear, agitation, or unusual excitement. Sometimes this can be attributed to having a history of prior negative dental experiences, especially in childhood. Some patients have phobias directly related to dental treatment.

Often, patients need assurance or perhaps a gentle touch on the forearm or shoulder to calm them. The dental assistant should exercise sensitivity and caution when a patient exhibits a specific difficulty when asked certain questions. Sometimes, the patient prefers to provide information to a caregiver of a particular gender; other times, patients feel timid about "wasting the dentist's time" asking questions that may be frivolous or unimportant but will confide in the dental assistant instead.

Patients may feel embarrassed about medical problems such as a weak bladder, incontinence, or wearing a colostomy bag. These sensitivities should be handled professionally and courteously by the dental assistant. Sometimes, patients simply feel socially insecure about having halitosis and request mouthwash prior to undergoing a dental examination.

Managing Sensitive Topics

During the course of completing a medical history form, some patients experience discomfort when asked about a previous or current history of

---

BOX 3-2

Helping Patients Feel at Ease During a Medical History Interview

The following guidelines may be helpful to the dental assistant when taking a medical/dental history on a new patient.

1. Provide a comfortable, private, well-lighted, well-ventilated area in which to interview the patient.
2. Position yourself facing the patient and maintain eye contact, especially when speaking with the patient.
3. Avoid using medical or dental jargon or terminology that may distance the patient.
4. Speak in a professional tone of voice; avoid slang and use proper grammar.
5. Postpone asking personal, sensitive, or lifestyle questions until you have established rapport with the patient.
6. Keep focused and avoid distractions such as phone calls and interruptions by other staff members or patients.
7. Do not chew gum, bite your nails, pick your cuticles, play with your hair, lick your fingers when turning pages, or exhibit nervous mannerisms such as finger drumming or foot shaking. (The latter behaviors suggest you are impatient, trying to speed up the interview, or that you would rather be somewhere else.)
8. Emphasize to the patient that all information is kept confidential and cannot be released without the patient's written permission.
9. Keep in mind that all patients should be treated as individuals.

---

sexually transmitted diseases, HIV/AIDS disease, venereal disease, lifestyle choices, or treatment for drug or alcohol addiction. They may also be reluctant to discuss a history of pregnancies, miscarriage, abortion, or use of oral contraceptives (Box 3–3).

RELATED FORMS

There are several forms that require the dental assistant's knowledge in preparing and completing prior to the patient's first clinical appointment. These forms include clinical charts, financial responsibility and insurance forms, and informed consent forms, as well as the medical history form.

All chart entries must be legible, dated, and initialed by the person making the entry.

BOX 3-3

Managing Sensitive Topics

The following guidelines may be helpful to the dental assistant in managing topics of a sensitive nature.

1. Ask these questions later on during the interview, after rapport has been established.

2. Maintain direct eye contact and do not allow phone calls or other staff members to interrupt.

3. Ask all questions in a matter-of-fact tone; do not make judgments or respond inappropriately.

4. Employ a technique called "normalizing" when asking sensitive questions, for example, *"Often, young women who are in the early states of pregnancy are reluctant to share this information with others. If you are pregnant or think you may be pregnant, this information is important because we will use additional protective measures when treating you or prescribing specific drugs. Might you be pregnant?"*

Clinical Records

The clinical record contains pertinent information that results from the oral examination conducted by the dentist, the patient's report of pain or other complaints or concerns (if any), and treatment required or that has been completed previously.

Whether using computer-generated records or manual records, the dental assistant must complete general information, such as the patient's name, the date, and any other information the dentist requires on this form prior to seating the patient. If entries are made by hand, the dental assistant and all other clinical staff should use black or blue ink. If a mistake is made, it should not be erased or obliterated with correction fluid. A single line should be made through the error and the correction made immediately after it, the person's initials and date noted. No financial information is ever recorded on clinical records. Financial records are made on a separate form.

Financial Responsibility and Insurance

All patients, whether those of record or new, must complete a **financial responsibility form** (Figure 3–3). This information includes the name, address, and phone number(s) of the patient and the responsible party (if different); specific insurance information such as the name of the carrier, the insured's group and/or policy number, and expiration date.

Additional information required includes the responsible party's Social Security number and place of employment. Often a signature is required

Welcome

We are pleased to welcome you to our practice. Please take a few minutes to fill out this form as completely as you can. If you have questions we'll be glad to help you. We look forward to working with you in maintaining your dental health.

Patient Information

Name _____ Soc. Sec. # _____
　　　　Last Name　　　　　　　First Name　　　　　　　Initial

Address _____

City _____ State _____ Zip _____ Phone _____

Sex ☐ M ☐ F Age _____ Birthdate _____ ☐ Single ☐ Married ☐ Widowed ☐ Separated ☐ Divorced

Patient Employed by _____ Occupation _____

Business Address _____ Business Phone _____

Whom may we thank for referring you? _____

Notify in case of emergency _____ Home Phone _____ Work Phone _____

Primary Insurance

Person Responsible for Account _____
　　　　　　　　　　　Last Name　　　　　　　First Name　　　　　　Initial

Relation to Patient _____ Birthdate _____ Soc. Sec. # _____

Address (if different from patient) _____ Home Phone _____

City _____ State _____ Zip _____

Person Responsible Employed by _____ Occupation _____

Business Address _____ Business Phone _____

Insurance Company _____ Phone _____

Contract # _____ Group # _____ Subscriber # _____

Name of other dependents under this plan _____

Additional Insurance

Is patient covered by additional insurance? ☐ Yes ☐ No

Subscriber Name _____ Relation to Patient _____ Birthdate _____

Address (if different from patient) _____ Soc. Sec. # _____

City _____ State _____ Zip _____ Phone _____

Subscriber Employed by _____ Business Phone _____

Insurance Company _____ Phone _____

Contract # _____ Group # _____ Subscriber # _____

Name of other dependents under this plan _____

FIGURE 3–3

Sample patient financial responsibility form. (*Reprinted courtesy of ©SmartPractice, Inc., Phoenix, AZ. All rights reserved. To order call 800-522-0800.*)

from the responsible party, with that person agreeing to pay fees not covered by insurance.

The financial responsibility form may also contain specific information about availability of financial payment plans and the office's policy regarding assessment of interest on extended or late payments.

Informed Consent

Before initiating treatment, the dentist should also have a completed, signed, and dated **informed consent form**, which is a written prior consent allowing the dentist to proceed with patient examination, diagnosis, and treatment. Examination, diagnosis, and treatment should *not* begin until this form is signed. Informed consent is addressed in *Chapter 4: Legal and Ethical Considerations of Infection Control.*

SKILLS MASTERY ASSESSMENT: POSTTEST

Directions: Select the response that best answers each of the following questions. Only one response is correct.

1. The medical/dental history form provides all of the following EXCEPT
   a. an opportunity to note patients' feelings and attitudes about their teeth.
   b. an opportunity to obtain financial responsibility and insurance information.
   c. the reason for the first appointment.
   d. the patient's current dental complaints or concerns.

2. The office manager or dental assistant should never be allowed to assist the new patient in completing medical history forms because this information is confidential and can be given only to the dentist.
   a. True   b. False

3. The dental assistant reviews a new adult patient's medical history form and notices that the patient has left blank spaces for information about her family physician as well as the name and phone number of the person to contact in case of emergency. The dental assistant should:
   a. question the patient in private regarding this information and enter it on the medical history form.
   b. hand the questionnaire back to the patient and tell her the dentist cannot treat her until all blank spaces have been completed.
   c. call the patient's insurance company to try to determine the name of the patient's physician.
   d. assume this is confidential information or that the patient does not have a family physician or family member to call in the event of a medical emergency and leave the spaces blank.

4. Before initiating treatment on any patient, the dentist must have the opportunity to review the patient's medical history for all of the following EXCEPT
   a. writing prescriptions for the patient.
   b. alleviating pain or infection.
   c. avoiding possible drug interactions or sensitivities/allergies.
   d. reviewing the patient's financial/insurance form.

5. When or how often should the dental assistant update the patient's medical history?
   a. At every appointment
   b. Once every year
   c. At each subsequent recall visit
   d. Once every 2 years

6. An example of an especially serious emerging disease is
   a. colitis.   c. coxsackievirus.
   b. poliomyelitis.   d. hepatitis C.

7. Allergic reactions to latex may be any of the following EXCEPT
   a. sclerodermic (type III).
   b. immediate hypersensitivity (type I).
   c. delayed hypersensitivity (type IV).
   d. irritant dermatitis (ID).

8. Vinyl gloves
   a. provide greater elasticity than latex gloves.
   b. are an acceptable alternative to latex gloves.
   c. offer greater protection against hepatitis B and HIV.
   d. are truly hypoallergenic.

9. Patients who are allergic to bananas, avocados, chestnuts, kiwi, passion fruit, or potatoes may have a higher risk for _____.
   a. asthma   c. latex sensitivity
   b. syncope   d. anaphylaxis

10. Information of a sensitive nature must be obtained by the dental assistant in a private office or in another area out of earshot of other patients.
    a. True   b. False

11. The dental assistant realizes he or she has made an error on a patient's medical history form. The dental assistant should
    a. rewrite the information in red ink.
    b. erase and correct the error.
    c. obliterate the mistake using correction fluid so no one will notice it.
    d. draw a single line through the error and make the correction immediately after it, noting his or her initials and the date.

12. In an attempt to demonstrate professionalism, the dental assistant should always speak to patients using medical or dental jargon and terminology.
    a. True   b. False

Legal and Ethical Considerations of Infection Control

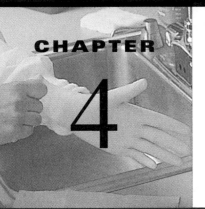

KEY TERMS

abandonment

Americans with Disabilities Act

burden of proof

disabled

ethics

impairment

jurisprudence

malpractice

negligent

risk management

standard of care

State Dental Practice Act

unprofessional conduct

LEARNING OBJECTIVES

Upon completion of this chapter, the student should be able to:

1. Describe legal and ethical responsibilities related to dentistry and the professional/ethical standards of the dental assistant.

2. Describe the legal importance of obtaining written informed consent prior to beginning treatment.

3. Be familiar with the importance of the concept of privileged communication and patient confidentiality.

4. Describe the legal considerations of treating and referring high-risk patients.

5. Be familiar with the content and implications of the American Dental Assistants Association's Principles of Ethics and Professional Conduct.

6. Describe the importance of risk management in preventing dental malpractice.

7. Describe necessary steps to dismiss a patient from the practice.

LEGAL AND ETHICAL RESPONSIBILITIES

As does every profession, dentistry carries with it legal and ethical responsibilities. The responsibility of carrying out sound infection control procedures is but a small part of that responsibility in ensuring the health, safety, and welfare of all patients.

Dental Jurisprudence

Dental **jurisprudence**, a philosophy of law or a set of legal regulations set forth by each state's legislature, describes the legal limitations and regulations related to the practice of dentistry and dental hygiene. All licensed dental personnel are legally bound to adhere to mandates of their respective **State Dental Practice Act**, which is a legally enforceable set of written rules and regulations set forth and enforced by the state Board of Dental Examiners.

Licensed dental personnel must be familiar with and follow these rules and be aware of dental duties legally allowable (and not allowable) in the state in which they practice. Failure to comply with these provisions may result in a malpractice suit filed by or on behalf of the patient or in a complaint filed by the patient or his or her representative with the Board of Dental Examiners.

While the majority of cases filed by patients are dismissed, those cases in which the dentist (and/or staff members) are found legally at fault may result in censure (discipline), restriction of practice, or loss of license. Sound jurisprudence includes following legally acceptable standards of infection control.

Dental Ethics

Dental **ethics** is a moral obligation that encompasses professional conduct and judgment imposed by the members of a particular profession. Ethical standards are developed by the professional organization; those who participate in the profession are morally obligated to act in an ethical or moral manner. Ethics is considered a higher standard (moral) than jurisprudence (legal) requirements. All members of the dental team have an ethical obligation to adhere to acceptable standards of infection control.

PROFESSIONAL STANDARDS OF THE DENTAL ASSISTANT

As a member of the dental team, the dental assistant is obligated to follow legal and ethical standards of the profession, including those required to maintain a safe, sanitary environment that reduces the potential for disease transmission. Failure to do so may result in the dental assistant's loss of employment or legal liability in a lawsuit or complaint filed by a patient.

For example, if a patient were to allege that he or she contracted an infectious disease as a direct result of care received in the practice, the dental assistant may be held liable for failure to prove that adequate infection control procedures were followed at the time of that patient's appointment. The burden of proof could fall on the dental assistant to be able to demonstrate that infection control procedures were maintained and that instruments were properly sterilized.

Vicarious Liability

Vicarious (secondhand) liability means the dentist or other employer of the dental assistant may be held liable for an action or deed of someone else working in the office, such as an employee or independent contractor.

Specific examples that lead to vicarious liability include a patient choking on an x-ray film, aspirating or swallowing a temporary crown, sustaining a burn, suffering visual impairment as a direct action of the dental assistant, or contracting an infectious disease as a result of a dental appointment. In any such incident, the dentist may be held liable for the dental assistant's action.

The dentist's liability may originate without the dentist having had any direct involvement with the party filing the claim. The dentist may never have seen or treated the patient and may still be named in a lawsuit or complaint.

In most cases, it is the owner of a dental practice who is named in a suit or complaint. This is called the *doctrine of respondeat superior* (Latin for "let the superior [person] respond") for the wrong that was allegedly committed.

ADAA Code of Ethics

The American Dental Assistants Association's Principles of Ethics and Professional Conduct is the standard by which all dental assistants, including clinical and managerial personnel, are expected to work (Box 4–1).

BOX 4–1

American Dental Assistants Association
Principles of Ethics and Professional Conduct

Each individual involved in the practice of dentistry assumes the obligation of maintaining and enriching the profession. Each member shall choose to meet this obligation according to the dictates of personal conscience based on the needs of the general public the profession of dentistry is committed to serve.

The member shall refrain from performing any professional service which is prohibited by state law and has the obligation to prove competence prior to providing services to any patient. The member shall constantly strive to upgrade and expand technical skills for the benefit of the employer and consumer public. This member should additionally seek to sustain and improve the local organization, state association and the American Dental Assistants Association through active participation and personal commitment.

MAINTAINING CONFIDENTIALITY OF PATIENTS' RECORDS

All patients' records are considered confidential. Failure to maintain a level of confidentiality may be cause for dismissal or legal liability for the dental assistant. This is especially true if a patient has a sexually transmissible disease or discloses a positive HIV/AIDS status.

Anything that is said, done, or written in the office is considered confidential. As such, names, addresses, telephone numbers, the nature of treatment, disclosure of infectious disease status, medical or financial history, and diagnosis are not generally disclosed to the public or to other private agencies.

Most insurance claim forms contain a statement and signature line stating that the patient or responsible party agrees to the release of treatment information, medical/dental history, and other pertinent information (such as Social Security number) for the claim to be processed. When in doubt, the dental assistant should always check with the doctor before releasing information.

If a patient requests release of treatment records or the dentist refers the patient to a specialist for further evaluation or treatment, the office must obtain a written, signed, and dated request from the patient or the new treating dentist of record. The office should release *copies* of the original clinical records and duplicates of dental radiographs, never the originals.

Patient Confidentiality and the Fax Machine

The introduction of the fax machine has caused healthcare professionals to be concerned about confidentiality, particularly regarding infectious disease status. The guidelines listed in Box 4–2 are helpful when considering whether to fax patients' records for timeliness.

Informed Consent

Prior to initiating examination or treatment, the practice must obtain a signed informed consent form (Figure 4–1) as part of the patient's complete records. If the patient is a minor or mentally incompetent, the dental assistant must obtain informed consent from a parent or guardian on behalf of the patient. (Implied consent, which, simply interpreted, means the patient sits in the dental chair and implies that he or she consents to whatever dental treatment is needed, is insufficient.)

Informed consent is more than obtaining permission to examine or treat a patient. It includes the ailment, disease, or problem; the recommended treatment and the risks involved; alternative treatments and the risks; inadequate or nontreatment risks; and estimated fees.

The practice's informed consent form should contain all of the following components:

- Reason for treatment
- Diagnosis
- Prognosis

BOX 4-2

Guidelines to Protect Patients' Privacy When Faxing Records

The dental assistant should use these guidelines when preparing to fax patients' records.

1. Have the patient or responsible party sign an authorization to release records before faxing information to another healthcare provider or insurance company.

2. Never fax financial information. Faxing on the basis of medical necessity or emergency can be justified in court; however, faxing of financial data a patient considers confidential is not justifiable.

3. Fax information only to other doctors' offices or designated insurance carriers.

4. Use a cover sheet with the following warning: "The information contained in this facsimile is medically privileged and confidential and is intended solely for the individual(s) and/or entities named herein. If you receive this message and are not the intended recipient, you are hereby notified that any dissemination, distribution, or reproduction of this communication is strictly prohibited. If you have received this communication in error, please notify us by telephone immediately and return the original message to us at the address given via U.S. mail. Thank you."

5. As soon as the fax transmission has been completed, call the recipient to confirm that the fax was received. If it was not, use the "recall" or "redial" button to find the last number dialed. Then fax an urgent alert to that number and ask, "All personnel of goodwill should immediately and effectively destroy all documents received in the previous transmission."

- Alternate plans of treatment
- Nature of care and treatment
- Inherent risks
- Expectancy of success
- Possible results (consequences) if treatment is not done

Privileged Communications

All communications between the patient and the office are considered privileged, and this information must not be repeated in any form—written, oral, or electronic—without the patient's express written consent.

As such, the dental assistant must ensure that all conversations regarding patients' diagnoses; treatment plans; health status, including history of any infectious diseases; and financial information are kept private. They may not be repeated within earshot of other patients, in the home, or in public.

DENTAL TREATMENT CONSENT FORM

*Please read and initial the items checked below
and read and sign the section at the bottom of form.*   Patient Name_____

☐ **1. WORK TO BE DONE**

    I understand that I am having the following work done: Fillings_____ Bridges_____ Crowns_____ Extractions_____
Impacted teeth removed _____ General Anesthesia_____ Root Canals_____ Other_____

(Initials_____)

☐ **2. DRUGS AND MEDICATIONS**

    I understand that antibiotics and analgesics and other medications can cause allergic reactions causing redness and swelling of
tissues, pain, itching, vomiting, and/or anaphylactic shock (severe allergic reaction). (Initials_____)

☐ **3. CHANGES IN TREATMENT PLAN**

    I understand that during treatment it may be necessary to change or add procedures because of conditions found while working on
the teeth that were not discovered during examination, the most common being root canal therapy following routine restorative
procedures. I give my permission to the Dentist to make any/all changes and additions as necessary. (Initials_____)

☐ **4. REMOVAL OF TEETH**

    Alternatives to removal have been explained to me (root canal therapy, crowns, and periodontal surgery, etc.) and I authorize the
Dentist to remove the following teeth _____ and any others necessary for reasons in paragraph #3. I
understand removing teeth does not always remove all the infection, if present, and it may be necessary to have further treatment. I
understand the risks involved in having teeth removed, some of which are pain, swelling, spread of infection, dry socket, loss of feeling
in my teeth, lips, tongue and surrounding tissue (Paresthesia) that can last for an indefinite period of time (days or months) or fractured
jaw. I understand I may need further treatment by a specialist or even hospitalization if complications arise during or following treatment,
the cost of which is my responsibility. (Initials_____)

☐ **5. CROWN, BRIDGES AND CAPS**

    I understand that sometimes it is not possible to match the color of natural teeth exactly with artificial teeth. I further understand that I
may be wearing temporary crowns, which may come off easily and that I must be careful to ensure that they are kept on until the
permanent crowns are delivered. I realize the final opportunity to make changes in my new crown, bridge, or cap (including shape, fit,
size, and color) will be before cementation. (Initials_____)

☐ **6. DENTURES, COMPLETE OR PARTIAL**

    I realize that full or partial dentures are artificial, constructed of plastic, metal, and/or porcelain. The problems of wearing these
appliances have been explained to me, including looseness, soreness, and possible breakage. I realize the final opportunity to make
changes in my new dentures (including shape, fit, size, placement, and color) will be the "teeth in wax" try-in visit. I understand that
most dentures require relining approximately three to twelve months after initial placement. The cost for this procedure is not included in
the initial denture fee. (Initials_____)

☐ **7. ENDODONTIC TREATMENT (ROOT CANAL)**

    I realize there is no guarantee that root canal treatment will save my tooth, and that complications can occur from the treatment, and
that occasionally metal objects are cemented in the tooth or extend through the root, which does not necessarily affect the success of
the treatment, I understand that occasionally additional surgical procedures may be necessary following root canal treatment
(apicoectomy). (Initials_____)

☐ **8. PERIODONTAL LOSS (TISSUE & BONE)**

    I understand that I have a serious condition, causing gum and bone inflammation or loss and that it can lead to the loss of my teeth.
Alternative treatment plans have been explained to me, including gum surgery, replacements and/or extractions. I understand that
undertaking any dental procedures may have a future adverse effect on my periodontal condition. (Initials_____)

    I understand that dentistry is not an exact science and that, therefore, reputable practitioners cannot fully guarantee results. I
acknowledge that no guarantee or assurance has been made by anyone regarding the dental treatment which I have requested and
authorized. I have had the opportunity to read this form and ask questions. My questions have been answered to my satisfaction. I
consent to the proposed treatment.

Signature of Patient_____ Date_____

Signature of Parent/Guardian if patient is a minor_____ Date_____

#21153 – Medical Arts Press 1-800-328-2179

FIGURE 4–1

Informed consent form. *(Reprinted courtesy of Medical Arts Press, Minneapolis, MN)*

Treating High-Risk Patients

The privilege of caring for a patient's oral health needs encompasses the patient's total health and well-being. Patients who are considered at high risk, for example those diagnosed with transmissible diseases such as HIV/AIDS, tuberculosis, hepatitis, and related sexually transmitted disease, are to be extended the same degree of dignity and privacy as all other patients. Members of the dental team must remember to withhold judgment as to the origin of the disease transmission and to focus on helping that patient reach and maintain as high a degree of dental health as possible.

Office Policy Statement on Treating Patients with HIV/AIDS

Awareness of the origin and sources of transmission of HIV/AIDS during the past decade has brought about an increased awareness of the potential for disease transmission and methods of preventing this transmission.

The dental assistant and all other clinical personnel should employ the same universal precautions while treating patients with known HIV/AIDS infection as when treating any other patients. Refusing treatment to known HIV/AIDS-infected patients is considered discrimination and may result in sanctions, penalties, or lawsuits.

To allay other patients' fears about the transmission of potentially fatal diseases from other patients or from potentially infected dental personnel, some offices have posted the dentist's personal HIV/AIDS test results in the reception area or printed these test results in the local newspaper.

Other practices take a more conservative approach, using plaques, signs, or notices on statements and in the practice newsletter. For further information on developing a written HIV/AIDS statement for the dental office manual or for patients to read, refer to *Chapter 16: Marketing Infection Control.*

Observe Applicable Laws

The dental office must observe all applicable laws and ordinances, such as zoning and parking ordinances, and secure the proper building permits, and fire extinguisher and elevator inspections. Failure to comply may result in a warning, followed by legal action, and fines may be imposed if violations are not corrected.

THE AMERICANS WITH DISABILITIES ACT

Approximately 43 million Americans have some degree of disability. Enacted in 1992, the **Americans with Disabilities Act** applies specifically to dental offices, requiring that facilities be accessible to disabled (physically or mentally compromised) patients, including those with infectious diseases.

Implications for the Dental Office

The Americans with Disabilities Act enumerates five categories of people who are protected from discrimination:

1. People with a physical or mental impairment that substantially limits one or more of the major life activities such as seeing, hearing, speaking, walking, breathing, performing manual tasks, learning, caring for oneself, or working. Also included in this category are people who have disabling conditions such as AIDS, HIV infection, heart disease, diabetes, cancer, learning disabilities, or mental retardation.

2. People who have a record of such an impairment such as a history of cancer or a person with a history of mental illness are included.

3. People who, while not actually disabled, are regarded as having such an impairment due to severe disfigurement but are fully functional are included.

4. People who are discriminated against because they have a known association or relationship with a disabled individual are included.

Impairment means any physiological disorder or condition, cosmetic disfigurement, or anatomical loss. It can also mean any mental or psychological disorder such as mental retardation, emotional or mental illness, or specific learning disabilities.

Disabled patients are those with neurologic or physical disabilities that impair function. Neurological handicaps can be motor, sensory, emotional, or intellectual in nature. The Act protects people who currently participate in or who have completed a drug or alcohol rehabilitation program. Advanced age and obesity do *not* qualify as impairments under the Act (Box 4–3).

Under Title I, a dentist who employs 15 or more people for a minimum of 20 weeks annually must comply with the applicable Title I requirements of the Americans with Disabilities Act. Title I specifically prohibits discrimination against a qualified individual (employment candidate) with a disability because of the disability.

Title III of the Act covers public accommodations (any facility operated by a private entity whose operations affect commerce, including a professional office of a healthcare provider). A dental office is a public accommodation under the Act. A public accommodation includes a private home to the extent it is used for a professional office of a healthcare provider, including a dental practice.

Under Title III, the dental office is a public accommodation and thus may not refuse to provide access and services to any person because he or she is disabled. The obligation to not discriminate is placed on anyone who owns, leases (or leases to), or operates a place of public accommodation.

The underlying principles of the nondiscrimination requirements of Title III include the following:

- Equal opportunity for the disabled to participate
- Equal opportunity for the disabled to benefit
- Opportunity for the disabled to receive benefits in the most integrated setting possible

---

BOX 4-3

What Is the Americans with Disabilities Act?

The Americans with Disabilities Act is a federal legal provision designed to prevent discrimination against disabled people. It provides a national mandate for the elimination of discrimination against individuals with disabilities and provides clear, strong, enforceable standards addressing discrimination against disabled people. The Act is broken down into five titles; *Titles I* and *III* have the greatest relevance to dental practices.

1. *Title I* eliminates discriminating employment policies.
2. *Title II* prohibits discrimination against the disabled in the use of public transportation.
3. *Title III* requires that public accommodations operated by private entities not discriminate against individuals with disabilities (including those with infectious/sexually transmissible diseases).
4. *Title IV* prohibits discrimination against the disabled in the area of communication, especially the hearing and speech impaired.
5. *Title V* contains miscellaneous provisions regarding the continued viability of other state or federal laws providing disabled persons with equal or greater rights than the Act. This section also prohibits state or local governments from discriminating against individuals with disabilities.

Violations of the Act may result in civil monetary penalties of up to $50,000 for the first violation and up to $100,000 for subsequent violations. In addition, a violator (dentist) may be ordered to provide services that are found to have been wrongfully denied (Box 4–4).

Necessary Office Renovations

The Americans with Disabilities Act does *not* require the dental practice to remove all barriers to accessibility as long as a plan of priorities is established. The Department of Justice recommends barriers be removed based upon the following priorities:

- Access to premises: Provide access from public sidewalks, parking, and public transportation. This can be done by providing wider entrances, ramps, and accessible parking spaces, including designated handicapped spaces.
- Access to service areas: Create physical access, as well as eliminate barriers for the visually and hearing impaired.
- Access to restrooms: Widen doorways, install ramps, add appropriate signage, widen toilet stalls, and install grab bars in restrooms.
- Access to other areas of the practice: Provide equal services to the disabled.

BOX 4–4

Equipping the Office to Accommodate Disabled Patients

The Department of Justice recommends the following modifications to barriers that may be readily achievable under the Americans with Disabilities Act:

- Installing ramps
- Installing curb cuts (areas where the sidewalk dips down to accommodate wheelchairs or vehicles)
- Designating handicapped parking spaces
- Installing raised letters and braille on elevator controls
- Providing visual alarms
- Widening doors and doorways
- Installing grab bars
- Installing raised toilet seats and large stalls
- Repositioning paper towel dispensers in restrooms
- Installing paper cup dispensers at existing water fountains
- Eliminating high-pile, low-density carpeting

Reception areas should feature built-in counters and patient interview areas accessible to accommodate disabled people. Providing a clipboard or table is an acceptable alternative if counter areas cannot be reached by wheelchair patients.

For access to treatment rooms, if steps exist between treatment and service areas, ramps must be provided for wheelchair patients. Portable ramps are acceptable if permanent ramps are not readily available. A portable ramp should be equipped with handrails and a slip-proof surface.

Office restrooms should have raised letters and braille symbols to designate men's and women's restroom doors. Widening of doors and doorways; installing grab bars, raised toilet seats, and full-length mirrors; and repositioning of paper towel dispensers are required to make restrooms accessible to the disabled. Water fountains must also be made accessible when readily achievable. If water fountains cannot be lowered, a paper cup dispenser must be installed within reach of a person sitting in a wheelchair.

A minimum of one wheelchair-accessible telephone must be made available when public telephones are provided inside the facility. If the public telephone is not accessible, a private telephone should be made available. Signs must be posted near the public telephone to indicate the location of the private telephone.

Audible alarms must be installed for the visually impaired, and visual alarms should be installed to alert the deaf. Directories should be posted to designate the location of visual alarms.

All attempts should be made by the dental team to integrate patients with disabilities into the practice. No service can be denied, nor can an individual patient be excluded, segregated, or otherwise treated differently than other patients simply because the patient has a disability.

Auxiliary aids and services named in the Americans with Disabilities Act include qualified interpreters, note takers, printed instructions and materials, telephone handset amplifiers, assistive listening devices, telephones compatible with hearing aids, or other effective methods of making visually delivered materials available to hearing-impaired patients. Auxiliary aids for visually impaired patients may include taped texts, braille materials, and large-print materials. Additional fees may *not* be charged by the practice for providing any auxiliary aid or service, barrier removal, or any other measures necessary to ensure compliance with the Act.

To help offset costs of upgrading or modifying physical structures in the office, Congress instituted the Disabled Access Credit (Form 8826), whereby 50 percent of eligible access expenditures up to $10,250 may be deducted or depreciated from taxes.

RISK MANAGEMENT AND QUALITY ASSURANCE STRATEGIES TO PREVENT MALPRACTICE

Dental legal and ethical concerns continue to grow as the number of dental **malpractice** suits rises, meaning professional negligence or implying failure to perform one's professional duties. The dental assistant must keep in mind that while lawsuits cannot be eliminated or prevented, the risk for potential must be kept to a minimum; having a quality assurance program may help. **Risk management** means having a preventive strategy to reduce this potential.

The wise dental assistant is alert to strategies for risk management and ways to reduce the potential for malpractice suits against the practice. The following concepts are important in maintaining a quality assurance program and in preventing malpractice suits.

Negligence

In most states, a dentist is **negligent** when he or she does an act within his or her profession that a responsible dentist would not do, or fails to do an act that a reasonable dentist would do. If a lawsuit is filed against the dentist, it must be shown that the dentist acted negligently and that this negligence was the cause of the patient's injury for an award to be made. While the dentist, as primary care practitioner and/or owner of the practice, is most often the one against whom a suit is filed, any member of the dental staff may also be held accountable for negligence or harm done to a patient.

Negligence with regard to infection control may come about if the patient or the patient's attorney can prove that instruments were improperly sterilized and the patient developed a resulting infection.

Standard of Care

An unsatisfactory treatment outcome does not confirm negligence on the part of the dentist. It must be proved that the dentist provided treatment that deviated from an applicable **standard of care**, which means treatment guidelines that a dentist with the same knowledge, skill, and care in the same community would provide, and that this departure resulted in the injury sustained by the patient.

In healthcare, there are no "absolute" standards of care but rather treatment guidelines that a dentist with the same knowledge, skill, and care in the same community would provide. Thus, the standard of care may be interpreted to mean, "Did the dentist act reasonably at the time and under the circumstances?"

An example of a dentist adhering to the standard of care regarding infection control would be if the dental office employed the equivalent methods, techniques, and equipment used to sterilize instruments as other dental practices in the area.

Abandonment

Abandonment, or failure to provide necessary dental treatment, is considered **unprofessional conduct**, which is defined as any act or deed that fails to uphold the State Dental Practice Act. Under this provision, the dentist may not withdraw treatment of a patient unless both reasonable notice of the withdrawal and replacement dentist(s) are offered to the patient. Failure to treat a patient whose needs are apparent and for which the opportunity to treat the patient exists may be considered negligence.

With regard to infection control, a patient may claim a communicable disease was contracted during the course of treatment, and the dentist did nothing to address this allegation. Another example would be if the dentist learned of a patient's AIDS/HIV status after initiating treatment, then refused to continue or to complete treatment or attempted to refer the patient out of the practice for this reason. The dental office must take great care in addressing all complaints or concerns raised by patients to avoid patient claims of abandonment or failure to complete necessary treatment.

Burden of Proof

In a malpractice case, the **burden of proof** means that the patient seeking to impose liability against the dentist must supply the more convincing evidence that the dentist's action caused resulting harm or injury.

In a case in which a patient alleges that harm was done to him—for example, he believes he contracted hepatitis B from an injection or during a procedure in the dental office—that patient must be able to prove convincingly that his evidence is more persuasive than the dentist's attempt to refute the claim.

Elements of Malpractice

All dental staff are legally obligated to adhere to the dental standards set forth in the State Dental Practice Act. As an example, many states require all dental staff to have cardiopulmonary resuscitation (CPR) certification with periodic updates. In addition to familiarity with the terms set forth in the State Dental Practice Act, the dentist and staff must possess an awareness of treatment procedures and protocols that fall within the standard of care. Failure to perform any of the following may be considered cause for malpractice:

The first element is a *duty to act*. A healthcare practitioner has a legal and ethical duty to respond when treatment is required.

The second element is an act of *omission* or an act of *commission*. The first means failing to carry out something that should be done to prevent harm or injury; the second means committing an act that contributes to or directly causes harm or injury. Failure to provide CPR to a patient in cardiopulmonary arrest would be an act of omission. Knowingly using an instrument contaminated from use on a prior patient would be an act of commission.

The third element is *proof of injury or harm* caused to a patient of record. This most commonly refers to physical injury but may include emotional or psychological harm.

The fourth element is *failure to act as a reasonable, prudent person would* was the proximate cause of the patient's injuries. An example would be spilling acid etch material on a patient's skin, resulting in burning.

Causes of Malpractice Suits

More than two-thirds of the claims made in healthcare malpractice suits are directly related to unexpected outcomes or unrealistic expectations perceived by the patient. The following sequence of events is often what leads up to a patient's filing of a malpractice suit:

1. A dental problem occurs that may be unexpected but not unusual under the circumstances.
2. The patient is unhappy with the situation or result.
3. The patient contacts the dentist for clarification or solutions.
4. The patient is dissatisfied with attempts or explanations made by the dentist about the perceived problem or the result associated with treatment.
5. The patient files a malpractice suit.

Another very common reason patients file malpractice is poor communication on the part of the dentist or staff.

Failure to diagnose/inform the patient of specific clinical findings is another common reason for filing a malpractice suit.

Failure to diagnose and treat or refer for treatment to a specialist is common cause for malpractice.

Failure to explain treatment options and the expected, realistic outcome and/or consequences of nontreatment is another cause of malpractice suits.

Steps to Prevent Malpractice

The following risk management steps are important to reduce the possibility of a lawsuit against the dentist. The dental assistant must ensure that these steps are followed and that all team members are familiar with them.

1. Always obtain informed consent—written, signed, and dated—prior to proceeding with treatment.
2. Always obtain a thorough medical and dental history, signed and updated. It is the dental assistant's responsibility to update this information at each recall visit or, at a minimum, annually.
3. Make sure all records are complete and accurate. These include up-to-date radiographs, a written treatment plan, diagnosis, and dated treatment progress notes. Also document that the reasons for recommended treatment were explained to the patient, including possible complications of delayed treatment or noncompliance with recommended treatment; document that all treatment options and their corresponding prognoses were explained to the patient. If the patient elects *not* to accept or proceed with recommended treatment, request that he or she sign a detailed, dated waiver rejecting treatment and stating that he or she understands the consequences.
4. Document all patient complaints, comments, and reasons for seeking treatment.
5. Always enter chart notations in ink. Never erase, cover up, use correction fluid on, or attempt to amend records. If an error is made, draw a *single line* through the error, initial and date the error, and make the correction immediately next to the original chart entry. All staff members, including the dentist, must initial chart entries.
6. If an additional treatment note is required, enter it on a new line in the chart, with *addenda* and the date.
7. Never discard inactive patient records. Store them in a separate, secured area and retain them for a minimum of 30 years.
8. Always keep treatment, financial, and personal patient documentation and records on separate forms.
9. Follow a uniform chart entry system to ensure conformity and lessen the likelihood of omission of relevant information.
10. If records are requested or subpoenaed, forward quality duplicates—never the originals.
11. Never berate another dentist's treatment. Clinical records and related discussion and documentation should include only the patient's condition as diagnosed, objective observations, patient's comments relating to the situation, and the recommended necessary treatment plan.
12. Document in the record all telephone conversations with patients, referring specialists, and authorized prescriptions.
13. Use sequentially numbered prescription pads with carbon paper or carbonless copies, and always place one copy into the patient's record.
14. Document all cancellations, late arrivals, and disappointments in the record.

15. Enter the dates of all radiographs and other diagnostic casts in the record.
16. Enter specific postoperative instructions or note that standard postoperative instructions were given to the patient.
17. Note the type (generic or brand name) of materials used for all dental procedures.
18. Never make treatment guarantees. Instead, educate patients that their active participation and cooperation have a substantial effect on the success of their treatment outcomes.

When an Accident Happens or a Patient Complains

If an accident occurs, especially resulting in undue injury or harm to a patient, or if there is a complaint by a patient, the dental assistant should say nothing. Instead, the assistant should alert the dentist to the nature of the patient's injury or complaint and let the dentist handle it appropriately.

When a Patient Declines or Discontinues Treatment

If a patient chooses to discontinue planned treatment, the doctor believes it is in the patient's best interest to seek dental treatment elsewhere, or the practice has been sold, great caution must be taken in releasing the patient from the doctor's care. This is to reduce the likelihood of the patient's claiming abandonment and also to ensure that the patient finds another treating dentist of record.

The practice should take the following steps in dismissing a patient:

1. Send a certified, return receipt request letter to the patient. Include two copies and request that the patient sign, date, and return one copy. This provides written documentation for the office files.
2. Include in the letter the reasons for treatment discontinuance, such as failure to comply with recommended treatment or home care or failure to pay for services.
3. The dentist should offer to be available to provide only emergency care for the next 30 calendar days, from the date of the certified letter.
4. The dentist should also offer to forward copies of the patient's records to the new treating dentist or to make copies available for the patient to pick up, upon receipt of a written, signed, and dated request. The office should provide legible copies and may charge a reasonable fee to provide these copies. The practice legally owns the records, although patients have access to them.
5. The dentist should also provide the names of several practitioners or clinics available to provide continued care.

SKILLS MASTERY ASSESSMENT: POSTTEST

Directions: Select the response that best answers each of the following questions. Only one response is correct.

1. Which of the following is true regarding dental jurisprudence?
   a. Dental jurisprudence represents a philosophy of law or a set of legal regulations set forth by each state's legislature.
   b. Dental jurisprudence describes the legal limitations and regulations related to the practice of dentistry and dental hygiene.
   c. Dental jurisprudence represents a moral or ethical standard of dentistry.
   d. a and b only
   e. All of the above

2. Dental licensees found at fault with regard to the State Dental Practice Act may be subject to which of the following?
   a. Censure (discipline)
   b. Restriction of practice
   c. Loss of license
   d. b or c only
   e. Any/all of the above

3. Dental ethics is a moral obligation that encompasses professional conduct and judgment imposed by the members of a particular profession.
   a. True
   b. False

4. Jurisprudence is considered a higher standard (moral) than ethics (legal) requirements.
   a. True
   b. False

5. Because dental assistants are not licensed in most states, they are not obligated to follow legal and ethical standards of the profession in the state of employment.
   a. True
   b. False

6. A dental assistant places acid etch on a lower first molar of a 6-year-old patient. The patient accidentally gags and receives a third-degree burn on his tongue. Although the dentist was not in the treatment room and did not participate in the incident, he or she may be found liable under a condition known as
   a. direct supervision.
   b. respondeat superior.
   c. vicarious liability.
   d. indirect supervision.

7. "Each individual involved in the practice of dentistry assumes the obligation of maintaining and enriching the profession. Each member shall choose to meet this obligation according to the dictates of personal conscience based on the needs of the general public the profession of dentistry is committed to serve . . ." is an excerpt from
   a. the ADAA's Principles of Ethics and Professional Conduct.
   b. the ADAA's Statement of Professional Conduct.
   c. the DANB's Task Analysis.
   d. None of the above

8. Which of the following pieces of information is the dental assistant allowed to disclose without the patient's permission?
   a. Patient's name, address, and telephone number
   b. Nature of treatment
   c. Disclosure of infectious disease status and diagnosis
   d. a and b only
   e. None of the above

9. A patient requests release of treatment records or the dentist refers the patient to a specialist for further evaluation or treatment. The dental assistant should do all of the following EXCEPT
   a. obtain a written, signed, and dated request from the patient or the new treating dentist of record.
   b. release copies of the original clinical records and duplicates of dental radiographs.
   c. request payment in full of any outstanding balance on the patient's account.
   d. release copies of the original clinical records and dental radiographs.
   e. a and b
   f. c and d

10. If a patient alleges he or she contracted a serious infectious illness as a direct result of an office visit, that patient may sue the office for failure to maintain sound infection control techniques.
   a. True   b. False

11. When faxing a patient's records, the dental assistant should do all of the following EXCEPT
   a. require the patient or responsible party to sign an authorization to release records before faxing information to another healthcare provider or insurance company.
   b. fax financial information.
   c. fax information only to other doctors' offices or designated insurance carriers.
   d. use an appropriate cover sheet with instructions to the recipient.

12. If the patient is a minor or mentally incompetent, the dental assistant may sign the informed consent form on the patient's behalf.
   a. True   b. False

13. Informed consent includes all of the following EXCEPT
   a. the ailment, disease, or related dental problem.
   b. the recommended treatment and its associated risks.
   c. alternative treatments and the associated risks.
   d. consequences of inadequate treatment or nontreatment.
   e. the name of the party financially responsible.

14. Refusing treatment to known HIV/AIDS-infected patients is considered discrimination and may result in sanctions, penalties, or lawsuits.
   a. True   b. False

15. Under the Americans with Disabilities Act, the term *disabled* means
   a. any physiological disorder or condition.
   b. any cosmetic disfigurement or anatomical loss.
   c. any mental or psychological disorder, such as mental retardation, emotional or mental illness, or specific learning disabilities.
   d. None of the above

16. The Americans with Disabilities Act _____ requires that public accommodations operated by private entities not discriminate against individuals with disabilities, including but not limited to infectious/sexually transmissible diseases.
   a. Title I
   b. Title II
   c. Title III
   d. Title IV
   e. Title V

17. Under the Americans with Disabilities Act, no service can be denied, nor can an individual patient be excluded, segregated, or otherwise treated differently than other patients, simply because the patient has a handicap.
   a. True
   b. False

18. During the course of extensive periodontal and crown and bridge treatment, the dentist notices a case of oral candidiasis developing on the patient's oral mucosa. Having reason to believe the patient may be of alternative lifestyle and possibly be HIV/AIDS positive, the dentist suddenly refers the patient to a specialist to complete treatment. The dentist may be found guilty of
   a. discrimination.
   b. abandonment.
   c. malpractice.
   d. a and/or b only
   e. All of the above

19. To help avoid the potential for a malpractice suit, the dental assistant should
   a. always enter chart notations in pencil for easy correction.
   b. never erase, cover up, use correction fluid on, or attempt to amend records.
   c. draw a single line through the error, initial and date the error, and make the correction immediately next to the original chart entry.
   d. b and c only.

CHAPTER 5

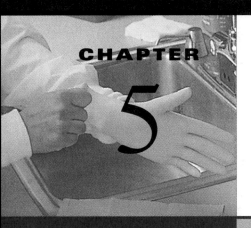

Regulatory Government Agencies and National Associations

KEY TERMS

American Dental Assistants
  Association (ADAA)

American Dental Association
  (ADA)

Centers for Disease Control and
  Prevention (CDC)

Dental Assisting National Board,
  Inc. (DANB)

Environmental Protection Agency
  (EPA)

Food and Drug Administration
  (FDA)

National Association of Dental
  Assistants (NADA)

Occupational Safety and Health
  Administration (OSHA)

Organization for Safety and
  Asepsis Procedures (OSAP)

other potentially infectious
  materials (OPIM)

LEARNING OBJECTIVES

Upon completion of this chapter, the student should be able to:

1. List and describe various government, national, and professional agencies associated with informing, educating, and protecting the general public and those affiliated with the practice of dentistry regarding infection control procedures.

2. Describe the purpose of personal protective equipment (PPE) and why it is necessary for dental employees to wear it.

3. Describe the purpose and scope of OSHA's Blood-borne Pathogens Standard and its importance to dental employees.

4. Relate the role of the American Dental Association (ADA) in informing, educating, and dictating policies regarding the containment of infectious diseases.

5. List organizations specific to dental assisting that may provide additional information on infection control, hazard communication, and certification in infection control.

THE ROLE OF GOVERNMENT AGENCIES

Many government agencies have responded to the demands of dental patients for protection from diseases and other potential hazards associated with dental care. New regulations, as well as stringent enforcement of older regulations, require dental practices to follow guidelines and recommendations set forth by several government regulatory agencies.

The purpose of these guidelines is to protect not only the public at large but also those employed in dental practice who may, in the performance of their clinical duties, contact potentially infectious diseases.

Some agencies dictate policies and guidelines. The Centers for Disease Control and Prevention (CDC), for example, is a federal agency that sets guidelines for healthcare practitioners. The Occupational Safety and Health Administration (OSHA) is a government agency that enforces guidelines for the protection of workers; OSHA has federal, regional, and state offices. OSHA enforces CDC guidelines and may impose fines or, in some cases, restriction of practice for noncompliance with required regulations.

COMPLYING WITH LOCAL, STATE, AND FEDERAL REGULATIONS

There are many government regulatory agencies that determine the way dental practices protect their employees and patients from potential hazards associated with dental treatment.

Some of these agencies are national; others are regional or statewide. It is the job of the dentist/owner of the dental practice to ensure that all regulations are met. Failure to do so may result in fines, citations, or restriction of practice.

DIFFERENCES AND DISTINCTIONS

Of the American Dental Association (ADA), the CDC, OSHA, and the Organization for Safety and Asepsis Procedures (OSAP), it is important that the dental assistant know that only OSHA has laws regarding infection control; the other organizations issue *recommendations.*

There is another significant difference between OSHA and the other groups: OSHA's Bloodborne Pathogens Standard addresses the protection of healthcare workers; the ADA, CDC, and OSAP guidelines for infection control, all of which are similar, address the protection of both healthcare workers and their patients.

Centers for Disease Control and Prevention

The **Centers for Disease Control and Prevention (CDC)** sets forth specific guidelines for infection control and disease containment. It studies and issues reports on a wide variety of data on diseases throughout the world and issues guidelines relevant to their containment.

Although the CDC does not have enforcement power over dental practices, as stated previously, OSHA is charged with investigation and enforcement of the CDC's guidelines.

Occupational Safety and Health Administration

It is the job of the **Occupational Safety and Health Administration (OSHA)** to enforce laws and regulations regarding safe dental practices. As an enforcement agency, OSHA has the legal right to enter a dental practice and to conduct an inspection for health and safety violations.

OSHA requires employers, including those in the healthcare profession to do the following:

- Establish and carry out a wide range of procedures designed to protect employees
- Implement and maintain employee exposure-incident records for the duration of employment plus 30 years
- Provide specific personal protective equipment (PPE) to protect staff from infectious diseases and other potential hazards

OSHA's Bloodborne Pathogens Standard applies to all dental employees who could reasonably anticipate coming into contact with blood, saliva, and **other potentially infectious materials (OPIM)**—those items considered contaminated that may have the potential to transmit disease—during the course of employment. It is designed to help them minimize occupational exposure to bloodborne illnesses and thus protect them from possible resulting illness.

OSHA inspectors may act upon the complaint of a patient or an employee of the practice. The name of the person filing the complaint is confidential.

The dentist/owner of the practice may request the OSHA inspector to return to conduct an inspection at a time when patients are not present in the office.

If issued a citation or citations, the dentist/owner of the practice may be supplied with a written report of the violation(s) and given a specific time frame to achieve compliance. Failure to comply may result in additional fines, citations, or restriction of practice, as well as undue negative publicity for the practice.

In some regions, OSHA will provide a free review of the office for potential health and safety violations and will make recommendations to resolve these violations. This is a complimentary service and the office cannot be issued fines or citations when the OSHA compliance officer has visited the office upon the request (invitation) of the dentist.

> *Note*
>
> The nature and intent of the law is *not* to cite or fine dental practices but rather to ensure the health, safety, and welfare of patients and staff.

Environmental Protection Agency

The **Environmental Protection Agency (EPA)** is a federal agency that regulates and registers certain products used in dental practices, including surface disinfectants; the EPA requires products to undergo and pass specific testing requirements prior to approval for registration.

For a product to be used for disinfection or sterilization procedures performed in the dental office, the product label must feature an EPA registration number.

Food and Drug Administration

The **Food and Drug Administration (FDA)** is a federal organization that regulates marketing of medical devices, including equipment and disposable items. The FDA reviews product labels for false or misleading information and sufficient directions for use and regulates many chemical germicides used as antiseptics, disinfectants, drugs, sterilizers, and latex-containing devices such as gloves and masks.

Manufacturers desiring FDA approval for their equipment, drugs, or devices must submit them to a significant review and scrutiny process prior to receiving approval.

Organization for Safety and Asepsis Procedures

The **Organization for Safety and Asepsis Procedures (OSAP)** is a national organization whose members include healthcare teachers, practitioners, dental healthcare workers, manufacturers, and distributors of dental equipment and products. OSAP develops and communicates standards and information on aseptic technique to dental practices and educational institutions to assist them in the efficacy of their infection control programs.

OSAP holds annual and regional meetings that address a variety of infection control and hazard communication topics of interest to the dental profession.

American Dental Association

The **American Dental Association (ADA)** is a national organization of licensed dentists. It releases a variety of publications to educate patients, establish protocols, and inform dentists regarding pertinent issues in dental practice. Although not a legal regulatory body, the ADA has a strong influence on dentistry by determining needs and setting policies, protocols, and standards of conduct for members of the dental profession.

In its publications, including the *Journal of the American Dental Association (JADA)*, and through press releases and a variety of media, the ADA provides information, position papers, directives, and statements regarding standards of dental care and protocols for ensuring a safe dental practice environment.

In addition to releasing publications for practicing dentists, the ADA releases many patient educational materials of interest to the public.

ORGANIZATIONS FOR DENTAL ASSISTANTS

There are a number of organizations specifically run for and by dental assistants. These organizations may be helpful as sources of information about infection control and hazard communication through continuing education seminars and home study courses.

The dental assistant should check with national and state dental agencies regarding continuing education requirements for national certification or state registration or licensure.

Dental Assisting National Board, Inc.

The **Dental Assisting National Board, Inc. (DANB)** is the national organization responsible for issuing the required task analyses for its national certification tests for dental assistants, including certification in infection control. Headquartered in Chicago, DANB administers national certification testing at designated state testing sites and dates.

American Dental Assistants Association

The **American Dental Assistants Association (ADAA)** is a national organization for dental assistants, which holds a national meeting annually in conjunction with the Academy of General Dentistry. Located in Chicago, its purpose is to promote the profession of dental assisting.

ADAA publishes *The Dental Assistant: Journal of the American Dental Assistants Association (JADAA)*, which provides valuable information on a variety of topics of interest to dental assistants, including infection control and hazard communication.

The continuing education department of the ADAA offers accredited home study courses for dental assistants to earn credits toward national annual certification renewal.

National Association of Dental Assistants

The **National Association of Dental Assistants (NADA)** is also a national organization dedicated to promoting the profession of dental assisting. NADA, located in Falls Church, Virginia, publishes a monthly newsletter, provides membership discounts and benefits, and also provides accredited home study courses for dental assistants to earn credits toward national annual certification renewal.

Constituent and Component Dental Assisting Societies

Constituent (the state level) and *component* (the local level) dental assisting societies provide a convenient source of information and continuing education programs on a variety of topics of interest to dental assistants, including infection control and hazard communication.

For information on meeting times and dates, the dental assistant may contact the local state dental association, dental assistant society, or a local dental assisting program.

SKILLS MASTERY ASSESSMENT: POSTTEST

Directions: Select the response that best answers each of the following questions. Only one response is correct.

1. OSHA requires employers, including those in the healthcare profession, to
   a. establish and carry out procedures to protect employees.
   b. implement and maintain employee exposure-incident records for the duration of employment plus 30 years.
   c. provide personal protective equipment to protect staff from infectious diseases and other potential hazards.
   d. All of the above

2. OSHA's Bloodborne Pathogens Standard covers all dental employees who could reasonably anticipate coming into contact with blood, saliva, and other potentially infectious materials during the course of employment.
   a. True   b. False

3. OSHA's Bloodborne Pathogens Standard is designed to help dental office employees minimize occupational exposure to bloodborne illnesses and thus protect them from possible resulting illness.
   a. True   b. False

4. The Environmental Protection Agency
   a. regulates and registers certain products used in dental practices.
   b. requires products to undergo and pass specific testing requirements prior to approval for registration.
   c. reviews product labels for false or misleading information and sufficient directions for use.
   d. All of the above

5. The role of the CDC is to enforce regulations set forth by OSHA to protect the health, safety, and welfare of the public and dental office personnel to ensure safe dental practices.
   a. True   b. False

6. All of these statements regarding OSAP are true EXCEPT for which of the following?
   a. OSAP is a national organization comprised of teachers, practitioners, dental healthcare workers, and manufacturers/distributors of dental equipment and products.

b. OSAP develops and communicates standards and information on aseptic technique to dental practices and educational institutions to assist them in the efficacy of their infection control programs.

c. OSAP has the authority to inspect dental offices and to issue citations and fines for noncompliance with government regulations.

d. OSAP holds annual and regional meetings that address a variety of infection control and hazard communication topics of interest to the dental profession.

7. All of these statements regarding the ADA are true EXCEPT for which of the following?

a. The ADA has a strong influence upon organized dentistry by determining needs and setting policies, protocols, and standards of conduct for members of the dental profession.

b. The ADA is a legal regulatory body.

c. The ADA provides information, position papers, directives, and statements regarding standards of dental care and protocols for ensuring a safe dental practice environment.

d. The ADA releases many patient educational materials of interest to the public.

8. The FDA reviews product labels for false or misleading information and sufficient directions for use.

a. True   b. False

9. The FDA has no power to regulate chemical germicides used as antiseptics, disinfectants, drugs, or sterilizers.

a. True   b. False

10. OSHA has the power to inspect dental offices and to enforce guidelines set forth by governmental regulatory agencies. It may impose fines, citations, or restriction of practice for noncompliance with required regulations.

a. True   b. False

11. Organizations that provide helpful information and education to the dental assistant, including information on infection control and hazard communication, include

a. DANB.   c. NADA.
b. ADAA.   d. All of the above

12. Certification in infection control for the dental assistant is available through testing offered by

a. DANB.   c. NADA.
b. ADAA.   d. All of the above

CHAPTER

6

The Dental Office Safety Supervisor

KEY TERMS

Bloodborne Pathogens Standard

Hazard Communication Standard

Material Safety Data Sheets (MSDSs)

office safety supervisor

LEARNING OBJECTIVES

Upon completion of this chapter, the student should be able to:

1. Describe the role of the dental office safety supervisor.
2. List the three minimum components of an office safety training program.
3. Relate who is responsible for conducting office safety training and when it should be conducted.
4. Describe ways to organize an office safety training program.
5. Describe record-keeping requirements related to staff safety training.
6. Describe the 12 essential tasks of office safety training.

ROLE OF THE OFFICE SAFETY TRAINER

OSHA requires minimum training of dental personnel in three areas. First, the OSHA **Bloodborne Pathogens Standard** is an OSHA regulation that covers all dental employees who could reasonably anticipate coming into contact with blood, saliva, and other potentially infectious materials (OPIM) during the course of employment. Second, the OSHA **Hazard Communication Standard**, or the Employee Right to Know Law, addresses the right of every employee to know the possible dangers associated with hazardous chemicals and related hazards in the place of employment; this law also requires employers to provide methods for corrective action. General safety standards require training of all new hires to be conducted as soon as reasonably possible and at least annually thereafter.

Further, training must be conducted at no cost to employees of the dental practice and must be conducted during normal working hours.

Because OSHA does not specifically name the dentist or practice owner as the responsible party for conducting safety training, the **office safety supervisor** is the staff member responsible for training other employees about infectious control and hazard communication; this responsibility often falls to the office manager with the greatest knowledge of infectious disease containment and government regulations regarding hazard communication. Training provided by the safety supervisor may be conducted in the office, or the staff may be sent to continuing education courses.

TRAINING ORGANIZATION

The office safety supervisor should develop training sessions that are organized and clear. The office safety supervisor may find it helpful to keep the end result in mind while planning and conducting training sessions and may find it helpful to follow these steps in organizing the office's training program:

1. Provide an overview of all the material to be learned.
2. Develop specific instructional objectives such as, "At the completion of this training session, team members should be able to . . ." and enumerate a list of measurable competencies such as, "Describe the proper method of sharps disposal and the required personal protective equipment (PPE)."
3. Reinforce incremental learning steps by summarizing what employees either already know or what they have learned as a result of new training.
4. Break down learning components into reasonably achievable time frames. For example, how often will training sessions be given and for how long? If training is to take place during weekly staff sessions, ensure that this is placed on the agenda and accomplished.
5. Keep learning paced to the individual. Encourage questions and practice sessions throughout the training.

Record Keeping of Training Sessions

It is the job of the office safety supervisor to maintain detailed records about the infection control/hazard communication training. Records must include the following:

- Dates on which the training sessions took place
- Content of each training session
- Names and qualifications of the trainer(s)
- Names and job titles of the trainees

Employees' training records must be maintained for a minimum of 3 years. These records must be available to employees upon request for review and for copying.

If the practice is sold or transferred, employee training records must be transferred to the new owner. If the practice is closed due to death or retirement of the practitioner, employee records should be offered to the National Institute for Occupational Safety and Health (NIOSH).

TWELVE TASKS OF THE OFFICE SAFETY SUPERVISOR

The office safety supervisor's job can be broken down into 12 tasks (Box 6–1), developed by Dr. Robert R. Runnells of the University of Utah.

Train Newly Hired Personnel

One of the immediate concerns of OSHA compliance inspectors is the assurance that all newly hired employees receive proper training in minimizing exposure to potential office hazards, preferably before they begin their assigned duties.

In fact, the dentist/owner of the practice may be subject to OSHA fines or penalties for failing to properly train an employee prior to the employee's assuming job-related duties, especially those associated with disease containment and hazard reduction.

Retrain All Personnel at Least Annually

While OSHA requires retraining of all staff annually, a minimum of semiannual retraining is often necessary in many practices. In a few instances, retraining may be necessary even more frequently than twice annually.

An example of this is when a new potentially toxic chemical is introduced into the practice for use in patient care or sanitation or disinfection.

Training must also include providing information in the form of **Material Safety Data Sheets (MSDSs)**, which contain written information about the content and potential hazard of specific products used in the dental office. Each product that has a potential hazard must have a corresponding MSDS on file in the office, on each product or chemical used in the office. These sheets must be easily accessible to all employees and to OSHA

Note

If the office takes student interns (those learning to be dental assistants and dental hygienists) who will assume clinically related duties, these students must also receive safety training prior to beginning duties in the operatory, including only observation.

BOX 6-1

The Twelve Tasks of the Office Safety Supervisor

1. Assist the employer in training newly hired personnel
2. Assist in retraining all personnel annually
3. Schedule regular review meetings with employer and team
4. Train janitorial service on sanitary maintenance of the office
5. Maintain records files
6. Perform (or delegate) hands-on daily functions
7. Perform inventory control
8. Supervise staff quality control and answer routine questions during the treatment day
9. Supervise proper handling and treatment of contaminated laundry
10. Check monthly to ensure that hazards signs and labels are posted prominently in the office and affixed to hazardous containers
11. Monitor publications for important infection control, chemical hazards, and waste disposal information
12. Prepare (or contribute to) patient communications on infection control, chemical hazards, and infectious waste educational information

From *Compliance Made Easy: Your Complete Procedures and Practices Training Manual for the Dental Office,* by R. R. Runnells, 1992, Phoenix, AZ: SmartPractice. Reprinted with permission of the author.

---

inspectors upon request. MSDSs may be stored in a binder or on the practice's hard drive.

Schedule Review Meetings

The office safety supervisor should schedule review meetings monthly to reinforce the annual retraining sessions. Review meetings are helpful in increasing efficiency of dental staff in the performance of assigned duties.

Staff should be encouraged to share their ideas for improving office safety during the training meetings, and, if helpful, these ideas should be incorporated into office procedures and protocols.

Train Janitorial Service Personnel

It is not unusual in an otherwise effective infection control program to have previously disinfected surfaces inadvertently contaminated by janitorial or maintenance personnel who have not been trained in the importance of maintaining minimal sanitary conditions while performing necessary cleaning tasks.

OSHA requires employers to maintain the work site in a clean and sanitary condition. It is the job of the office safety supervisor to train janitorial service personnel about office cleaning and sanitation in compliance with OSHA mandates.

Maintain Records Files

Current copies of infection control guidelines (Hazard Communication Standard) and EPA, state, or other infectious waste disposal standards must be available for employees and other parties to review as necessary. It is the job of the office safety supervisor to maintain and make these records accessible at all times.

Perform Hands-on Daily Functions

A comprehensive office safety program requires that repeatable actions be taken each day as the office is prepared to receive patients, during and between each appointment, and in preparation for closing the office. It is the job of the office safety supervisor to ensure that these functions are either performed personally or delegated to other staff members.

Perform Inventory Control

Inventory control has become more important to dental practices in view of the increased concern for office safety and compliance with regulatory mandates. It is essential that a minimum of all critical products and supplies necessary to practice universal precautions and to protect staff from hazards and accidents be maintained at all times. It is the responsibility of the office safety supervisor to ensure these are kept in inventory.

Maintaining minimal required inventory also contributes to cost containment for the dental practice.

Efficiently administered, inventory control can recoup some of the additional expense incurred as a result of operating dental office safety programs by purchasing sufficient minimal quantities as needed or by buying in bulk for large practices that consume significant amounts of supplies.

Supervise Staff Quality Control

The technical aspects of complying with a well-rounded office safety program require that a knowledgeable person be available during the workday to answer routine questions in the absence of the employer or dentist. Unless they are of an emergency nature, special questions should be referred to the safety supervisor. It is the responsibility of the office safety supervisor to supervise staff for quality control matters.

> **Note**
>
> Replacing old products with new ones requires procurement of a new MSDS and retraining of all personnel who may be exposed to such products if the products contain potentially toxic chemicals as defined by OSHA. It is the responsibility of the office safety supervisor to obtain MSDSs and keep them on file for employee access and review at all times. A new MSDS must replace an existing one if the chemical makeup of the product changes.

Supervise Handling and Treatment of Contaminated Laundry

Employers are required to furnish personal protective equipment (PPE) and, in some instances, other personal items for employees; laundering of reusable gowns may be the responsibility of the employee.

OSHA guidelines suggest that laundering of all reusable gowns or lab coats should be the responsibility of the employer to ensure that the equipment is rendered noninfectious.

It is the responsibility of the office safety supervisor to ensure that contaminated laundry is properly handled and processed.

Conduct Monthly Compliance Inspections

Under the provisions of OSHA's Hazard Communication Standard, all potentially dangerous containers, storage areas, and workrooms must be labeled or posted to ensure that employees are cautioned against potential hazards. It is the responsibility of the office safety supervisor to develop a list to ensure compliance with posting of hazard signs and labels. This inspection should occur monthly, and written records of verification must be maintained in the office.

Monitor Infection Control Publications

OSHA and other federal and state agencies do not normally inform employers and employees of changes in standards. Therefore, it is the responsibility of the dental safety supervisor to keep current on publications for notification of such changes.

This information is available in dental periodicals, newsletters, and continuing education programs and over the Internet at a variety of sites.

Prepare Patient Communications

It is the responsibility of the office safety supervisor to prepare communications on infection control, chemical hazards, and infectious waste and to be able to communicate accurate information to patients and staff (see *Chapter 16: Marketing Infection Control* for further information). This is done for the following reasons:

- To make the requirements more understandable and therefore more useful
- To make the requirements less threatening
- To lay the groundwork for the necessity of increased fees charged to patients to cover a portion of the cost

In the media, dentistry has been identified as a potential source of HIV transmission during patient treatment. Dentistry is taxed with the responsibility of adopting a more aggressive program of patient communication to place the proper perspective on disease transmission during the provision of treatment.

The duties of an office safety supervisor are best organized supervised and performed most efficiently in busy practices by one person. By organizing infection control, hazard communication, and waste disposal tasks in an integrated manner, the confusion of assigning such tasks to personnel already performing other unrelated tasks is often avoided.

Dental staff members become more efficient when they are assigned tasks that are related and similar in execution.

SKILLS MASTERY ASSESSMENT: POSTTEST

Directions: Select the response that best answers each of the following questions. Only one response is correct.

1. OSHA requires a *minimum* of training of dental personnel in all of the following areas EXCEPT
  a. the Bloodborne Pathogens Standard.
  b. the Hazard Communication Standard.
  c. specialty safety standards.
  d. general safety standards.

2. Training of dental personnel must be conducted
  a. as soon as reasonably possible for all new hires.
  b. at least weekly.
  c. at any time when a new product or chemical is introduced into the practice.
  d. a and b only
  e. a and c only

3. To be effective, the office's training program should
  a. provide an overview of all the material to be learned.
  b. provide specific instructional objectives and measurable competencies.
  c. reinforce incremental learning steps by summarizing what employees either already know or what they have learned as a result of new training.
  d. break down learning components into reasonably achievable time frames.
  e. All of the above

4. Office training records must include all of the following EXCEPT
  a. individuals' Social Security numbers.
  b. dates on which the training sessions took place.
  c. the names and qualifications of the trainer(s).
  d. the content of each training session.
  e. the names and job titles of the trainees.

5. Employees' training records must be
   a. maintained for a minimum of 3 years.
   b. available to employees upon request for review and for copying.
   c. transferred to the new owner in the event the practice is sold.
   d. transferred to the National Institute for Occupational Safety and Health (NIOSH).
   e. a, b, and c only
   f. All of the above

6. The dentist/owner of the practice may be subject to OSHA fines or penalties for failing to properly train an employee prior to the employee's assuming job-related duties, especially those associated with disease containment and hazard reduction.
   a. True   b. False

7. Training must include providing information in the form of a Material Safety Data Sheet on each product or chemical used in the office. MSDSs must be safely stored away and made available only to OSHA inspectors.
   a. True   b. False

8. Review meetings should be held _____ to reinforce the annual retraining sessions.
   a. daily   c. monthly
   b. weekly   d. bimonthly

9. Current copies of infection control guidelines (Hazard Communication Standard) and EPA, state, or other infectious waste disposal standards must be available for employees and other parties to review as necessary.
   a. True   b. False

10. A comprehensive office safety program requires that repeatable actions be taken at all of the following times EXCEPT
   a. each day as the office is prepared to receive patients.
   b. during and between each appointment.
   c. in preparation for closing for the lunch hour.
   d. in preparation for closing the office.

11. Replacing an old product with a new one requires procurement of a new MSDS and retraining of all personnel who may be exposed to such products if the products contain potentially toxic chemicals as defined by OSHA.
   a. True   b. False

12. For proper cost containment, it is not necessary to keep minimums of all "critical" products and supplies required to practice universal precautions or to protect staff from hazards and accidents; these items need only be on order.
   a. True   b. False

13. OSHA requires employers to furnish all of the following PPE EXCEPT

a. gloves.

b. masks.

c. ventilation hoods.

d. eye protection.

e. protective attire.

14. The office safety supervisor should

a. make sure all potentially dangerous containers, storage areas, and workrooms are labeled or posted to ensure that employees are cautioned against potential hazards.

b. develop a list to ensure compliance with posting of hazards signs and labels.

c. perform a monthly inspection and maintain written records in compliance with OSHA's Hazard Communication Standard.

d. All of the above

15. The office safety supervisor should stay current on notification of changing OSHA regulations through a variety of sources, including

a. dental periodicals.

b. dental newsletters.

c. continuing education programs.

d. the Internet.

e. All of the above

16. An office that accepts dental assisting student interns is not required to provide safety training because the student is not an employee of the practice and has already received training at school.

a. True

b. False

Infection Control Techniques in the Dental Office

CHAPTER 7

Personal Safety and Barrier Protection

LEARNING OBJECTIVES

Upon completion of this chapter, the student should be able to:

1. Determine vaccinations required for employment in the dental office.
2. Identify staff members who may be at risk by determining employee categories of all personnel.
3. Describe OSHA-mandated universal precautions and examples of the required components.
4. Describe the types of gloves most commonly used for dental procedures and the inherent risk of latex sensitivity associated with glove use.
5. Describe recommended guidelines for wearing and removing other forms of clinical attire, including masks and eyewear.
6. Relate acceptable methods of handling disposable and reusable outer protective clinical attire and recommended steps for handling washable wear.
7. Describe the emergency use of eyewash stations in the dental office.
8. Describe the measures required for handling sharps.
9. Explain the necessary measures to be taken in the event of an accidental exposure.

HEPATITIS B AND OTHER RECOMMENDED VACCINATIONS

It is the responsibility of the dental assistant to maintain a high level of personal health and well-being. This includes getting the recommended vaccinations and boosters. OSHA requires members of the dental team who are full-time employees and who may be at risk for occupational exposure to bloodborne pathogens to be vaccinated against hepatitis B.

The dentist/employer must make the vaccination available to all full-time employees at no cost. In rare instances in which the employee refuses the vaccination, the employee should sign a waiver acknowledging his or her refusal of the vaccine and that he or she does not hold the employer liable for possible consequences.

Recommended vaccinations for dental healthcare workers are listed in Table 7–1.

IDENTIFYING EMPLOYEES AT RISK: EXPOSURE DETERMINATION BY CATEGORIES

OSHA requires all dental practices having 11 or more employees to evaluate an employee's potential for an occupational exposure to bloodborne pathogens. An **accidental exposure** is a specific eye, mouth, or other mucous membrane, nonintact skin, or parenteral contact with blood or other potentially infectious materials (OPIM) that results from the performance of an employee's duties directly related to the nature of employment.

Task Categorization

To determine an employee's potential for an occupational exposure to any bloodborne pathogen through contact with any OPIM, all employees must be provided with a list of tasks associated with their respective job classifications. They must then identify their **employee category**, which is a method of identifying employees at risk for exposure to bloodborne pathogens based upon the nature of employment-specific tasks under which they fall. Categories are explained in the following discussion.

Category I

Category I includes all tasks involving exposure to blood, body fluids, or body tissues. It includes all chairside personnel, such as the chairside assistant, the dental hygienist, the dental laboratory technician, and the dentist.

TABLE 7–1

RECOMMENDED VACCINATIONS FOR DENTAL HEALTHCARE WORKERS

Generic Name	Primary Booster Schedule	Precautions and Contraindications
Hepatitis B recombinant	Two doses IM, 4 weeks apart, third dose 5 months after second dose*	Previous anaphylaxis to baker's yeast; pregnancy is not a contraindication
Rubella live virus	One dose SC, no booster required*	Pregnancy; immunocompromised condition; history of anaphylaxis with neomycin
Measles live virus	One dose SC, no routine boosters	Pregnancy; immunocompromised condition; history of anaphylaxis after eating eggs or taking neomycin
Influenza vaccine	Annual vaccination with current vaccine	Pregnancy; history of anaphylaxis associated with eating eggs
Tetanus-diphtheria toxoid	Two doses IM 4 weeks apart, third dose 6 to 12 months after second dose, booster every 10 years	Pregnancy; history of neurologic reaction or immediate hypersensitivity reactions after a previous dose
Enhanced-potency inactivated poliovirus (E-IPV); live oral polio vaccine (OPV)	E-IPV is preferred for primary vaccination of adults, two doses SC 4 to 8 weeks apart, a third dose 6 to 12 months after the second; in adults with a completed primary series and in whom a booster is indicated, either OPV or E-IPV may be administered	E-IPV should not be given to immunocompromised patients with known or possible immunocompromised family members
Varicella live virus	One dose SC ages 12 months to 12 years, second dose 4 to 8 weeks after first dose for ages 13 and above	Pregnancy; allergies to neomycin or gelatin; history of anaphylaxis to previous dose; immunocompromised condition; corticosteroids; receipt of blood transfusion during previous 5 months

*IM: intramuscular; SC: subcutaneous

Category II

Category II includes all work-related tasks involving no exposure to blood, body fluids, or body tissues, but may occasionally involve unplanned tasks from Category 1. Category II most often includes nonclinical personnel such as the receptionist, the office manager, or the insurance secretary.

Category III

Category III includes all work-related tasks involving no exposure to blood, body fluids, or body tissues. This category includes the office's accountant, or the tax preparer.

For additional information on exposure determination, see *Chapter 12: Hazard Communication.*

UNIVERSAL PRECAUTIONS: GLOVES, MASKS, EYEWEAR, AND OUTER PROTECTIVE CLOTHING

To be protected and to be in compliance with OSHA mandates and CDC guidelines, all members of the dental team who, as a routine part of their job, do or may encounter exposure to body fluids such as blood or saliva (Category I and Category II workers) must employ **universal precautions**. Universal precautions is an OSHA standard requiring dental staff to treat all patients as potentially infected with a communicable disease and to wear **personal protective equipment (PPE)** when treating patients (Figure 7–1). Minimal PPE includes gloves, a face mask, eyewear, and protective outer garments.

TYPES OF GLOVES USED IN DENTISTRY

The dental assistant must complete proper handwashing technique before putting on (donning) and removing (doffing) gloves. For detailed information and instructions about proper handwashing technique, refer to *Chapter 2: Disease Prevention in the Dental Office.*

Gloves are the single most important factor in controlling the spread of infectious disease between the dental healthcare worker and the patient. The dental assistant is required to wear gloves during all dental patient care procedures involving direct hand contact with saliva, blood, or other body fluids; gloving is also required when handling items contaminated with body fluids or OPIM.

The dental assistant should be familiar with the different types of gloves available to the dental profession, their uses, their advantages, and their disadvantages. Gloves are available in a variety of sizes, from extra small to extra large, and must be made available to employees in sizes that reasonably fit their hands.

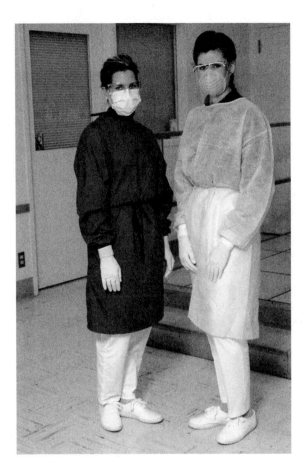

FIGURE 7–1
Two dental team members wear required PPE, which includes gloves, masks, eyewear, and outer clinical attire.

Disposable (Nonsterile) Examination Gloves

Disposable examination gloves are intended for single-procedure use and should be appropriately discarded following the conclusion of each chairside procedure. The most common types of disposable gloves are made from either vinyl or latex (Figure 7–2).

Examination gloves are supplied nonsterilized, and most manufacturers make them equally suited to adapt to either the right or left hand. Though latex examination gloves are the most commonly used type in dentistry, vinyl gloves have come to replace latex when hand irritations—usually called contact dermatitis—are present.

Overgloves

Overgloves are intended for one-time use, are made of inexpensive clear plastic, and are often referred to as food-handler's gloves. The overglove (Figure 7–3) is so named because it is placed over the treatment glove for temporary use, then removed when chairside duties are resumed on the same patient. Overgloves are not a suitable replacement for latex or vinyl gloves.

FIGURE 7–2
Examination gloves made of
(A) vinyl and (B) latex.

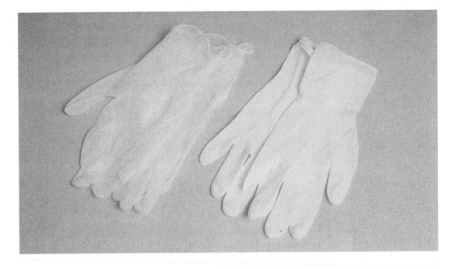

Common instances when an overglove might be worn by the dental assistant include when making chart notations, when making a denture or orthodontic appliance adjustment in the laboratory, or when taking a telephone call.

Sterile Gloves

Sterile gloves are intended for single use during oral surgery and involved periodontal surgical procedures. They are packaged presterilized and labeled for left and right hands.

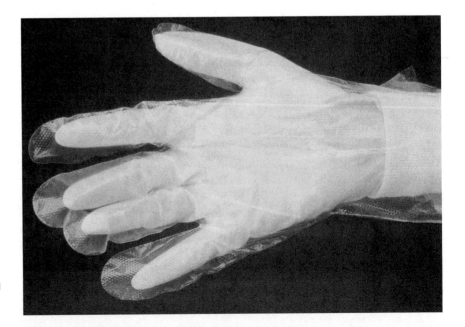

FIGURE 7–3
Overgloves are used for
opening a drawer or making
chart notes. *(Courtesy of
Biotrol, Louisville, CO)*

Nitrile Utility Gloves

Nitrile utility gloves are intended for multiple use and are to be worn during treatment room disinfection, instrument scrubbing and preparation, and other nontreatment procedures. Protective, heavy nitrile gloves (Figure 7–4) are puncture resistant, autoclavable, and reusable. Each staff member should have a pair of utility gloves designated with his or her name.

Nitrile gloves are not to be confused with nor substituted for the less expensive household cleaning gloves sold in grocery or hardware stores.

Nonallergenic Gloves

Nonallergenic gloves are available to the dental professional; however, they are not routinely used because of the expense. Nonallergenic gloves are indicated when dental healthcare workers have a severe allergic reaction to latex or vinyl gloves. The term *hypoallergenic,* while similar in meaning to *nonallergenic,* is no longer allowed by the FDA for labeling latex products because it is not necessarily accurate.

Proper Use of Gloves

According to the CDC guidelines, gloves are to be worn when treating every patient. Universal precautions means treating every patient as though he or she has an infectious, deadly disease. Before putting gloves on, the dental assistant must thoroughly scrub with an antimicrobial skin cleanser that has residual activity because this reduces the skin's transient microbial count and helps keep microbial growth to a minimum while wearing gloves.

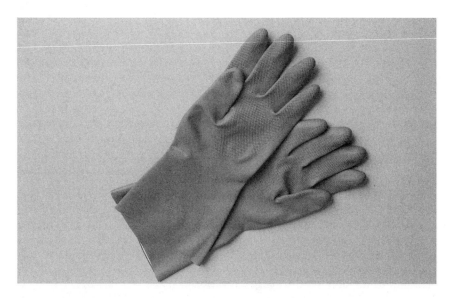

FIGURE 7–4
Utility gloves worn by the dental assistant during infection control procedures.

Gloving Procedure

The dental assistant must remove all hand and wrist jewelry, including rings and watches, because they harbor pathogenic microorganisms and may cause tearing, ripping, or puncturing of gloves. Thoroughly rinsing the hands with cool or cold water after washing closes the pores and makes the hands less susceptible to microbial infection and dermatitis. The hands should be thoroughly dried before gloving.

When gloving, the dental assistant should pick up the glove, using the fingers of the opposite hand to scoop up the glove at the outside of the cuff. (The fingers of the opposing hand should never touch the inside of the fresh glove.)

Some dental assistants experience perspiration under their gloves. This can be alleviated by lightly dusting the hands with cornstarch. (Most gloves are supplied from the manufacturer or dealer with either talc or cornstarch.) After putting on gloves, the dental assistant should rinse them with cold water to remove any excess cornstarch.

The assistant should not wear gloves that are visibly torn or punctured. If, during the course of a procedure, the glove is punctured, ripped, or torn, the dental assistant must remove the glove at once, thoroughly wash his or her hands with antimicrobial hand soap, and replace the glove with a new one.

Sometimes gloves will develop a sticky or tacky surface texture. This occasionally occurs during lengthy procedures (more than 1 hour duration). If this happens, the dental assistant should remove the soiled gloves, rewash the hands with antimicrobial cleanser, and reglove.

> *Note*
>
> Do not attempt to wash or reuse latex or vinyl gloves. Strong soaps or alcohol can have a deleterious effect on gloves.

Glove Storage

Gloves should be stored within easy access of all dental personnel. A cool, dark place is best for glove storage because prolonged exposure to heat, sun, or fluorescent light increases the likelihood of perforations, tears, or glove decomposition. Many glove distributors also offer a variety of glove dispensers that fit into the operatory decor with either a wall mount or countertop fitting. Gloves also have an expiration date on the box that should be checked before they are worn.

Latex Warnings

As of September 1998, all manufacturers of medical/dental devices containing natural rubber latex (NRL) are required to include a warning on their products' labels that such products may pose a significant health risk to some consumers or healthcare providers who are sensitized to natural latex proteins.

Most often, it is the protein used during the glove manufacturing process, rather than the NRL, that causes skin irritation on the hands associated with glove use.

All medical/dental devices that contact the hands and contain NRL or dry natural rubber require one or more of four new FDA labeling statements warning of potential allergic reactions.

MASKS

Surgical face masks (Figure 7–5) must be worn when splashing or spattering of blood, saliva, or other body fluids is likely. CDC guidelines recommend that surgical disposable masks be replaced between patients or during extended procedures when the mask becomes visibly wet or soiled with bioburden (blood, saliva, and spatter).

Most masks are formfitting over the bridge of the nose to minimize fogging and to fit under prescription eyewear or goggles. Commercially available styles of face masks include preformed dome-shaped masks, pliable pleated masks, and mask-eyewear combinations with elastic strap and tieback options. Masks made of glass fiber mat and synthetic fiber mat provide the highest filtration rate. The FDA recommends that surgical masks have a 95 percent or greater bacterial filtration efficiency.

The dental assistant should avoid handling the body of the mask, instead handling the mask at the periphery. The assistant should also refrain from pulling the mask down to rest against his or her neck because the patient's bioburden on the outside of the mask could inadvertently contact the dental assistant's skin.

EYEWEAR

Protective eyewear is also OSHA mandated as part of PPE. Protective eyewear is designed to safeguard the eyes from diseases such as herpes simplex viruses and Staphylococcus aureus; eyewear also protects against contact with caustic chemicals, radiographic solutions, dental lab materials, and flying particulates such as pieces of scrap amalgam and tooth fragments.

The dental assistant may wear goggles (Figure 7–6A), eyeglasses with side shields (Figure 7–6B), or a plastic face shield for eye protection (Figure 7–6C).

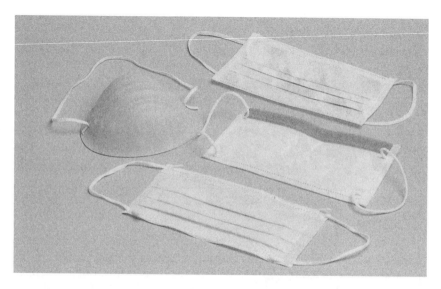

FIGURE 7–5

Masks are available in a variety of styles, including dome and pleated.

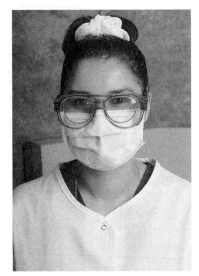

FIGURE 7–6A
The dental assistant wears goggles and a pleated face mask.

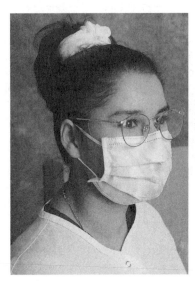

FIGURE 7–6B
The dental assistant wears prescription eyeglasses with clear plastic side shields and a pleated mask.

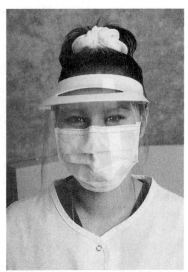

FIGURE 7–6C
The dental assistant wears a chin-length face shield and a pleated mask.

Goggles must have both front and side shields for use during exposure-prone procedures. Goggles, available with or without prescription lenses, provide the highest level of protection against front and side splashes, and impacts.

Regular glasses with side shields also offer some degree of protection and often have desirable features such as replaceable lenses (in case of scratching), antifogging properties, and heat tolerance to allow autoclaving.

Chin-length face shields, which should be worn in combination with a face mask to reduce exposure to blood, saliva, or other body fluids, may be worn instead of goggles or glasses. If a face shield is used to protect against damage from solid projectiles, the protective eyewear should meet the American National Standards Institute (ANSI) Occupational and Educational Eye and Face Protection Standard and be clearly marked as such.

Eyewear must be thoroughly washed with soap and hot water and rinsed well after each patient. Eyewear may be decontaminated and disinfected using a spray-wipe-spray method before reuse. The dental assistant should exercise extreme care to ensure that residual disinfectant is thoroughly removed before placing the glasses, goggles, or face shield near his or her eyes.

SCRUBS OR PROTECTIVE OUTER GARMENTS

Scrubs or protective outer garments (Figure 7–7) must also be worn by the dental assistant when contact with spray, splashes, or body fluids can be reasonably anticipated to contaminate the torso, forearms, or lap of chair-

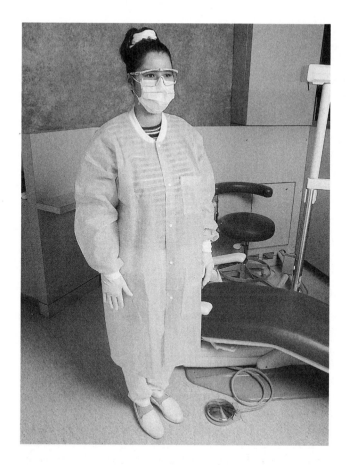

FIGURE 7–7
The dental assistant wears complete PPE, including disposable outer garment.

side personnel. Suitable protective garments, worn over street clothes, undergarments, or the clinic uniform as a protective outer layer, prevent organisms on nonclinical attire from shedding into ambient air over patients with open tissues. Protective garments should be long-sleeved and high-necked and should also be free of ornamentation such as buttons or jewelry.

For routine dental procedures, disposable dental gowns are worn once and then discarded. They must be properly discarded and replaced if they become visibly contaminated, soiled, or wet.

Reusable cotton or cotton-polyester lab coats, clinic jackets, aprons, or gowns, donned at the beginning of the treatment day, are acceptable alternatives to disposable protective garments. The dental assistant may not wear these articles of clothing to and from the office, nor outside the office, when leaving the office for lunch or running errands.

LAUNDERING OF REUSABLE PPE

Reusable protective garments may not be laundered by employees in their home laundry with their own personal clinic attire or with other family members' clothing.

OSHA's Bloodborne Pathogens Standard clearly states that the laundering of protective garments is the responsibility of employers and prohibits contaminated clothing and linens from being laundered by employees in their homes. Instead, protective garment laundry must be done either on site in the office or through a commercial laundering service or dry cleaner, provided that universal precautions are applied and PPE is in place.

The standard laundry cycle recommended by detergent and machine manufacturers is considered sufficient for decontaminating reusable clinic attire.

Unless the laundry service employees practice universal precautions in handling all laundry, contaminated laundry transported away from the practice for laundering must be packaged in leakproof bags appropriately marked or labeled with the universal biohazard symbol.

GUIDELINES FOR PUTTING ON AND REMOVING PPE

The dental assistant must always follow a consistent routine when donning (Box 7–1) and doffing (Box 7–2) PPE. This is to ensure that all steps are followed correctly and in the proper sequence.

At the conclusion of the appointment, the dental assistant removes contaminated PPE, taking great care. PPE must be removed and discarded in such a manner that it reduces the potential for cross-contamination and prevents the spread of disease to other areas of the office.

After dismissing the patient, the dental assistant gathers all instruments and related materials used for the procedure. Instruments on the tray that were not used should also be considered contaminated and thus must be recycled with the contaminated instruments. Contaminated instruments are removed to the instrument recycling area and submerged in a presoak

---

BOX 7-1

Procedure Into Practice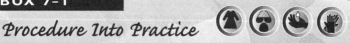

Donning PPE

After seating the patient and completing proper handwashing technique, the dental assistant should do the following:

1. Gather all PPE needed for the procedure.
2. Don outer protective clothing.
3. Don clinical protective footwear, if required.
4. Apply face mask.
5. Don eyewear.
6. Don gloves.
7. Open sealed sterilized instrument cassette, tray, or pouch in front of the patient.

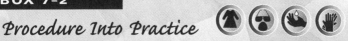

BOX 7–2

Procedure Into Practice

Removing PPE

At the conclusion of the appointment and after dismissing the patient, the dental assistant should do the following:

1. Carry contaminated instruments to the recycling area.

2. Remove and dispose of contaminated gloves.

3. Remove and dispose of—or wash, dry, and disinfect—contaminated face and eye protective coverings.

4. Remove contaminated outer clinical wear.

5. Remove clinical footwear.

6. Wash and dry hands and don jewelry and clothing to be worn home.

7. Place marked contaminated laundry bag (for reusable clinical attire) in a designated pickup area.

---

solution (see *Chapter 8: Instrument Recirculation* for instrument sterilization steps).

The dental assistant should remove the gloves, one at a time, grasping the opposing glove by the outer cuff (Figure 7–8A), with fingertips under the cuff, inverting the glove as it is removed. To avoid cross-contamination, the dental assistant must take care not to touch the exposed skin to the contaminated outer surface of the glove. This procedure is repeated to remove the other glove (Figure 7–8B). Gloves should be disposed of according to area, state, or regional specifications and are considered contaminated medical waste (Figure 7–8C).

Next, the dental assistant unties the mask ties or lifts off the elastic mask and drops it into the same waste disposal container. When removing the mask, the dental assistant should take care not to touch the outside of the mask because this may cause cross-contamination. If the dental assistant has worn a face shield, goggles, or eyeglasses, these are removed and placed with the contaminated instruments in the recycling area to be disinfected and thoroughly rinsed prior to reuse.

When removing disposable protective outer clinical attire, the dental assistant must discard it appropriately. When removing the outer garment, the dental assistant should turn it inside out to avoid cross-contamination, taking care not to let the cuff or edge of the sleeve touch the skin. A paper towel should be used to pull the cuff over the hand. The dental assistant unbuttons or unties the lab coat or other upper garment (Figure 7–9A). The article of clothing is unwrapped around the body folding the contaminated surface to the inside to avoid contact with the body. When removing the second arm, the dental assistant folds the item (Figure 7–9B). Paper and other disposable attire is dropped into the biohazard-labeled waste receptacle.

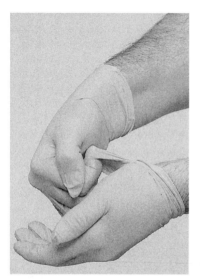

FIGURE 7–8A
The dental assistant grasps the outside cuff of the first glove and lifts it off, holding the removed glove in the opposite gloved hand.

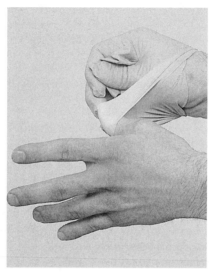

FIGURE 7–8B
The dental assistant inserts the fingers of the freed hand inside the cuff of the other glove, pulling it down and off, capturing the first glove inside.

FIGURE 7–8C
The dental assistant drops both contaminated gloves into the bio-hazard-labeled contaminated waste receptacle.

Reusable clothing to be laundered is placed in a marked laundry bag (Figure 7–9C).

The dental assistant removes contaminated pants by pulling them off inside out to avoid contamination. Pants are also placed in a marked laundry bag. The dental assistant should take great care to remove contaminated outerwear slowly to avoid the inadvertent spread of pathogenic microorganisms by accidentally letting the contaminated side touch his or her skin or surrounding areas.

If special shoes are worn, they must be stepped out of and hose or stockings should be slipped off, leaving them inside out. Shoes worn only in the office should not be worn home—they must stay in the office. Hose are placed with other contaminated laundry; shoes are wiped off using a disposable paper towel saturated with disinfecting solution. The dental assistant should hold and use the towel in such a manner that it acts as a barrier between the ungloved hand and the surface of the shoe. The towel is disposed of properly, taking care to avoid touching the contaminated side with the bare hands.

After removal of contaminated PPE, the dental assistant washes the hands with antimicrobial soap and redons jewelry and street clothes to be worn home. The marked laundry bag is placed in a designated area for pickup and removal.

FIGURE 7–9A
The dental assistant removes the first arm and folds the outside of the lab coat inward to capture the pathogens inside.

FIGURE 7–9B
The dental assistant removes the lab coat using a slow, deliberate movement to avoid spreading bloodborne pathogens.

FIGURE 7–9C
The dental assistant places the contaminated lab coat into a properly labeled container. If reusable, the lab coat is placed in a separate, marked laundry bag and washed in a separate area or is sent to a commercial laundry service.

EYEWASH STATIONS

Because it is sometimes necessary to handle hazardous chemicals in the dental office, an eyewash station and sink (Figure 7–10) must be readily available in case there is an accidental exposure of the chemicals to the eye(s).

The eyewash station should be appropriately labeled, and the office should have a formal procedure for the disposal of hazardous chemical waste. It should be located in a central treatment room, easily accessible from the laboratory and all other treatment rooms.

As part of the annual training/refresher, the office safety supervisor should include use and demonstration of the eyewash station in the event of an emergency (Box 7–3).

The eyewash station should be checked monthly to ensure it is in proper working order.

SHARPS MANAGEMENT AND DISPOSAL

The term **sharps** refers to all sharp, invasive objects and instruments used to directly inject or cut into soft or hard tissue of the oral cavity. Management and disposal of sharps are vital roles of the dental assistant. In dental

FIGURE 7–10
Eyewash station.

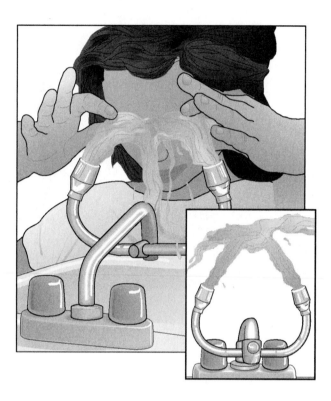

practice, the most commonly used sharps items include disposable needles, scalpel blades (or disposable scalpels), burs, orthodontic wires, and extracted teeth.

According to OSHA, sharp items should be considered potentially infective and must be handled with extraordinary care to prevent unintentional injuries. Disposable syringes and needles, scalpel blades, and other sharp items must be placed into puncture-resistant containers (Figure 7–11) located as close as is practical to the area in which they are used.

BOX 7-3

Procedure Into Practice

Emergency Eyewash Procedure

In the event of an accidental exposure, the dental assistant should do the following:

1. Hurry to the nearest eyewash station.

2. Remove mask and gloves.

3. Flush the eye(s) for 30 to 60 seconds under comfortably warm water.

4. If necessary, repeat step 3.

5. If an object has become embedded in the eye, the area should be covered with an eye patch or bandage and the assistant should be transported to the nearest medical emergency room for treatment.

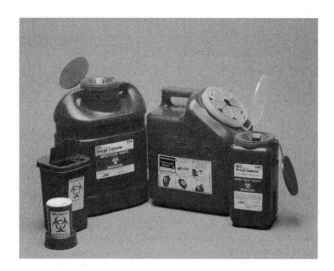

FIGURE 7–11
Puncture-resistant
sharps containers.

The key phrases of importance to the dental assistant are *puncture resist-ant* and *as close as is practical to the area in which they were used. Puncture resist-ant* is important because anyone handling the container, from dental personnel to janitorial or disposal services, must be protected from inadvertent sticks or cuts if the container drops, breaks, or tips over. *As close as practical to the area in which they were used* is important because some OSHA inspectors may interpret this as meaning one sharps disposal container for each operatory.

Recapping Contaminated Needles

OSHA specifically states that recapping of a needle increases the risk of unintentional needlestick injury; thus, needles should not be recapped, bent, or broken before disposal (Box 7–4).

OSHA advises, especially when dental procedures on an individual patient may require multiple injections from a single syringe, that it is more prudent to place the unsheathed needle into a sterile field between injections rather than to recap the needles between injections—such as slipping it between two sterile 2 x 2 gauzes—than to recap the needle.

Thus, needles should not be recapped manually because this may cause unintentional parenteral (penetrating the skin) needlestick injuries.

There are at least three alternatives to traditional, two-handed needle recapping. The first is to use one hand to slip the needle cover back on. To do this, the dental assistant simply wiggles the cover back onto the needle loosely, then secures the cover tightly by pushing down vertically on the syringe.

A second method involves using a needle holder or hemostat to hold the needle cap, instead of using the other hand.

A third option is the use of a disposable cardboard needle shield (Figure 7–12) to prevent inadvertent sticking.

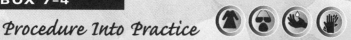

BOX 7-4

Procedure Into Practice

Minimizing Personal Injury from Contaminated Sharps

The dental assistant should employ the following guidelines to help minimize the risk of personal injury sustained from sharps injuries:

1. Always point the sharp end of the instrument away from the body.

2. Always pass scalpels and syringes with the sharp end(s) away from the body and the intended recipient.

3. Avoid using a two-handed technique to debride instruments at chairside with gauze sponges, patients' bibs, or paper towels. As an alternative, take two or three cotton rolls and wet one or two with clean water. Then tape the cotton rolls to the bracket tray. To remove debris and visible bioburden from sharp instruments, insert the sharp end into the wet cotton roll and remove remaining loose debris and excess moisture.

4. Avoid picking up sharp instruments by the handful.

5. Keep fingers clear of rotating instruments.

6. Dispose of used needles and other sharps immediately after the procedure and properly in a biohazard-labeled, leakproof, puncture-resistant container kept in close proximity to the point of use. Whenever possible, avoid transporting reusable contaminated sharps to the instrument recirculation area in a folded tray cover.

7. Never overfill a sharps container; start a new one.

8. Always wear puncture-resistant utility gloves during instrument and treatment room cleanup. (Note: household gloves are not to be used.)

9. If an accidental exposure occurs, follow the OSHA/CDC protocol for postexposure management and follow-up.

Updated Safety Needle Management Regulations

In July 1999, the Cal/OSHA Bloodborne Pathogens Standard requires all healthcare employers to begin providing sharps safety devices. Many other states have since enacted or introduced similar legislation to protect employees from accidental exposure to bloodborne pathogens. The new legislation has resulted in a shift from traditional needles to safety needles with engineered built-in safety mechanisms.

The newly enacted measure means that if a safety needle is available for a given procedure, such as dental anesthetic administration, it must be used. The law defines engineered sharps protection as a physical attribute built into a needle device used for withdrawing body fluids, accessing a vein or artery, or administering medications or other fluids that effectively reduces the risk of an exposure incident with a barrier creation, blunting, encapsulation, withdrawal, or other effective mechanism.

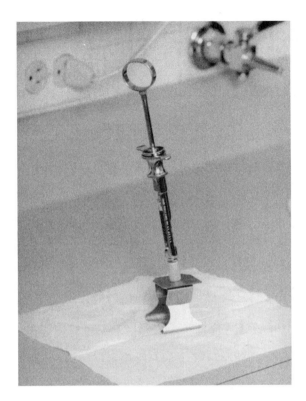

FIGURE 7-12
Needle-recapping device prevents accidental exposures.

This engineering control is not required in the following cases:

- If it is not available in the marketplace
- If it will jeopardize the patient's safety or the success of the procedure (this must be documented)
- If the employer can demonstrate through objective evaluation criteria that the engineering control is not more effective in preventing exposure incidents
- If reasonable, specific and reliable information is not available about the safety performance

HANDLING AN ACCIDENTAL EXPOSURE

If the dental assistant or any other member of the dental team sustains an accidental exposure, the dentist/employer is required by law to follow specific steps. Details of the exposure must be documented on an Exposure Incident Report Form (Box 7–5).

The most common examples of occupational exposures occurring in the dental office are accidentally cutting oneself with a contaminated dental instrument, sustaining a needlestick injury from a contaminated anesthesia syringe, or scratching oneself on a contaminated bur.

BOX 7-5

Exposure Incident Report Form

Employee: _____

Date: _____

Place and time of incident: _____

Those present: _____

Route of exposure: _____

Description of the exposure incident: _____

_____

_____

Engineering controls in place: _____

_____

Work practice controls employed: _____

_____

List PPE used at time of exposure incident: _____

_____

Source patient: _____

Was source patient tested?   [ ] Yes   [ ] No

HIV status: [ ] Positive   [ ] Negative

Name of lab: _____

Date of testing: _____

Employee tested?   [ ] Yes   [ ] No

If employee refused, was waiver signed: [ ] Yes   [ ] No

Explain: _____

Postexposure prophylaxis: _____

Physician's follow-up: _____

Physician's written opinion on file?   [ ] Yes   [ ] No

The dental practice must have a proactive written policy statement regarding the postoperative management and follow-up of accidental exposures. The policy statement should do the following:

- Include measures the practice will take to prevent accidental exposures
- Promote prompt reporting of accidental exposures
- Ensure confidentiality of all concerned
- Be consistent with CDC guidelines and OSHA enforcement policies
- Include prevention strategies
- Include postexposure management principles
- Include the name of the preselected healthcare provider to treat and manage postexposure follow-up and counseling

If the dental assistant sustains an accidental exposure, the incident and all action taken regarding it must be recorded in the hazard communication manual. Box 7–6 lists what the dental assistant must do in the event of an accidental exposure. Box 7–7 lists what the dentist or employer must do in the event of an accidental exposure.

BOX 7-6

Procedure Into Practice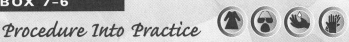

What the Dental Assistant Must Do in the Event of an Accidental Exposure

In the event of an accidental exposure, stop immediately and report the incident to the office manager and to the dentist. If the exposure involves the hands, remove the gloves and treat the injury employing the following scrupulous first-aid measures:

1. If the affected area is bleeding, squeeze it gently until a small amount of blood is released.

2. Wash the hands thoroughly using antimicrobial soap and comfortably warm-to-hot water. Do *not* expose the injured area to harsh chemicals or submerge it in bleach.

3. After drying the hands, apply a small amount of antiseptic to the area and cover it with a bandage.

If the patient being treated is a known AIDS or HBV victim, the following three measures *must* be taken:

1. A physician must be contacted regarding the exposure.
2. A gamma globulin shot may be administered and/or any other diagnostic tests performed.
3. Appropriate counseling must be provided for the staff member.

BOX 7-7

Procedure Into Practice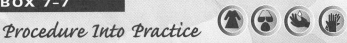

What the Dentist/Employer Must Do in the Event of an Accidental Exposure

The employer must follow specific OSHA guidelines, including providing an independent medical evaluation of the exposure incident at no charge to the employee:

1. Document the route or routes of exposure as well as how and when the incident occurred.

2. Attempt to identify the source individual (the patient who was treated using the specific instruments or needle) if possible.

3. Obtain the results of that patient's blood tests, if available.

4. With informed consent of the dental assistant, have the assistant's blood collected and tested.

5. Ensure that the assistant receives medically necessary injections, such as gamma globulin, hepatitis B vaccine booster, and/or possibly a tetanus booster.

6. Ensure that appropriate postexposure counseling is provided for the dental assistant.

7. Ensure that any additional follow-up is completed as recommended by the attending physician.

A dental assistant who sustains an exposure incident may choose to decline the exposure incident follow-up but must sign a disclaimer waiving the employer's responsibility for future results or side effects. This documentation must be recorded on an OSHA 200 log form in offices having more than 10 employees. In those with fewer than 10 employees, the event must nonetheless be documented. The office with fewer than 10 employees may use a similar form.

SKILLS MASTERY ASSESSMENT: POSTTEST

Directions: Select the response that best answers each of the following questions. Only one response is correct.

1. Which of the following is a contraindication to hepatitis B vaccine?
   a. Pregnancy
   b. History of anaphylaxis associated with neomycin
   c. Previous anaphylaxis to baker's yeast
   d. Previous allergic dermatitis associated with latex

2. Minimal PPE required to be worn by the dental assistant during all invasive procedures includes all of the following EXCEPT
   a. gloves.
   b. face mask with hepafiltration.
   c. eyewear.
   d. protective outer garments.

3. _____ are the single most important factor in controlling the spread of infectious disease between the dental assistant and the patient.
   a. Masks   c. Goggles
   b. Face shields   d. Gloves

4. Overgloves are a suitable, inexpensive alternative to latex or vinyl examination gloves.
   a. True   b. False

5. The FDA recommends surgical masks have a _____ or greater bacterial filtration efficiency.
   a. 90 percent   c. 95 percent
   b. 93 percent   d. 98 percent

6. Chin-length face shields, which reduce exposure to blood, saliva, or other body fluids, can be worn by the dental assistant in place of a face mask and goggles.
   a. True   b. False

7. The dental assistant has worked at chairside all morning. The last procedure involved periodontal surgery. Upon dismissing the patient, the assistant notices that his or her mask and washable, cotton-polyester

lab coat worn over scrubs are splattered with traces of blood and saliva. After dismissing the patient, and before seating the next patient, the dental assistant should
   a. remove and discard only disposable PPE and begin decontaminating the treatment room.
   b. remove and discard disposable PPE and don a clean lab coat.
   c. remove and discard only disposable PPE and remove the soiled cotton-polyester lab coat and not replace it.
   d. remove and discard only disposable PPE and go home at lunchtime to wash and dry the cotton-polyester lab coat.

8. Laundering of reusable outer protective garments is the responsibility of _____.
   a. employers   b. employees

9. The CDC recommends that disposable face masks must be replaced
   a. after each patient.
   b. during extended procedures when the mask becomes visibly wet or soiled with bioburden.
   c. every morning and afternoon.
   d. a and b only

10. According to OSHA, the dental assistant may do which of the following prior to depositing a contaminated needle in a designated puncture-resistant container?
   a. Recap it.
   b. Bend it.
   c. Break it.
   d. None of the above are acceptable according to OSHA.

11. All dental practices are required to have a proactive written policy statement regarding the postoperative management and follow-up of accidental exposures. The policy statement should include
   a. measures the practice will take to prevent accidental exposures.
   b. prompt reporting of accidental exposures.
   c. prevention strategies.
   d. postexposure management principles.
   e. a and b only
   f. All of the above should be included.

12. By law, the dentist/employer is entitled to the results of the employee's blood test resulting from an accidental occupational exposure.
   a. True   b. False

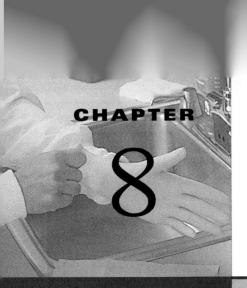

CHAPTER 8

Instrument Recirculation

KEY TERMS

autoclave

biological monitor

chemical vapor sterilization

critical items

cycle time

disinfection

dry heat sterilization

ethylene oxide sterilization

flash priority sterilizer

holding/presoaking solution

instrument recirculation

noncritical items

process indicators

semicritical items

steam under pressure (autoclaving)

sterilization

ultrasonic cleaner

LEARNING OBJECTIVES

Upon completion of this chapter, the student should be able to:

1. Describe and discern the difference between critical, semicritical, and noncritical items with relation to sterilization/disinfection techniques in the dental office.

2. Describe how to maintain a sterile field when handling dental instruments.

3. List the stages of processing contaminated instruments and how these instruments become resterilized.

4. Describe the process and rationale for instrument precleaning/soaking relevant to sterilization/disinfection techniques in the dental office.

5. Describe the techniques, the pros, and the cons of manual versus mechanical instrument scrubbing.

6. Define, describe, and differentiate between the terms *disinfection* and *sterilization;* list the different levels of chemical disinfection available to the dental assistant and relate their applications.

7. List and describe the uses and processes for each of the ADA- accepted forms of sterilization used in the dental office.

continues

LEARNING OBJECTIVES *continued*

8. Describe the process of packaging instruments for sterilization and how to properly load the sterilizer.

9. Describe the need for biological monitors and discuss the difference between process indicators and spore testing; relate the importance of third-party verification.

10. Describe the accepted procedure for cleaning, lubricating, and sterilizing dental handpieces.

11. List common reasons for sterilizer failure.

INTRODUCTION TO INSTRUMENT RECIRCULATION

A crucial responsibility of the dental assistant is **instrument recirculation**, which includes all of the steps required to properly transfer, handle, soak (preclean), scrub, and sterilize contaminated instruments and related items following a dental procedure to make them sterile again.

In the ideal clinical environment, everything that comes into contact with the patient's mouth should be sterilized and should remain within a sterile field (not come into contact with anything that could contaminate the working area) throughout the procedure. However, not all things that come in contact or that are associated with dental treatment can be sterilized. Whenever possible, it is most desirable to sterilize *all* instruments, handpieces, and other devices that are used for invasive procedures inside the oral cavity. When working in a sterile field, the chairside dental assistant should remember to keep all instruments and other armamentarium—all instruments and equipment required for the procedure—within that sterile field. Failure to do so results in the breaking of the chain of sterility.

The CDC, the ADA, and OSAP have mandated that all critical and semicritical dental instruments that are heat stable should be sterilized routinely between uses by steam under pressure (autoclaving), dry heat, or by chemical vapor, following the instructions of the manufacturers of the instruments and sterilizers.

CRITICAL, SEMICRITICAL, AND NONCRITICAL CLASSIFICATIONS

With regard to instrument recirculation, there are three categories of dental hand and rotary instruments and related items: critical, semicritical, and noncritical items.

Critical Items

Critical items are those instruments and related items used to perform invasive procedures and that come into direct contact with soft or bony tissues of the oral cavity. These include, but are not limited to, scalpels, surgical forceps, bone chisels, manual cutting instruments, handpieces, and burs. These items must be sterilized.

Semicritical Items

Semicritical items are those instruments and related items *not* intended to penetrate oral soft or hard tissues but that may come into contact with oral tissues. These include amalgam condensers, plastic instruments, and dental dam frames. These instruments should be sterilized when possible. If they cannot be sterilized, they should be high-level disinfected using an EPA-registered product such as glutaraldehyde.

Noncritical Items

Noncritical items are those instruments and items that do *not* come into direct contact with body fluids. For example, they may come into contact with intact skin or working surfaces but are not used directly in the mouth. These items do not necessarily require sterilization or high-level disinfection and include such items as medicament jars, cavity liners, unit tubings, and restorative materials. These items should be sanitized or cleaned using a low-level disinfectant such as household bleach and water.

PROCESSING CONTAMINATED INSTRUMENTS

To better understand the overall concept of instrument recirculation (processing), it is helpful for the dental assistant to keep in mind all the steps required to transform a contaminated tray of instruments into a sterile instrument setup ready for reuse (Box 8–1).

AFTER COMPLETION OF A CHAIRSIDE PROCEDURE

After the patient has been dismissed and escorted to the front desk, the dental assistant dons PPE consisting of puncture-resistant, heavy-duty utility gloves (nitrile), a mask, protective eyewear, and a gown. Using one hand, the dental assistant can use the leftover 2 x 2 gauzes or cotton rolls (which will be discarded anyway because they are considered contaminated, even if not used) to carefully wipe off visible bioburden and other items, such as dental cement, from contaminated instruments remaining on the tray. Contaminated disposables such as paper cups, used floss, cotton rolls, and 2 x 2 gauze sponges are discarded. The dental assistant carries the tray with contaminated instruments to the instrument recycling area.

Next, the dental assistant submerges the instruments into the **holding/ presoaking solution**, a solution in which the dental assistant submerges

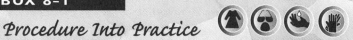

BOX 8–1

Procedure Into Practice

Processing Contaminated Instruments

The dental assistant should follow these steps in processing contaminated dental instruments:

1. After dismissing and escorting the patient to the front desk, return to the treatment room and discard all disposables.

2. Continuing to wear personal protective equipment (PPE), carefully wipe off excess visible bioburden from contaminated instruments remaining on the tray using a one-handed technique (such as securely placing a 2 x 2 gauze or taping several cotton rolls to the edge of the tray) and transport the tray to the instrument recycling area. (To prevent accidental contamination or sticking injuries, the dental assistant should never attempt to wipe excess bioburden from contaminated instruments using a two-handed technique.)

3. Submerge contaminated instruments in the holding/precleaning solution.

4. After returning from other chairside duties, rinse instruments for 1 minute under running water and scrub them, either manually or ultrasonically.

5. Following scrubbing, rinse instruments for 60 seconds under running tap water and blot dry.

6. Determine the appropriate method of processing, that is, which instruments will be disinfected with sterilant and which will be heat sterilized.

7. If steam under pressure is indicated, dip sharp and hinged instruments into protective emulsion.

8. If chemical vapor or dry heat is indicated, dry instruments thoroughly before processing.

9. If cold chemical processing (disinfection or cold sterilant) is indicated, place instruments into the designated container, making sure all instruments are completely submerged in the solution. Do not add instruments during the cycle time. If additional instruments are added, the cycle time must be restarted.

10. Wrap or prepare instruments correctly according to the type of sterilization process that is to be used. Load into the sterilizer, allowing for appropriate circulation to occur.

soiled or contaminated instruments until they are properly processed, either in a metal basket, such as an ultrasonic instrument basket, or in a plastic instrument cassette.

INSTRUMENT PRECLEANING/SOAKING

Dental instrument precleaning/soaking (Box 8–2) prior to sterilization is a crucial step performed by the dental assistant in the instrument processing cycle because it reduces the number of microbes present and removes blood, saliva, and other materials that may insulate pathogenic microbes from the sterilizing agent.

BOX 8-2

Benefits of Precleaning/Soaking Dental Instruments

There are numerous benefits to the dental assistant of using a holding/presoak solution. Presoaking does the following:

- Helps minimize drying or caking of contaminants such as encrusted dental materials (cements) and patients' dried body fluids
- Makes instruments easier to clean later on
- Allows the dental assistant to proceed with other time-sensitive procedures such as disinfecting and preparing the treatment room to seat the next patient

---

Note

The dental assistant should be advised that manufacturers of some plastic/resin cassettes do not recommend presoaking. To avoid corrosion of instruments, instrument presoaking should be limited to several hours, and the instruments should *never* be left overnight.

In a busy office or clinic, it is often not practical or time efficient for the dental assistant to prepare instruments for sterilization immediately after dismissing each patient. In this instance, the dental assistant submerges contaminated instruments in a holding/enzyme presoak or holding solution until he or she has time to process them correctly. This solution may be sudsy warm water, a diluted solution of household bleach and water, or the same solution used in the ultrasonic instrument cleaner reservoir.

INSTRUMENT SCRUBBING

After the instruments have been submerged in the precleaning/presoaking solution and when the dental assistant has time to process them, he or she thoroughly rinses the instruments under running water and then scrubs them. Scrubbing contaminated instruments removes remaining visible bioburden, making sterilization more effective.

There are two forms of instrument scrubbing: manually or using an **ultrasonic cleaner**, a mechanical scrubbing device. Although manual scrubbing is not the preferred method because of the potential for an accidental exposure, the dental assistant should be familiar with the method in case the office does not have an ultrasonic cleaner or the ultrasonic cleaner breaks down.

Procedure Into Practice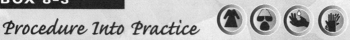

Manual Instrument Scrubbing

The dental assistant should follow these steps when manually scrubbing contaminated instruments:

1. Don necessary PPE, including nitrile gloves.
2. Remove instruments from holding/presoak solution while wearing nitrile gloves.
3. Grasp the instruments firmly and rinse them under a steady stream of warm-to-hot water for 1 minute.
4. Resubmerge the instruments; still holding the instruments in one hand, use a designated scrubbing brush with the other to scrub instruments free of visible bioburden

and dental materials. Pay special attention to scrub the working ends of the instruments: scrub one end first, then the other.

5. Rinse instruments again.
6. Pat dry, if necessary (depending upon the type of sterilization that will take place).
7. Instruments are now ready to place into either sterilizer wrapping, pouches, or cassettes.
8. The contaminated scrub brush is sterilized at the end of the clinical day (if it can withstand the heat of sterilization). Otherwise, the brush is soaked in disinfectant overnight.

Manual Instrument Scrubbing

When scrubbing contaminated instruments by hand (Box 8–3) it is imperative that the dental assistant wear all required PPE and especially important to don nitrile utility gloves, which are stronger than exam gloves and impervious to most sharp instruments. Needlestick or puncture wounds to the hands are all-too-frequent injuries that may cause serious—even fatal—bloodborne infections.

When manually scrubbing instruments (Figure 8–1), the assistant holds the contaminated instruments beneath the surface of the holding solution to prevent unnecessary splashing. The assistant uses one hand to grasp a complete instrument setup and the other to use a scrubbing brush made specifically for cleaning dental instruments.

After hand scrubbing the instruments, the assistant thoroughly rinses them under running water, still holding a complete set used for a specific procedure. Some dentists prefer the instruments to be banded using an elastic stretch material or a large twist tie; others prefer the instruments to be bagged, with the type of tray setup marked on the outside for ready recognition; others prefer a color-coded system in which all instruments used for a specific tray setup are placed inside a color-coded cassette.

FIGURE 8–1
Dental assistant hand
scrubbing contaminated
instruments. (Note the
heavy nitrile gloves worn.)

Ultrasonic Instrument Cleaning

The ultrasonic cleaner (Figure 8–2) is a mechanical device containing a basket and/or beakers that fit inside a chamber filled with cleaning solution manufactured especially for ultrasonic cleaning. Ultrasonic cleaning is different from other forms of debris and bioburden removal because it employs a system of *implosion* (an inward burst—the opposite of *explosion*) to gently remove contaminants from soiled instrument surfaces.

Ultrasonic instrument scrubbing (Box 8–4) is preferred over hand scrubbing because it has been clinically demonstrated to clean instruments 16 times more effectively. Ultrasonic cleaning also reduces the likelihood of sustaining a parenteral exposure (stick through the skin) to bloodborne pathogens, which occurs more often during hand scrubbing. Ultrasonic cleaning also frees up the assistant to perform other tasks such as decontaminating and preparing the treatment room for the next patient.

Most dental instruments can be scrubbed using the ultrasonic cleaner, with the exception of high-speed handpieces, which must be hand cleaned. Both loose instruments and those in cassettes should be suspended within the ultrasonic solution, not touching the bottom of the chamber.

Monitoring the Ultrasonic Instrument Cleaner

It is the dental assistant's responsibility to periodically monitor the ultrasonic cleaner for effectiveness. To do this, the dental assistant holds a 3-inch-square piece of aluminum foil partially in the cleaning solution at the beginning of the workday, then runs the unit for 60 to 90 seconds and removes the foil. If significant pitting (appearance of pinholes) occurs, the unit is operating properly.

To increase cleaning efficiency, the dental assistant should limit the number of loose instruments ultrasonically cleaned at a time. Again, keeping together all instruments common to a specific procedure makes setting up clean trays when they come out of the sterilizer much easier.

FIGURE 8–2
The dental assistant prepares a plastic instrument cassette for submersion in the ultrasonic cleaner. (Note the assistant is wearing proper PPE, including nitrile gloves, which prevent accidental needlestick and puncture wounds.)

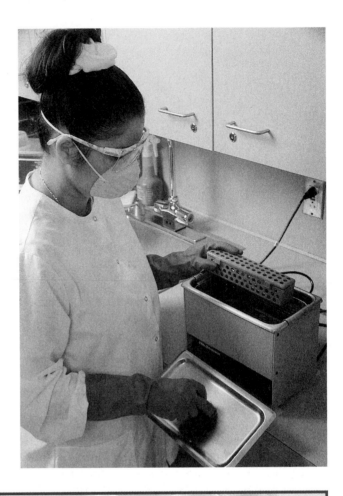

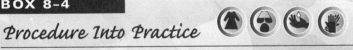

BOX 8-4

Procedure Into Practice

Ultrasonically Scrubbing Instruments

The dental assistant should follow these steps when ultrasonically scrubbing contaminated instruments:

1. Don PPE, including nitrile gloves.

2. Remove instruments from holding/presoak solution.

3. Grasping instruments firmly, rinse them under a steady stream of warm-to-hot water for 1 minute.

4. Keep instruments in groupings according to procedure and place them into the color-coded instrument cassette.

5. Carefully and gently submerge instruments into the ultrasonic basket, taking care not to touch the sides of the chamber or to splash the cleaning solution.

6. Place the lid on the ultrasonic cleaner.

7. Turn timer switch to desired number of minutes.

After removing the instruments from the holding/presoak solution, the dental assistant thoroughly rinses them and either places the instruments into a color-coded cassette or groups them together and submerges them into the ultrasonic cleaner basket.

Ultrasonic cleaning usually takes place within 3 to 6 minutes. The dental assistant places the lid on the ultrasonic cleaner and turns the dial to the desired number of minutes.

If the dental assistant works in an office that uses instrument cassettes, from 10 to 20 minutes may be required when using metal cassettes; plastic/resin cassettes may require a longer ultrasonic cleaning time. The dental assistant should always check the manufacturer's instructions when using any instrument cleaning or cassette system.

After the ultrasonic timer has sounded, the assistant removes the instruments, rinses them thoroughly under a heavy stream of warm-to-hot water, and prepares them for **sterilization**, which will destroy of all forms of microbial life, including mycotic spores.

DISINFECTION VERSUS STERILIZATION

Heat sterilization is required for all dental instruments and related items that go into a patient's mouth, providing they can withstand repeated exposure to high temperatures. Thus, the resulting rule is: Do not disinfect when you can sterilize. Sterilization is the preferred form of instrument processing on critical items.

Disinfection, which is the inhibition or killing of pathogens, may be used in place of sterilization on items that are considered semicritical or noncritical.

Chemical Disinfection of Instruments

Disinfection refers to the inhibition or killing of pathogens. *Spores* are not killed during disinfection procedures; with some classes of disinfectants, certain groups of nonsporulating pathogens also are not destroyed. Thus, disinfection represents a compromised, lower level of infectious disease control, far below the goals of sterilization. Items that cannot withstand prolonged, repeated exposure to high temperatures may need to be disinfected.

Two types of disinfectants used in dentistry are *immersion disinfection* and *surface disinfection*. Immersion disinfection is used on items that can be immersed in a covered, cold disinfection (meaning without the use of heat) pan for the time specified by the manufacturer for the intended purpose. Surface disinfectants are used as a spray on countertops and other surfaces that cannot be immersed or sterilized. For a complete list of disinfectants used in dentistry and how to perform barrier disinfection techniques, refer to *Chapter 9: Environmental Surface and Equipment Asepsis*.

Instruments and related items that cannot withstand the heat of sterilization should be rinsed and dried (following the presoak) and then submerged into the cold sterilant/disinfectant solution for the time required by the manufacturer for the intended use (Box 8–5). After the required time has passed, the dental assistant, wearing appropriate PPE, removes the items and rinses them under running water for 60 seconds. These items are then stored until required.

Disinfectants can be further differentiated as high level, intermediate level, and cleaner/sanitizer only. In some cases, when instruments are submerged for long periods, high-level disinfectants may be used as instrument sterilants. Multipurpose disinfectants may also be used as hard-surface cleaning and sanitizing agents.

BOX 8-5

Procedure Into Practice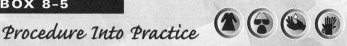

Chemical Disinfection of Instruments That Cannot Be Heat Sterilized

Chemical disinfection is used to achieve asepsis for instruments and related items that cannot withstand heat sterilization.

1. After precleaning/soaking instruments, rinse them under running water for 60 seconds to remove bioburden.

2. Prepare solution following the manufacturer's instructions; indicate the date of opening or preparation of the solution and mark your initials on the container of solution. Note the expiration date on the label of the solution.

3. Pour the prepared solution into a Bard-Parker or equivalent cold sterilization pan; take care to avoid splashing the solution because chemical disinfectants should not be left exposed in open air. The rationale for this is to prevent accidental inhalation, poisoning, or spilling. Splashing solution may cause inhalation, skin, or mucous membrane contact with possible injury.

4. Submerge instruments into the chemical solution, making sure the instruments are completely covered and that the pan is not overfilled. Take care not to splash the solution when adding the instruments to the pan.

5. Close the container; label the container with the name of the solution, the exposure time, and your initials. Start a timer for the amount of time recommended by the manufacturer to ensure proper cycle time.

6. Avoid opening the lid or adding more instruments during the disinfection cycle time. Adding instruments during the cycle time limits the overall efficacy of the disinfectant solution and increases the time necessary to complete disinfection or cold sterilization.

7. Following the required exposure time, and still wearing PPE, lift the items from the container using transfer forceps and rinse the instruments well under running water for 60 seconds.

8. Place instruments on a disposable paper towel and dry them thoroughly. Put away in a closed cupboard or storage area until required for use.

STERILIZATION

Sterilization is the destruction of all forms of microbial life. The ultimate requirement is the inactivation of high numbers of bacterial and mycotic spores. Note: Proof of spore destruction is the ultimate criterion for sterilization because these are the most heat-resistant microbial life forms.

ACCEPTED METHODS OF STERILIZATION

There are a number of ADA-accepted methods of dental instrument sterilization: liquid chemical sterilants, ethylene oxide, dry heat, steam under pressure (**autoclave** and flash priority sterilization), and saturated chemical vapor (chemiclave) (see Table 8–1).

Regardless of the type of accepted sterilizer used, the following three sterilization cycle components are universal:

1. Heat-up period: The dental assistant must allow the sterilizer to reach proper temperature.
2. Exposure period: The dental assistant must allow the full cycle time required for sterilization of the load.
3. Cooldown period: The dental assistant must allow sufficient cooling for handling and for removal of excess moisture.

Liquid Chemical Sterilants

Liquid chemical sterilants are not generally used routinely in dentistry, except when an item cannot withstand any type of heat sterilization. Liquid chemical sterilants are often impractical because of the time required for sterilization to take place. Glutaraldehyde, for example, requires 10 hours of immersion to achieve sterilization.

Ethylene Oxide Sterilization

Ethylene oxide sterilization is a form of gas sterilization usually reserved for hospital use. It is an ADA-accepted form of sterilization for the dental practice (Figure 8–3); however, because of the long cycle time, it is not practical. **Cycle time** refers to the amount of time required during instrument sterilization to attain the combination of proper temperature, time, and/or pressure to kill all forms of microbial life, in this case 10 to 16 hours, which requires running overnight all the instruments used throughout the day.

This is impractical and expensive in terms of number of instruments required. Ethylene oxide sterilizers are large, expensive, and require special ventilation because of the vapors released. They are most often used in hospitals.

Dry Heat Sterilization

Dry heat sterilization refers to any form of sterilization that uses time and heat to kill all forms of microbial life, including microbial spores; it includes

TABLE 8-1

ADA-ACCEPTED METHODS OF STERILIZATION					
Method	**Temperature**	**Pressure**	**Cycle Time**	**Advantages**	**Disadvantages**
Steam autoclave	250°F (121°C) 273°F (134°C)	15 psi 30 psi	15–20 min. 3–5 min.	Rapid turn-around time; low cost per cycle; no toxic/hazardous chemicals	May corrode instruments; cannot be used with many plastics
Dry heat oven	320°F (160°C) 340°F (170°C)		2 hours 1 hour	Does not corrode instruments; no toxic/hazardous chemicals, low cost per cycle	Long cycle time; cannot be used with plastics; paper products may char
Rapid heat transfer	250°F (121°C) 270°F (132°C)	15 psi 15 psi	15 min. (for wrapped items) 3 min. (for unwrapped items)	Short time; items are dry after cycle	Cannot sterilize liquids; may damage plastic and rubber items; door cannot be opened before end of cycle; small capacity per cost; unwrapped items quickly contaminated after cycle
Unsaturated chemical vapor	270°F (132°C)	20 psi	30 min.	Good turn-around time; less corrosive to instruments	Uses toxic/hazardous chemicals; requires fume ventilation; cannot be used with many plastics
Ethylene oxide	Room temperature		10–16 hours	Can be used with almost all materials, including dental appliances and instruments	Very long cycle time; uses toxic/hazardous chemicals; requires special ventilation

FIGURE 8–3
Ethylene oxide sterilizer.
(Courtesy of 3M Health Care, St. Paul, MN)

standard or rapid heat transfer (Figure 8–4). Dry heat sterilization is an ADA-acceptable form of instrument sterilization. The unit requires little maintenance and does not corrode or rust most instruments. Before using the dry heat sterilizer, the dental assistant must bring the dry head sterilizer to the proper temperature by employing an initial preheat time of 20 minutes.

The sterilization cycle requires 1 hour at 340°F (170°C), or 2 hours at 320°F (160°C). As when using all equipment, the dental assistant should check the manufacturer's instructions for operating the dry heat sterilizer.

FIGURE 8–4
Dry heat sterilizer.

Note

Household toaster ovens and convection ovens are *not* approved by the FDA as medical devices and are therefore inappropriate for dental instrument processing; household dishwashers should not be used for instrument cleansing.

Plastic instruments and materials should *not* be placed in the dry heat sterilizer because they may melt during cycle time. Another disadvantage of the dry heat sterilizer is that loads must be carefully wrapped and organized inside the chamber to allow proper air circulation to complete the sterilization cycle. Instruments placed inside the dry heat sterilizer must be completely dry to prevent rusting or corrosion; solder joints of some instruments cannot tolerate the heat of a dry heat sterilizer.

Newer forms of dry heat sterilizers operate on long electromagnetic radiation waves, heated moving air/convection, or conduction.

Acceptable wraps for dry heat sterilization of dental instruments include paper, aluminum foil, metal and glass containers, and certain heavy nylon bags. Cloth wrappings should be avoided because they may char.

Steam under Pressure (Autoclaving)

Steam under pressure (autoclaving) refers to a process of instrument sterilization that uses time, temperature, and pressure to kill all forms of microbial life, including spores (Figure 8–5). Autoclaving is one of the most widely used types of sterilization in dental practices (Box 8–6).

Autoclaving uses steam under pressure, which kills all forms of microorganisms, including spores. For steam to be an effective form of sterilization, it must penetrate all surfaces and areas of the instruments and related items placed inside the chamber. Thus, the dental assistant must be sure to load all instrument pouches, tray setups, or cassettes in such a manner as to allow

FIGURE 8–5

Autoclave. *(Courtesy of MDT Corporation, Torrance, CA)*

BOX 8-6

Procedure Into Practice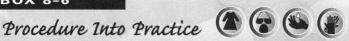

Instructions for Operating the Autoclave

1. Use distilled water to fill the reservoir to within 2½ inches below the opening or to the "fill level" indicated on the autoclave. Always use distilled water in the autoclave because it prevents the collection of mineral deposits and prolongs the life and efficacy of the autoclave.

2. Check the pressure gauge to ensure it is at zero. Remember: Never open the autoclave door unless the pressure is at zero.

3. Open the door; some autoclave doors require an upward and inward pressure; others require a side-pressure technique.

4. Load instrument packs, bags, pouches, or cassettes, taking care not to overfill the chamber and ensuring adequate circulation inside the chamber. Always ensure that there is sufficient space between the packs to allow steam to circulate. Place larger pouches or packages on the bottom of the chamber.

5. Close the door firmly and lock it securely; turn the control valve from "fill" to "steril-ize." Remember that the cycle does not start until temperature has been reached.

6. When the cycle has been completed and the steam on the pressure gauge has gone back to zero, the autoclave has adequately vented. Slowly open the chamber door one half-inch to allow any remaining excess steam to vent. Do *not* touch the autoclave metal parts or instrument packs at this time—wait until they have had sufficient time to cool.

7. When removing packs or pouches, use transfer forceps or wear heavy gloves.

8. Note: The dental assistant should always check to ensure there is sufficient distilled water in the water chamber prior to running a load. Take care not to overfill the chamber and do not add additional water during the sterilization cycle time because this will cause flooding after the remaining steam has converted back to water.

9. If the sterilizer drips or leaks, it may require a replacement gasket around the door to the chamber.

adequate steam penetration. The dental assistant should never overload an autoclave. If necessary, an additional load should be run instead.

To ensure sterilization, autoclaving requires a minimum of 250°F (121°C) with steam pressure of 15 pounds per square inch (psi), for 15 minutes. (Bacterial spores are more resistant to heat than hepatitis viruses and are destroyed in 15 minutes.) Note: Larger loads require an additional 5 to 15 minutes. Because timing is critical in autoclaving, the dental assistant should also note that the true sterilization cycle time does not begin until the autoclave has reached the proper temperature and pressure. Failure to attain these criteria may result in unsterile instruments being used in a patient's mouth.

There are several disadvantages of autoclave sterilization, including rusting, corroding, or dulling of some instruments. To prevent this, the dental assistant can dip rust-prone instruments into a milky emulsion of oil in water or into a fresh solution of 1 percent sodium nitrite prior to sterilization. (The milky emulsion will not leave noticeable residue on the instruments.) Rust inhibitor is also available in spray form.

Some portable electric autoclaves also require that a volatile alkaline solution be used to prevent rusting. To do this, the dental assistant places an open beaker containing 15 ml of fresh household ammonia solution into the autoclave chamber with each load of the oil-emulsion-treated instruments.

Another disadvantage of autoclaving is that instrument packs come out of the completed cycle damp as a result of the steam inside the chamber. Thus, the wise dental assistant plans ahead to allow sufficient time for the steam to dry, as well as for the instruments to cool.

The following are acceptable wraps for autoclaving dental instruments: muslin, paper instrument bags, and steam-permeable plastic or nylon pouches. If an instrument wrap is found to have holes, rips, punctures, or tears, it should be discarded and not reused.

Note
The dental assistant should *not* use impermeable or closed containers in the autoclave because this may cause an explosion inside the chamber.

Autoclave Cleaning and Maintenance. Like any other piece of equipment used in the dental office, the autoclave requires periodic cleaning and maintenance. The frequency required depends upon how often the autoclave is used.

If the autoclave is used every day, the dental assistant should wash the inner chamber with a mild detergent and cloth, and wash and dry the chamber daily. The outside of the autoclave should be wiped clean of dust and oil. The dental assistant should always follow the manufacturer's instructions for cleaning and maintenance.

At least weekly, the dental assistant should drain the autoclave water reservoir and clean it thoroughly. Cleaning requires that the dental assistant drain, fill with cleaning solution and run a 20-minute heated cycle, then drain the solution, fill the reservoir with distilled rinse water, and rerun for another 20-minute heated cycle.

The dental assistant should also remove and scrub the inner shelves or racks and wipe the inner chamber clean. Because cleaning and maintenance take time, the assistant should plan time in the weekly schedule when the autoclave will not be needed for processing instruments.

When cleaning the autoclave, the assistant should also check the rubber gasket (seal) for cracks or wear and tear. A replacement rubber door gasket should be kept on hand.

Flash "Priority" Sterilization

Although technically a form of steam autoclaving, the **flash priority sterilizer** (Figure 8–6) is a device that uses steam under pressure to quickly sterilize items used in the dental office. Items may be placed loosely or wrapped for processing.

The sterilization chamber in the flash priority sterilizer is considerably smaller than that of a traditional autoclave and thus may be better suited

FIGURE 8–6
Steam (flash sterilizer). *(Courtesy of Sci-Can)*

for smaller loads or specialty items such as individual handpieces and forceps.

The requirements to attain sterilization are 15 minutes of cycle time at 250°F (121°C) at 15 pounds of steam pressure at sea level. For unwrapped items, the cycle time is shorter: 270°F (132°C) at 15 pounds of steam pressure for 3 minutes. If instruments are wrapped, the time increases to 8 minutes.

The dental assistant must take great care in loading instruments into the flash priority sterilizer to ensure that steam can penetrate all surfaces of contaminated instruments. Plastics may melt due to high temperatures, metals may corrode or rust, and instrument tips may become dulled when using a flash priority sterilizer.

The dental assistant must take care to lubricate handpieces and wrap them prior to sterilization to extend their life span. Because many flash priority sterilizers require that only distilled water be used, the dental assistant must be sure to read and follow the manufacturer's directions carefully.

Chemical Vapor Sterilization

Chemical vapor sterilization (Figure 8–7) uses a combination of heat, water, chemicals, and pressure to kill all forms of microbial life on contaminated instruments. The dental assistant fills the sterilizer reservoir with a chemical solution provided by the manufacturer. The cycle time for chemical vapor sterilization is 20 minutes plus, and the pressure rise time is 3 to 8 minutes. To sterilize effectively, the chemical vapor sterilizer must reach sterilization temperature of 270°F (132°C) with a minimum of 20 psi.

Advantages of the chemical vapor sterilizer include fast cycle time and less damage to carbon steel, knives, burs, and other sharp instruments. Disadvantages of the chemical vapor sterilizer include irritation to the eyes caused by

FIGURE 8–7
Chemical vapor sterilizer. *(Courtesy of Barbstead/Thermolyne Harvey Chemiclave)*

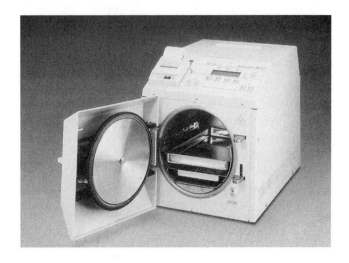

the solution and a mild odor, also emitted from the solution. Thus, adequate ventilation in required when using chemical vapor sterilization.

Acceptable wraps for unsaturated chemical vapor sterilization of dental instruments include muslin, paper, and steam-permeable plastic and nylon.

Uncovered tubes or other vessels should be tipped on their sides during processing. The dental assistant should avoid using closed, impermeable containers in a chemical vapor sterilizer because this may cause an explosion. The dental assistant should avoid using paper and autoclavable tape with a high sulfur content because sulfur causes the sterilizing chamber to turn black; it may also damage internal components of the chemical vapor sterilizer.

PROCESSING HIGH-SPEED DENTAL HANDPIECES

While technically a form of hand instrument, expensive high-speed dental handpieces must be handled and processed with great care to extend their use life (Box 8-7). Following is a standard protocol for sterilizing and maintaining most air-powered handpieces (Table 8–2). Note: Do not use this in lieu of the specific manufacturer's instructions.

Before removing the handpiece from the hose following the completion of the procedures, the bur should remain in the handpiece chuck because running a handpiece without a chuck could cause permanent damage to the turbine. The dental assistant wipes all visible debris from the handpiece and runs it for 20 to 30 seconds to flush the air and water lines.

The dental assistant removes the bur from the handpiece, then removes the handpiece from the coupler. Using a brush and manufacturer-recom-

---

BOX 8-7

Procedure Into Practice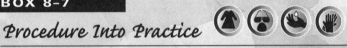

Handpiece Sterilization Steps

Following are the general steps to complete dental handpiece sterilization. Always check the manufacturer's instructions first.

1. Flush handpiece air-water lines before removing from the hose. (Note: Leave the bur in the handpiece.)

2. Thoroughly clean and dry the handpiece.

3. Apply handpiece cleaner and/or lubricant (if required by the manufacturer).

4. Expel excess lubricant with the bur in the handpiece.

5. Clean fiber optics (if handpiece has this feature).

6. Bag and heat process the handpiece.

7. Flush air-water lines for 20 to 30 seconds before attaching handpiece.

8. Open bag and if necessary lubricate handpiece with separate lubricant, attach handpiece to hose, and briefly operate it to expel the excess lubricant with the bur in.

---

mended soap or detergent, the dental assistant scrubs the handpiece thoroughly under hot running water, then thoroughly rinses and dries it.

If the manufacturer of the handpiece recommends ultrasonic cleaning of either the head or the entire handpiece, the dental assistant should do the following: Drain well, attach to hose, and briefly operate to expel debris. The dental assistant should *not* use an ultrasonic cleaner unless specifically recommended by the manufacturer.

Next, the dental assistant internally cleans and lubricates the handpiece only if it is one that requires pre-heat-processing lubrication (some do not). The dental assistant must carefully follow the manufacturer's directions and use the proper lubricant for each type of handpiece. The assistant should not attempt to use one manufacturer's lubricant or cleaner on another handpiece in an attempt to economize because this may invalidate the manufacturer's warranty.

Next, the dental assistant reattaches the handpiece to a hose or uses a flushing device in the air system to blow out excess lubricant from the moving parts. Failure to do this step before processing may result in excess lubricant gumming up the rotating assemblies, which may eventually lead to slowing or stopping of the handpiece. Most manufacturers do not recommend running a handpiece without a bur or blank in the chuck.

Processing Fiber-Optic Handpieces

The dental assistant flushes the excess cleaner/lubricant out of the handpiece and uses a cotton swab dampened (not saturated) with isopropyl alco-

Note

Do *not* soak the handpiece unless specifically recommended by the manufacturer.

TABLE 8-2

MANUFACTURERS' RECOMMENDATIONS FOR HANDPIECE STERILIZATION

Brand	Ultrasonic Cleaning	Cleaning/ Lub. Type	Lube Time	Maximum Temp.	Dry Heat
Adec	Yes	Spray	B & A	250°F	No
Adec H&W	No	Assistinia	B	275°F	No
Bien Air	No (but grease air bearing)		B & A	270°F	No
Bien Air	Air bearing	Gyro-cleaner	B (cleaner only)		
Dabi-Atlanta	No	Cleaner/lube	B & A	275°F	No
Luckman Corp. Encore	No	Encore cleaner	B & A	260°F	Yes
Kavo/all	No	KaVo spray	B	275°F	No
Kinetics/all	Yes	Spray	A	275°F	No
Lares	No	Spray	B & A	275°F	Yes
Midwest	Yes	HS-pump LS-drop oil	B (Life cycle)	275°F	No
NSK/all	No	NSK oil	B & A	275°F	No
Star	No	HS-spray LS-drop oil	B	275°F	No

B & A = Before and After
HS = High speed
LS = Low speed

hol to remove all excess material from the fiber-optic interfaces and exposed optical surfaces. If the fiber-optic interfaces are not properly cleaned, lubricant and dirt can be forced in between individual strands of the fiber during pressure processing. This may ultimately darken or dim the fiber-optic bundle.

To prepare the handpiece for processing, the dental assistant seals it in a sterilization bag or pouch and heat processes according to sterilizer instructions (Box 8–8). When the heat cycle has been completed, time must be allowed for cooling and drying. The bag or pouch should be kept sealed until the handpiece is needed for use on the next patient.

BOX 8–8

Procedure Into Practice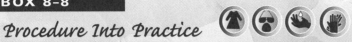

Packaging Instruments and Loading the Sterilizer

It is the job of the dental assistant to properly package or wrap instruments prior to loading them into the sterilizer. Following are the general steps for packaging and loading instruments into the sterilizer.

1. Wrap and place all instruments inside the sterilizer changer loosely enough to allow sufficient steam, heat, or chemical penetration during cycle time.

2. Prepackage all instruments prior to sterilization. Keep individual tray setups together in one package, pouch, or cassette, for example, a basic setup, a composite restoration setup, a prophylaxis setup. Surgical forceps are often packaged separately for individual use and selection by the dentist or oral surgeon.

3. Carefully seal instrument pouches, bags, and cassette wraps and list the contents and date of sterilization on the outside. Make notations with a lead pencil rather than a pen or felt-tip marker (Figure 8–8A).

FIGURE 8–8A The assistant uses a pencil to indicate the contents and date of sterilization on the outside of the bag.

4. Insert the instruments into the bag or pouch and double-fold the open end of the bag (Figure 8–8B) to ensure the instruments will not accidentally fall out.

FIGURE 8–8B The assistant double-folds the end of the sterilization bag to protect the instruments from falling out.

5. Affix autoclave tape to seal the bag before placing it into the sterilizer chamber (Figure 8–8C).

FIGURE 8–8C The dental assistant seals the instrument bag with autoclave tape.

6. If the practice uses instrument cassettes, the cassettes are most often color-coded by procedure; for example, a blue cassette may contain an amalgam setup, or a red cassette may contain a composite setup. It is essential that all clinical staff be familiar with the instrument identification procedure to maintain sterility at all times. Wrap cassettes as necessary.

7. Carefully load the instrument bags, pouches, or cassettes into the sterilizer chamber.

STERILIZER MONITORING

An important role of the dental assistant in instrument recirculation is sterilizer monitoring, which ensures that sterilization has taken place in each and every load of instruments run. Many states now require periodic sterilizer testing with proof of verification. The dental assistant or safety supervisor should keep a written log of sterilizer testing results, including the initials, date, and results of test load, in case an OSHA inspector requests to see verification records (Box 8–9).

In specialty practices, such as oral surgery or periodontics, or in special cases such as dental implant procedures, the dentist or specialist may require verification on every load of surgical instruments as an added precaution. Note: Valid test results are a vital step in risk reduction in the event of an allegation by a patient or patient's attorney in a malpractice suit of claim filed with the State Board of Dental Examiners regarding cross-contamination during a dental procedure.

Biological Monitors

Use of a **biological monitor**, which is a commercially prepared device that provides confirmation that sterilization has taken place (Figure 8–9), is the most accurate method to confirm that true sterilization has been attained during a sterilization cycle. Biological monitors are packaged by the manufacturer in three strips or sealed glass ampules impregnated with *nonpatho-*

BOX 8-9

Procedure Into Practice

Maintaining a Sterilization Monitoring Log

An important role of the dental assistant or safety supervisor is creating and maintaining a sterilization monitoring log and retaining the files. This provides third-party proof of sterilization and helps reduce risk. The sterilization log should be filled in with the following information:

Name of Patient(s)	Processing Date	Assistant's Initials	Result	Date Entered

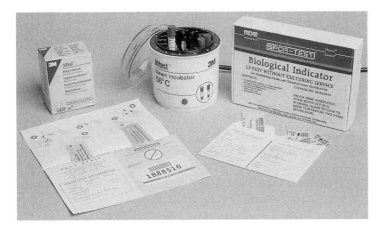

FIGURE 8–9
Biological monitor testing kit.

genic (non-disease-causing) spores. The test spores most often used are *Bacillus stearothermophilus* or *Bacillus subtilis* (Table 8–3).

To use the biological monitor testing kit, the dental assistant or infection control coordinator removes two strips from one side of the envelope. (The third strip always remains sealed in the envelope as the control.) The dental assistant places the two test strips removed from the envelope inside instrument packs in the test load. After running the load, the dental assistant returns the two original test strips to the original (same) side of the envelope, seals them, and sends them to an outside testing agency for verification. These testing services are available through private companies and through microbiology departments in several dental schools around the country.

When the verification is received, the dental assistant or safety supervisor records the date and result on the original tracking sheet and keeps this information on file. A negative report indicates sterilization took place; a positive report indicates corrective procedures must be taken immediately.

Process Indicators

Process indicators are heat-sensitive tapes or inks most often used on autoclave bags. Some manufacturers imprint autoclave bags (Figure 8–10)

TABLE 8–3

SPORE TYPES USED FOR EVALUATING STERILIZATION		
Sterilization Method	Spore Type	Incubation Temperature
Autoclave chemical vapor	*Bacillus stearothermophilus*	132°F (56°C)
Dry heat Ethylene oxide	*Bacillus subtilis*	98°F (37°C)

FIGURE 8–10
Proceses indicators.

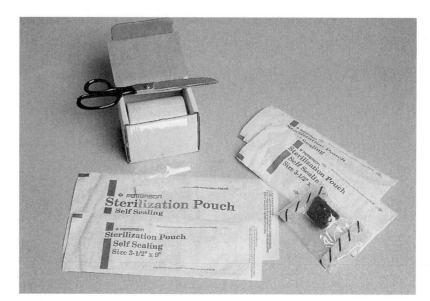

with indicator ink, which turns color upon completion of the cycle. Processor tape is a special form of masking tape impregnated with heat-sensitive dye strips manufactured to withstand the heat of a sterilizer.

The significant difference between a process indicator and a biological monitor is that the process indicator turning color does not verify that either sterility or spore kill has taken place—only that the required temperature level was achieved.

While process indicators are helpful in a sterilization program, they should be used with other biological monitors to ensure that sterilization actually took place.

STORAGE OF STERILIZED INSTRUMENTS

While steps of instrument recirculation are important, storage of sterilized instruments and tray setups should not be overlooked. Once allowed to cool down and dry out, instrument packs, pouches, and cassettes should be handled as little as possible. They should be stored in a closed cabinet and remain in the sterilization area until they are needed.

Instrument setups for a particular procedure should be removed from the cabinet using an old principle of storage: "First in, first out," sometimes referred to as "FIFO." Simply stated, this means that if a tray setup is required for a crown and bridge preparation, the instrument pack having the oldest date of sterilization should be used. Instruments not used for 30 days should be reprocessed through the sterilizer, with the new date noted.

Another important concept in maintaining the chain of sterility—and also a marketing "plus"—is to wait until the patient has been properly seated and draped before the instrument packet or cassette is opened. It is opened in front of the patient after the assistant has completed handwashing and has donned appropriate PPE.

MOST COMMON REASONS FOR INSTRUMENT STERILIZATION FAILURE

Following are the most common causes of sterilizer failure:

- Operator failure
- Sterilizer malfunction
- Type of packaging materials
- Instrument wrapping technique
- Sterilizer overloading
- Test kit may be outdated or may have been accidentally subjected to extreme temperatures

Autoclave Sterilization Errors

Following are the most common autoclave sterilization errors:

- Inadequate precleaning of instruments
- Improper packaging: steam cannot penetrate pack or too many instruments are included per package
- Improper loading: packs are not properly spaced
- Inadequate sterilization time or inadequate temperature and pressure
- Faulty seals, heating coils, traps, and exhaust lines.
- Air in the chamber
- Wet steam and/or inadequate drying

Unsaturated Chemical Vapor Sterilization Errors

Following are the most common unsaturated vapor sterilization errors:

- Improper operation of unit
- Use of sterilization wraps not designed for chemical vapor units (instruments must be wrapped loosely to allow vapor to penetrate packaging; sealed containers, foil, and cloths cannot be used)
- Wet instruments placed inside sterilizer chamber
- Inadequate spacing of packs
- Worn door gasket or seals
- Inadequate ventilation

Dry Heat Sterilization Errors

Following are the most common dry heat sterilization errors:

- Inadequate or excessive temperatures
- Inadequate sterilization time

- Interrupted sterilization cycle
- Exposure of heat-sensitive materials to dry heat
- Packages too bulky or improperly spaced
- Use of sterilization wraps not suitable for dry heat, resulting in destruction of packaging
- Use of inappropriate equipment (conventional household or toaster ovens)

Sound instrument sterilization techniques are the basis of cross-contamination prevention in the dental office. Thus, it is imperative that all dental assistants and infection control coordinators follow scrupulous procedures of instrument sterilization to help ensure a healthy environment for their patients and the entire dental team.

SKILLS MASTERY ASSESSMENT: POSTTEST

Directions: Select the response that best answers each of the following questions. Only one response is correct.

1. Critical items are those instruments and related items that
   a. are not intended to penetrate oral soft or hard tissues but may come into contact with oral tissues.
   b. are used to perform invasive procedures.
   c. can be scrubbed, sanitized, and returned to the cupboard.
   d. are used only by dental specialists.

2. Instruments that cannot be sterilized should be high-level disinfected using an EPA-registered product such as glutaraldehyde.
   a. True   b. False

3. After the patient has been dismissed and escorted to the front desk, the dental assistant accomplishes which of the following steps in the correct order?
   a. Discards soiled paper disposables, wipes off visible bioburden from contaminated instruments, carries the remaining contaminated instruments on the tray to the recycling area, and dons PPE
   b. Removes the contaminated instruments from the tray, submerges the instruments into the holding/presoaking solution, and removes PPE
   c. Dons PPE, discards soiled paper disposables, wipes off visible bioburden from contaminated instruments, and carries the remaining contaminated instruments on the tray to the recycling area
   d. Discards paper disposables, dons PPE, and carries the remaining contaminated instruments on the tray to the recycling area

4. Instrument precleaning prior to sterilization is a crucial step in the instrument processing cycle because it
   a. allows the dental assistant time to take an extra break.
   b. eliminates the need to scrub instruments.

   c. reduces the amount of sterilization cycle time.

   d. reduces the number of microbes present and removes blood, saliva, and other materials that may insulate pathogenic microbes from the sterilizing agent.

5. Why should the dental assistant wear heavy nitrile gloves when manually scrubbing contaminated instruments?

   a. They protect his or her fingernails from breakage.

   b. They prevent potentially serious needlestick or puncture wounds.

   c. They allow the assistant to avoid touching water that is too hot or too cold.

   d. They last longer than latex or vinyl gloves and are less expensive.

6. Why should the dental assistant hold the contaminated instruments below the surface of the solution when scrubbing them?

   a. To reduce the amount of time required to scrub the instruments

   b. To avoid potential allergic reactions to the solution

   c. To better be able to identify the instruments by tray setup

   d. To avoid unnecessary splashing of the solution

7. Ultrasonic instrument scrubbing is preferred over hand scrubbing for all of the following reasons EXCEPT

   a. it has been clinically demonstrated to clean instruments more effectively.

   b. it reduces the likelihood of sustaining a parenteral exposure to bloodborne pathogens.

   c. it takes the place of using a holding/presoaking solution.

   d. it frees up the assistant to decontaminate and prepare the treatment room for the next patient.

8. Disinfection refers to the inhibition or killing of pathogens.

   a. True   b. False

9. Spores are killed during the disinfection process.

   a. True   b. False

10. Chemical disinfectants in dentistry are used for

   a. sterilizer solution.

   b. oral preoperative rinses.

   c. immersion and surface disinfection.

   d. fixing laboratory cultures.

11. Chemical disinfection

   a. takes less time than heat sterilization.

   b. replaces heat sterilization.

   c. is used to achieve asepsis for instruments and related items that cannot withstand heat sterilization.

   d. is most effective when the lid is left off the pan.

12. Proof of spore destruction is the ultimate criterion for sterilization because spores are the most heat-resistant forms of microbial life.

   a. True   b. False

13. The three universal sterilization cycle components, in the correct order, are
a. exposure period, heat-up period, and cooldown period.
b. cooldown period, exposure period, and heat-up period.
c. heat-up period, exposure period, and cooldown period.
d. presoak, scrub, and sterilize.

14. All of these statements are true of dry heat sterilization EXCEPT which of the following?
a. Plastic instruments and materials may melt during cycle time.
b. Loads must be carefully wrapped and organized inside the chamber to allow proper air circulation to complete the sterilization cycle.
c. Instruments placed inside must be completely dry to prevent rusting or corrosion.
d. Solder joints of most instruments can tolerate the heat of a dry heat sterilizer.

15. Household toaster ovens and convection ovens are approved by the FDA as medical devices and are therefore appropriate for dental instrument processing.
a. True   b. False

16. For sterilization to occur, which of the following is required when using an autoclave?
a. 250°F at 15 psi for 15 minutes
b. 350°F at 15 psi for 20 minutes
c. 400°F at 20 psi for 30 minutes
d. 150° at 25 psi for 35 minutes

17. To sterilize effectively, which of the following is required when using a chemical vapor sterilizer?
a. 270°C at 20 psi for a minimum of 20 minutes
b. 350°F at 15 psi for a minimum of 15 minutes
c. 270°F at 20 psi for a minimum 20 minutes
d. 400°F at 20 psi for 30 minutes

18. Process indicators are the most accurate method to confirm that true sterilization has been attained during a sterilization cycle.
a. True
b. False

19. Reasons for sterilization failure may include all of the following EXCEPT
a. sterilizer malfunction.
b. the test kit may be outdated or accidentally exposed to extreme temperatures.
c. the type of packaging materials used.
d. reading and following the manufacturer's recommended instructions.

CHAPTER 9

Environmental Surface and Equipment Asepsis

LEARNING OBJECTIVES

Upon completion of this chapter, the student should be able to:

1. Describe the reasons and rationale for environmental surface disinfection in the dental office and the role of the dental assistant.

2. List and compare chemical disinfectants used for environmental surface and equipment disinfection.

3. List and define the classifications of environmental surfaces.

4. Be thoroughly familiar with and be able to describe and demonstrate the spray-wipe-spray technique for disinfection of environmental surfaces that cannot be sterilized.

5. Describe and demonstrate the role of the dental assistant in placing and removing protective (environmental) barriers in the dental operatory.

6. Describe the importance of front (business) office barriers and their role in preventing cross-contamination.

THE NEED FOR SURFACE DISINFECTION

OSHA requires employers to protect dental office employees from contacting bloodborne diseases in the workplace. The Bloodborne Pathogens Standard considers decontamination as the use of physical or chemical means to remove, inactivate, or destroy bloodborne pathogens from a surface or item so that they are no longer capable of transmitting infectious particles and the surface or item is rendered safe for handling, use, or disposal.

Although it is most desirable to sterilize everything that comes into direct contact with patients and their body fluids, this is neither reasonable nor practical when considering surfaces such as countertops and equipment, the dental chair, stools, x-ray machines, tubings, and the dental unit.

The dental assistant provides a valuable service in removing or eliminating bloodborne pathogens and other potentially harmful substances from environmental surfaces and equipment.

Thus, the need exists to either surface disinfect these items or to cover them with a barrier, which is any physical device that provides a layer of protection to eliminate or reduce the transfer of harmful pathogens.

Classification of Environmental Surfaces

Environmental surfaces are classified as follows.

- *Touch surfaces* are those surfaces usually touched and contaminated during the course of an invasive dental procedure. Examples include dental light handles, dental unit handles and controls, headrest adjustment buttons, dental chair switches, and x-ray exposure buttons. Touch surfaces should be used minimally and should be cleaned and disinfected at the end of the clinic day.

  If a surface must or might be touched during the course of providing invasive treatment, the dental assistant must clean and disinfect it or cover it with a protective barrier impervious to liquid.

- *Transfer surfaces* are not touched but are usually contacted by contaminated instruments. Examples include instrument trays, dental unit handpiece brackets, or the x-ray viewbox. To ensure proper and consistent asepsis, the dental assistant must treat transfer surfaces in the same manner as touch surfaces.

- *Splash, spatter, and aerosol surfaces* include all surfaces in the treatment room other than touch or transfer surfaces. Splash and spatter surfaces need not be disinfected but must be decontaminated at least daily.

Decontamination of Environmental Surfaces

Each dental office is required to have a written cleaning and maintenance schedule for environmental surfaces and other areas that may become contaminated with blood or saliva. This description should outline how equipment and treatment rooms are decontaminated.

The CDC guidelines require that, at the completion of daily work activities, countertops and environmental surfaces that may have become contaminated with blood or saliva be wiped with absorbent toweling to remove extraneous organic material and disinfected with a suitable chemical germicide.

When selecting a surface disinfectant, the dental assistant should look for the ADA Seal of Acceptance and the EPA's registration number on the label. To meet these criteria the disinfectant must be "hospital level," which means it inactivates the polio 2 virus and tuberculosis. As when working with any potentially hazardous material, the dental assistant should wear PPE, in this case, utility gloves, a mask, and eyewear.

CHEMICAL DISINFECTANTS

A number of chemical disinfectants are available to the dental assistant for use on environmental surfaces and equipment that cannot be sterilized.

Chlorine Dioxide Compounds

These are EPA-registered, high-level chemical disinfectants (and sterilants) that can be used only on instruments, environmental surfaces, and equipment not susceptible to corrosion. Items that are noncorrodible are those made of or containing high amounts of stainless steel, carbide steel, copper, or brass. Because of this corrosive property, chlorine dioxide disinfectants should be stored only in plastic or glass containers. As when using any disinfectant, the dental assistant should always follow the manufacturer's instructions for handling and storage, as well as disposal.

Chlorine dioxide compounds may also be used for processing instruments; when they are used as an instrument sterilant, from 6 to 10 hours is required, which may not be practical.

Glutaraldehydes

These EPA-registered, high-level disinfectants (and sterilants) may also have a corrosive effect upon certain metals. Thus, the dental assistant must exercise caution when using them.

Glutaraldehyde may also be used for processing instruments; disinfection time with glutaraldehydes takes from 10 to 90 minutes; sterilization takes 6 to 10 hours, which may not be practical. (It does not have a residual effect.)

The dental assistant must note that if additional instruments or related items are added to the glutaraldehyde solution, the "start" time must begin again. Glutaraldehydes retain efficacy for 28 days from the time of mixing, even if not used.

> **Note**
>
> When working with chemical sterilants, the dental assistant must be careful to avoid directly touching the solutions, unnecessarily splashing the solutions, or breathing in their vapors to minimize health risks.

> **Note**
>
> Glutaraldehyde fumes are highly toxic, thus the dental assistant should avoid contact with these solutions with exposed skin or eyes and must not inhale the vapors.

As when handling, mixing, storing, and disposing of all chemicals, the dental assistant must follow the manufacturer's instructions.

Iodophors

Iodophors are intermediate-level disinfectants. The dental assistant must take care when handling and diluting the solutions to derive the correct concentration. As the name suggests, iodine is a main ingredient of an iodophor and thus may cause staining of light-colored chair covers, countertops, and other surfaces with repeated use. A second disadvantage of iodophors is they are apt to corrode some metals; they also have a short life span and must be changed as often as every 3 days. They are also irritating to the ungloved skin.

Iodophors may also be used for dental instrument processing, requiring from 5 to 25 minutes upon contact.

Sodium Hypochlorite

Sodium hypochlorite is another intermediate-level disinfectant and is derived from a common household bleach; it is usually supplied in a concentration of 5.25 percent.

For general-purpose disinfection, the dental assistant may use a 1:10 dilution, adding ¼ cup of bleach to 1 gallon of water. Because of rapid deterioration, sodium hypochlorite used as a disinfectant must be discarded at the end of the workday and a fresh solution made the next morning.

Sodium hypochlorite may be corrosive to some metals and is irritating to the skin and eyes. The dental assistant must take care not to contact sodium hypochlorite with clothing because it may cause moderate to severe bleaching and in some cases may eat through clothing.

As when mixing, handling, using, or storing other chemical disinfectants, the dental assistant must take care to wear proper PPE and to avoid inhaling the toxic fumes.

Phenolics

Phenolics are also used for intermediate-level chemical disinfection. An advantage to phenolics is that the surface contact time is generally only 10 minutes.

Disadvantages of phenolics are that they are irritating to the eyes and skin; they are also destructive to plastic surfaces.

Isopropyl Alcohol

This is also called isopropanol and was once used as a surface disinfectant because of its low cost and quick surface drying time. A disadvantage of isopropyl alcohol is that it has only limited disinfection properties; because it has a fast drying time, it does not provide sufficient time to be efficacious in many applications. Isopropyl alcohol is no longer recommended for disinfection in the dental office. Table 9–1 provides a comparison of the various

TABLE 9–1

DISINFECTANT COMPARISON

Disinfectant	Level	Advantages	Disadvantages	Time Required for Effectiveness
Chlorine dioxide	High	Rapid disinfection	Corrosive to metals Requires ventilation Irritating to eyes and skin	5–10 minutes
Glutaraldehyde	High	Used to disinfect some impressions Instrument can be submerged Many have a 28-day useful life.	Some are corrosive to metal Requires ventilation Irritating to eyes and skin	10–90 minutes
Iodophors	Intermediate	Used as holding solution for impressions	May discolor white or pastel vinyls Irritating to eyes and skin	10 minutes on surfaces
Sodium hypochlorite	Intermediate	Rapid disinfection	Corrosive to metals Irritating to skin and eyes Diluted solution unstable, must be mixed daily	5–10 minutes
Phenolics	Intermediate	Available as sprays or liquids	Skin and mucous membrane irritation Cannot be used on plastics	10 minutes
Alcohol	Cleaner only	NA	NA	NA

From *Dental Assisting: A Comprehensive Approach*, by D. J. Phinney and J. H. Halstead, 2000, Albany, NY: Delmar.

disinfectants. Guidelines for mixing, handling, and discarding chemical sterilants and disinfectants can be found in Box 9–1.

SPRAY-WIPE-SPRAY TECHNIQUE

The spray-wipe-spray theory of environmental disinfection requires a three-step process. The first step involves mechanical removal of the organic debris—this step is called precleaning. The second step involves wetting of the surface by wiping thoroughly with the appropriate disinfectant solution. The third step requires allowing time for residual effect of the disinfectant.

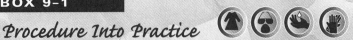

BOX 9-1

Procedure Into Practice

Guidelines for Mixing, Handling, and Discarding Chemical Sterilants and Disinfectants

The dental assistant must always take special care when handling chemical sterilants and disinfectants because of their toxicity.

1. Always wear appropriate PPE.
2. Always follow the manufacturer's instructions for storing, diluting, handling, and disposal.
3. Never allow solutions to touch the skin, to contact the eyes, or to be inhaled.

4. Follow instructions for proper shelf life and use life (term of usage) and dispose of all solutions according to local statutes and government requirements.
5. Keep necessary cleanup and spill-kit materials handy in the event of an accidental spill or splashing of solutions.

While it may seem time consuming, the spray-wipe-spray technique is the recommended way for the dental assistant to kill viable pathogenic microorganisms on environmental surfaces and equipment that cannot be sterilized.

The dental assistant should use the spray-wipe-spray method on any environmental surfaces and equipment contacted in the treatment room, or that have the potential for splash or splatters of OPIM. Examples include the following:

- Light handles and switches
- Chair switches and stool levers
- Tubing attached to handpieces, air-water syringes, and high-velocity systems
- X-ray tubehead
- Tray, tray arm, and bracket table
- Countertops, cabinet surfaces, mobile cabinets, and carts
- Handles on cabinets and drawers

The dental assistant should not spray electrical switches or the x-ray master control with disinfectant because this may cause short-circuiting. Box 9-2 lists the spray-wipe-spray procedure.

PLACEMENT OF PROTECTIVE BARRIERS

To prevent the spread of infectious diseases, the dental assistant must place disposable barriers (Figure 9-2, Figure 9-3) to protect environmental surfaces likely to be contaminated during routine treatment of patients. Pro-

BOX 9-2

Procedure Into Practice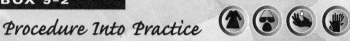

Guidelines for the Spray-Wipe-Spray Technique

The dental assistant should follow the spray-wipe-spray procedure (Figure 9–1) when disinfecting environmental surfaces and equipment that cannot be sterilized.

FIGURE 9–1 The dental assistant disinfects the dental chair using the spray-wipe-spray technique.

1. *Spray surfaces.* Spray the disinfectant onto the environmental surface to initially clean visible gross debris. Proper disinfection cannot occur without proper cleaning. Spraying the solution allows sufficient disinfectant to adequately clean the environmental surface.

2. *Wipe surfaces.* Wipe the environmental surface to remove gross soil, debris, or residue that remains on splash surfaces. Use 4 x 4 gauze squares or paper towels in overlapping strokes in a systematic pattern to wipe all surfaces.

3. *Spray surfaces again.* Then spray the environmental surface again and allow the disinfectant to dry for 10 minutes.

FIGURE 9–2
Disposable plastic barriers and sleeves protect the dental light handles, handpieces, air-water syringes, and the dental chair from cross-contamination with infectious diseases. *(Reprinted courtesy of Perio Support Products, East Irvine, CA)*

FIGURE 9–3
Disposable plastic tubing pro-
tects the air-water syringe
and oral vacuum tubings.
*(Reprinted courtesy of Perio
Support Products, East
Irvine, CA)*

tective barriers consist of plastic sleeves placed over dental tubings and covers on dental light handles, light switches, patients' chairs, and x-ray
machine tubeheads, master control, and switches.

Barriers must be single-use and must be replaced to avoid cross-
contamination. More specifically, the dental assistant should place new
barriers before the first patient each clinic day. These must be discarded
after the patient has been dismissed and replaced before seating the next
patient.

The dental assistant should be aware that protective barriers add nonbiodegradable plastic to the environment and may give a less aesthetic
appearance to treatment rooms. However, barriers provide the advantage of
saving the dental assistant time and help eliminate the presence of strong
odors associated with chemicals used for disinfection.

Another time-saving benefit of protective barriers is that the dental
assistant need not disinfect environmental surfaces after each patient if they
were not touched or used during that procedure. As long as the barrier stays
intact, the dental assistant can simply remove and replace the contaminated
barrier.

At the end of the clinic day or following any contact between the surface and blood or OPIM, the dental assistant must follow appropriate disinfection procedures.

The next morning the dental assistant places fresh barriers prior to
seating the first patient. Another benefit to placing and removing protective
barriers is that there is no need for the assistant to don PPE because no

chemicals are used. The dental assistant only has to have clean hands when applying protective barriers.

Because of these factors, most offices choose barriers for at least some of their operatory surfaces. For surfaces that are difficult to access or time consuming to clean, the dental assistant should use protective barriers designated for touch and transfer surfaces. Guidelines for placing and removing environmental surface barriers are listed in Box 9-3.

Front Office Barriers

With growing concerns about the spread of infectious bloodborne diseases, some dental practices have expanded the use of environmental barriers to the front (business) office, sometimes called the reception area. The rationale is to prevent potentially infectious bloodborne microorganisms from being transferred from the treatment areas to the front desk.

The dental assistant and front office staff must be especially careful when transferring such items as patient treatment charts and outer file covers, pens, pencils, lab cases, and prescriptions from clinical areas to the business area.

BOX 9-3

Procedure Into Practice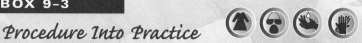

Guidelines for Placing and Removing Environmental Surface Barriers

The dental assistant should follow these steps when placing and removing protective barriers.

1. Apply appropriate surface covers before environmental surfaces become contaminated with patients' bioburden. If the treatment surface to be covered has already been contaminated, preclean and disinfect the surface, remove gloves, and wash hands before applying the surface cover.

2. Place each surface barrier in such a manner that it protects the entire surface and does not dislodge when touched.

3. Wear gloves when removing contaminated surface barriers following patient care.

4. Remove contaminated barriers from environmental surfaces and equipment using care to avoid touching the underlying surface. If a contaminated surface is accidentally touched during removal of a barrier, preclean and disinfect the surface.

5. Discard used covers in regular office trash unless local laws or regulations classify these items as regulated waste, in which case they must be disposed of as per local regulations.

6. Remove and discard contaminated gloves, wash hands, and apply fresh barriers prior to seating the next patient.

SKILLS MASTERY ASSESSMENT: POSTTEST

Directions: Select the response that best answers each of the following questions. Only one response is correct.

1. The Bloodborne Pathogens Standard considers _____ as the use of physical or chemical means to remove, inactivate, or destroy bloodborne pathogens from a surface or item so that they are no longer capable of transmitting infectious particles and the surface is safe for handling, use, or disposal.
   a. disinfection
   b. asepsis
   c. decontamination
   d. sterilization

2. All of these statements regarding touch surfaces are true EXCEPT which of the following?
   a. They are those surfaces usually touched and contaminated during the course of an invasive dental procedure.
   b. They need not be disinfected but must be cleaned at least daily.
   c. They generally include dental light handles, dental unit handles and controls, headrest adjustment buttons, dental chair switches, and x-ray exposure buttons.
   d. These surfaces should be used minimally.

3. All of these statements are true of transfer surfaces EXCEPT which of the following?
   a. They are usually touched during an invasive procedure.
   b. They are usually contacted by contaminated instruments such as instrument trays, dental unit handpiece brackets, or the x-ray viewbox.
   c. For proper and consistent asepsis, they should be treated in the same manner as touch surfaces.
   d. All of the above statements are true.

4. When selecting and using an environmental surface disinfectant, the dental assistant should
   a. look for the ADA Seal of Acceptance and the EPA's registration number on the label.
   b. make certain it inactivates the polio 2 virus and tuberculosis as a "hospital level" disinfectant.
   c. wear appropriate PPE, including utility gloves, a mask, and eyewear.
   d. a and b only
   e. All of the above

5. Chlorine dioxide compounds are EPA-registered, high-level chemical disinfectants and sterilants that can be used only on instruments, environmental surfaces, and equipment not susceptible to corrosion.
   a. True
   b. False

6. Glutaraldehyde is an EPA-registered, _____ disinfectant and sterilant.
   a. uncategorized
   b. low-level
   c. intermediate-level
   d. high-level

7. The dental assistant should avoid contact with glutaraldehyde and must not inhale the vapors because its fumes are highly toxic.
   a. True   b. False

8. All of these statements about sodium hypochlorite are true EXCEPT which of the following?
   a. For general-purpose disinfection, the dental assistant may use a 1:10 dilution, adding ¼ cup of bleach to 1 gallon of water.
   b. Used as a disinfectant, sodium hypochlorite has a 28-day shelf life.
   c. It may be corrosive to some metals and is irritating to the skin and eyes.
   d. Because it is a bleach, the dental assistant must take care not to contact sodium hypochlorite with clothing because it may cause moderate-to-severe bleaching and in some cases may eat through clothing.

9. Because of its low cost and quick surface drying time, isopropyl alcohol is highly recommended as a disinfectant in the dental office.
   a. True   b. False

10. When handling and discarding chemical sterilants and disinfectants, the dental assistant should always follow instructions for proper shelf life and use life (term of usage) and dispose of all solutions according to local statutes and government requirements.
   a. True   b. False

11. Which of the following is the proper sequence for environmental surface disinfection?
   a. Wet surface with disinfectant solution by thoroughly wiping; spray to preclean; spray again to allow time for residual effect of the disinfectant.
   b. Spray to preclean; spray again to allow time for residual effect of the disinfectant; wet surface with disinfectant solution by thoroughly wiping.
   c. Spray to preclean; wet surface with disinfectant solution by thoroughly wiping; spray again to allow time for residual effect of the disinfectant.
   d. Spray for residual effect of the disinfectant; wet surface with disinfectant solution by thoroughly wiping; spray to reclean.

12. All of these are advantages to using barriers in the treatment rooms EXCEPT for which of the following?
   a. Barriers save the dental assistant setup time and help eliminate the presence of strong odors associated with chemicals used for disinfection.
   b. The dental assistant need not disinfect surfaces after each patient if they are not touched or used during that procedure.
   c. Protective barriers add nonbiodegradable plastic to the environment.
   d. There is no need for the assistant to don PPE because no chemicals are used. The dental assistant need only have clean hands when applying protective barriers.

Dental Laboratory Asepsis

LEARNING OBJECTIVES

Upon completion of this chapter, the student should be able to:

1. Describe the importance of infection control in the dental laboratory areas, including necessary asepsis technique in the shipping/receiving areas of the office.

2. Describe the components of a dental lab prescription or work order and the role of the dental assistant in maintaining a tracking system for all lab cases.

3. Relate the importance of using PPE when handling and disinfecting dental prostheses and appliances.

4. Describe necessary asepsis technique for disinfection of countertops and work surfaces, as well as disinfection techniques for specific types of impressions and prostheses.

5. Describe necessary asepsis technique in the treatment room and dental lab areas regarding pumice materials and related equipment.

6. Describe waste management procedures that are necessary when working in the dental office laboratory.

THE IMPORTANCE OF INFECTION CONTROL PROCEDURES IN THE DENTAL OFFICE LABORATORY

For many years, asepsis in the dental office laboratory was often overlooked. More recently, however, controlling cross-contamination in the lab area has become equally as important as disease containment in the treatment rooms.

CDC guidelines specify that blood and saliva must be thoroughly and carefully cleaned from laboratory supplies and materials that have been used in the mouth, especially before polishing and grinding intraoral devices.

Communication with the Commercial Dental Lab

Communication between a dental office and the commercial dental laboratory regarding handling and decontamination of supplies and materials is of the utmost importance. This communication most often is the responsibility of the dental assistant, upon the direction of the dentist.

Logging and Tracking Lab Cases

In addition to maintaining asepsis of cases, the dental assistant must also manage the flow of dental cases in and out of the office by maintaining a tracking system as to the type and nature of lab cases, the name of the patient, the date sent out, anticipated due date, and information about the status of the case.

A dental lab prescription, sometimes referred to as a *work order* is written in duplicate: one copy goes to the lab with the case and the other is retained in the patient's chart. The prescription's dual parts are usually labeled "lab copy" and "office copy" or "doctor's copy."

To maintain current information on the status of all lab cases, it is helpful to set up a dental lab tracking system to enable the dentist and chairside assistant to know at any given time the location and status of every lab case sent out of the office.

This tracking system may be a notebook, a dry-wipe board in the office laboratory, or a program logged into the practice's computer database (Table 10–1).

TABLE 10–1

SAMPLE LAB TRACKING FORM						
Patient's Name	Date Sent Out	Lab	Work Ordered	Date Needed	Date Returned	Patient's Appointment
Mary Smith	10/3	Smile Dental	PFG 4-unit bridge	10/17	10/15	10/24
Harold Roberts	10/5	Dental Works	FU/FL denture	10/12	10/10	11/3
Ralph Garcia	10/7	Dental Works	PU metal framework	10/18	10/17	10/20

It is also essential that the dental assistant keep a schedule of the required number of "turnaround" working days required by each respective lab to complete the procedure requested and to entrust the office manager to schedule the patient accordingly for subsequent, sequential appointments, if necessary.

It is beneficial to the practice that one dental assistant be charged with the responsibility of tracking and maintaining status on lab cases; a backup staff member should have training as well.

Most dental labs provide their own printed prescription pads for convenience. The following information should appear on the outgoing lab prescription:

- Patient's name (or sometimes a patient's case number or Social Security number)
- Type of service, prosthesis, or appliance required
- Type of material required, such as porcelain or metal
- Shade (tooth color) required by the dentist to match the patient's original or existing dentition and a mould number for denture teeth
- Date required for the case to be returned to the office (usually 1 to 2 days prior to the patient's reappointment time)
- Dentist's name, address, telephone number, license number, and signature or initials

Often, a member of the dental staff may write dental lab work orders and sign the dentist's name or initials, as directed by the dentist.

> **Note**
>
> The clinician must allow sufficient time when setting up appointments for the lab to complete the work and return it to the office prior to the patient's next scheduled appointment.

Management of Outgoing Lab Cases

Prior to sending out a case, the dental assistant must carefully disinfect, dry, wrap, and mark the impression, prosthesis, or appliance for shipment or pickup (Figure 10–1). The laboratory prescription is completed with instructions for the lab technician. The patient's name must also be included; some offices assign a patient number, often the patient's Social Security number, to the case as well.

It is also helpful when communicating with commercial dental labs to include a Laboratory Asepsis Form, which ensures accountability in infection control practices and procedures for both the dental office and the laboratory (Box 10–1). The dental assistant should store a copy in the practice's office manual or hazard communication manual.

Management of Incoming Lab Cases

When a case comes in from the commercial laboratory, the dental assistant opens the box, noting the condition of the contents, the patient's name, and the type of lab work completed.

Incoming commercial lab materials, impressions, and intraoral appliances should be cleaned and disinfected before being handled, adjusted, or inserted into a patient's mouth. These items should also be cleaned and

FIGURE 10–1

The outgoing lab case contains the items for fabrica-
tion or repair; the completed, signed, and dated work
authorization form; the disinfection notice; and protective wrapping to prevent damage during transport.

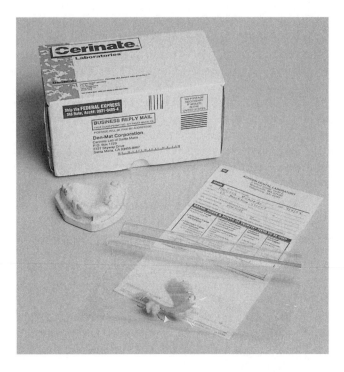

BOX 10–1

Sample Laboratory Asepsis Forms

This form will help the dental assistant keep track of incoming and outgoing laboratory cases. These completed records should be kept on
file as a permanent part of the practice's infection control program.

Impressions and Outgoing Cases

In accordance with CDC and OSHA guidelines, our office uses
_____ for _____ minutes prior to handling or pouring
models and impressions. We do this to prevent cross-contamination to
laboratory personnel, to our patients, or to ourselves.

Incoming Cases

We use _____to disinfect/sterilize cases returning from the
dental laboratory for _____ minutes prior to placing prostheses in the
mouth. We do this to prevent cross-contamination from laboratory
personnel, patients, and ourselves.

_____   _____
Doctor's Signature   Date

disinfected when returned from the dental laboratory and before placement in the patient's mouth.

The CDC requires that a chemical germicide be used that is EPA-approved as a hospital disinfectant and that has a label claim for micobactericidal (e.g., tuberculocidal) activity.

The dental assistant should discard packaging materials immediately upon opening. To reduce the likelihood of cross-contamination, do not save and reuse laboratory packaging materials.

When the lab case is returned, it should be compared to the original work order or prescription for accuracy and quality. The returned case will include a copy of the prescription, which the office manager files to later compare to the monthly statements sent by the various labs with which the doctor works.

Asepsis in the Shipping/Receiving Areas of the Office

Smaller dental offices generally do not have a specific area for shipping and receiving. Cases delivered and picked up from an outside dental lab are usually left at a back entrance to the office or at the front desk. Shipping and receiving areas should be kept clean and free from contaminants and debris. Incoming cases should not be opened or unnecessarily handled and should be transferred immediately to the designated lab area.

Likewise, outgoing lab cases should be transferred to the designated pickup area in the office and handled by dental personnel as little as possible to maintain aseptic conditions.

Appropriate PPE in the Lab

When working in the dental lab areas, on dental impressions or on prosthetic or orthodontic cases, the dental assistant must employ universal precautions. Wearing PPE not only aids in prevention of disease transmission, it provides additional protection for the assistant against inhaling dangerous substances such as pumice and fumes or sustaining accidental splatters, burns, or injuries that may result from flying objects such as tooth fragments or pieces of acrylic.

Disinfection of Lab Counters and Work Surfaces

When working in the dental lab area all counters and work surfaces must be kept clean and free of debris daily. The dental assistant should use the same environmental disinfection techniques as in the dental treatment rooms. The technique called spray-wipe-spray is detailed in *Chapter 9: Environmental Surface and Equipment Asepsis*. If unfamiliar with this technique, the dental assistant should review this chapter.

Frequently used lab drawers, exposed equipment, and work surfaces should be cleaned daily, using an appropriate disinfectant. Large sheets of paper work well as a surface barrier. These must be disposed of immediately after use.

Any instruments, attachments, items, or materials used with new prostheses or appliances should be maintained separately from those to be used with prostheses or appliances that have already been inserted into the mouth and are thus contaminated. This separation procedure includes separate pumice pans for new and existing prostheses, as well as separate polishing burs.

Disinfection of Removable Prosthetics and Orthodontic Appliances

Items to be inserted into the patient's mouth should be handled carefully and as little as possible; prior to the try-in, they must be cleaned and disinfected (Box 10–2). All dental prostheses carry potentially infectious microorganisms, but most are unable to withstand heat sterilization; other considerations of heat sterilization include the sterilization cycle time required and cooldown time.

Other alternatives, such as disinfection, are more practical. A thorough cleaning, followed by immersion in a disinfectant, is the preferred technique. The dental assistant should place the prosthesis or appliance in a disposable plastic cup, plastic container, or zip-type plastic bag and submerge it in a nontoxic disinfectant for a minimum of 15 minutes. The item should then be rinsed; if heavily soiled or contaminated with visible bioburden, the prosthesis should then be placed in the ultrasonic cleaner in a basket or beaker especially designed to hold prosthetic appliances.

Next, the assistant sets the ultrasonic cleaner timer for 3 minutes. After the 3 minutes has elapsed, the assistant removes the appliance from the ultrasonic cleaner and rinses it under body-temperature, running water for 30 seconds.

BOX 10-2

Procedure Into Practice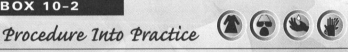

Disinfection of a Dental Prosthesis or Orthodontic Appliance

The dental assistant should use the following steps to disinfect dental prostheses and orthodontic appliances.

1. Place the item in a disposable plastic cup, plastic container, or zipped plastic bag; make sure it is submerged in a nontoxic disinfectant, such as glutaraldehydes, iodophors, or sodium hypochlorite may also be used (see Table 10–2).

2. If the prosthesis is heavily soiled, ultrasonically clean it for 3 minutes. Throughout

the appointment, transport and store the prosthesis in its original container of disinfectant.

3. Thoroughly rinse the item before insertion into the patient's mouth.

4. If the appliance or prosthesis is to be sent back to the commercial laboratory, soak it for 10 to 30 minutes in a sodium hypochlorite solution.

5. To prevent cross-contamination, discard the disinfectant solution after use.

TABLE 10-2

RECOMMENDED DISINFECTANTS FOR PROSTHETIC APPLIANCES AND DEVICES			
Device	**Glutaraldehydes**	**Iodophors**	**Sodium Hypochlorite**
Plastic or porcelain full dentures	No	Yes	Yes
Removable plastic partials	No	Yes	Yes (use a 1:10 solution and do not exceed 10 minutes)
Fixed prostheses	Yes	No	Yes (use a 1:10 solution and do not exceed 10 minutes)
Stone casts	No	Yes	Yes
Wax rims, bites	No	Yes	No

If the appliance or prosthesis must be returned to the commercial dental lab for further adjustment, the dental assistant should soak it for 10 to 30 minutes in a disinfecting solution. If the appliance or prosthesis contains metal, the dental assistant should not use sodium hypochlorite because this will cause corrosion.

DISINFECTION OF DENTAL IMPRESSIONS

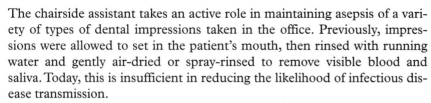

The chairside assistant takes an active role in maintaining asepsis of a variety of types of dental impressions taken in the office. Previously, impressions were allowed to set in the patient's mouth, then rinsed with running water and gently air-dried or spray-rinsed to remove visible blood and saliva. Today, this is insufficient in reducing the likelihood of infectious disease transmission.

All dental impressions are contaminated with the patient's blood and/or saliva and thus carry the potential for cross-infection to other dental team members and to dental laboratory personnel. Some microorganisms may exist for extended times outside of the human mouth and can be transferred from contaminated impressions to dental cases. Oral bacteria can remain viable in set gypsum for up to 7 days! If improperly handled, impressions can be a source of cross-contamination.

PPE must be worn by all clinical personnel or any other personnel who may have the potential for contact with contaminated impressions while performing their job.

Impressions are best decontaminated and disinfected (Table 10–3) at chairside immediately after removal from the oral cavity.

TABLE 10–3

RECOMMENDED DISINFECTANTS FOR DENTAL IMPRESSION MATERIALS			
Impression Material	Glutaraldehydes with Phenolic Buffer	Iodophors	Sodium Hypochlorite
Alginates	Yes	Yes	Yes
Polysulfides	Yes	Yes	Yes
Silicones	Yes	Yes	Yes
Polyethers	No	Yes	Yes
Reversible hydrocolloids	No	Yes	Yes
Compounds	No	Yes	Yes

Because some dental impression materials are more sensitive than others and need to be handled using a specific technique or disinfecting solution, it is important that the office have a written policy or procedure that it employs with the commercial dental laboratory.

Elastomeric Impressions

Polysulfides and silicone impression materials are relatively stable and can withstand disinfection without adverse effects by immersion in most disinfectants. Hydrophilic, polyether impressions can also be disinfected by immersion; however, exposure time should be no more than 10 minutes.

Immersion in acid glutaraldehyde has been shown to improve the surface detail reproduction in elastomeric impressions.

Alginate (Irreversible Hydrocolloid) Impressions

Immediately after the impression is removed from the mouth, it is rinsed gently under tap water and sprayed with an ADA-recommended disinfectant (Figure 10–2) before it is placed in a zip-locked plastic bag (Figure 10–3). The ADA recommends disinfection of alginate impressions by spraying and wrapping in diluted hypochlorite, iodophor, or glutaraldehyde with phenolic buffer.

Hydrocolloid (Reversible) Impressions

Reversible hydrocolloid impressions may be disinfected by immersion in an iodophor diluted 1:213 (5.25 percent); sodium hypochlorite diluted 1:10 (2

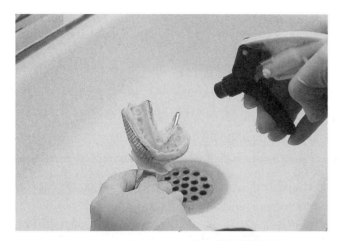

FIGURE 10–2
The dental assistant sprays the alginate impression with an ADA-approved disinfectant prior to placing it in a zip-locked plastic bag for pouring up later on.

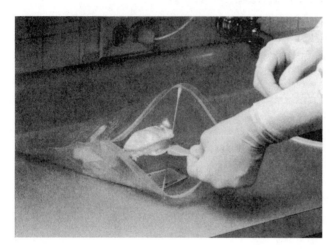

FIGURE 10–3
The dental assistant carefully inserts the disinfected alginate impression into a plastic bag. After the gloves are removed, the assistant closes the bag by touching the outside only.

percent); acid glutaraldehyde diluted 1:4; or glutaraldehyde with phenolic buffer diluted 1:16.

DISINFECTION OF RELATED DENTAL LABORATORY ITEMS

The dental assistant is responsible for disinfecting a number of laboratory items used at the chairside related to dental impressions.

Wax Rims and Wax Bites

The dental assistant disinfects wax rims and wax bites using the spray-wipe-spray technique (see *Chapter 9: Environmental Surface and Equipment*

Asepsis) with an iodophor recommended by the ADA. For disinfection to be most effective, the item should remain wet with disinfectant for the time recommended for tuberculocidal disinfection.

Wax rims and bites can also be immersed in sodium hypochlorite or iodophor.

Bite Registrations

Bite registrations of ZOE (zinc-oxide and eugenol) or compound can also be disinfected in the same manner with an EPA-registered, hospital-level tuberculocidal disinfectant in spray form. Chlorine compounds should be avoided on ZOE impressions. Following disinfection, the dental assistant should rinse again to remove any residual disinfectant solution.

Custom Acrylic Impression Trays

The dental assistant disinfects custom acrylic impression trays by spraying with a surface disinfectant or immersion in either 1:213 iodophor or 1:10 sodium hypochlorite. The tray should be rinsed thoroughly to remove residual disinfectant, then allowed to dry completely prior to use.

Dental Casts

The dental assistant disinfects dental casts only after the final set has been reached. Stone models should be disinfected with a spray of iodophor used according to the manufacturer's instructions.

Miscellaneous Chairside Lab Items

Miscellaneous lab items used at chairside that cannot withstand sterilization or that may not fit inside a sterilizer also require disinfection. Articulators, facebows, plane guides, Boley gauges, torches, and shade guides can become contaminated with saliva.

The dental assistant scrubs them with an iodine-containing disinfectant, alternately spraying the instrument with the disinfectant, maintaining wetness for at least 2 minutes. Then the assistant wipes them dry.

If iodophors are used to disinfect shade guides, the dental assistant should wipe them with water or alcohol following exposure time to remove any residual disinfectant. If glutaraldehyde or phenolics are used on any of the above items that may come into contact with mucous membranes or skin, the items must be thoroughly rinsed afterward.

ASEPSIS IN THE DENTAL OFFICE LAB

As at chairside, the dental assistant is responsible for disinfecting a number of laboratory items also used in the lab area of the office. When handling dental appliances and prostheses, the dental assistant must wear appropriate PPE.

Pumice

For many years, the pumice pan was a functional piece of equipment that held polishing material used by the dentist, laboratory assistant, or lab technician to polish removable appliances or dentures. A small amount of water was added to the pumice to aid in polishing as needed, over and over, for the denture or appliance adjustment for many patients. Little thought was given to the pumice pan as a breeding ground for pathogenic microorganisms. This thinking has changed significantly.

These organisms (opportunistic pathogens) rarely produce disease in healthy patients; however, they may cause secondary infection in certain predisposed or immunocompromised, debilitated patients.

If this contaminated pumice is used to polish an immediate denture, the possibility exists for a potential infectious fungal, bacterial, or viral infection to be transmitted into open wounds (sockets), cross-contaminating the patient.

To reduce the likelihood of cross-contamination when adjusting any removable appliance or prosthesis, the operator should wear protective gloves, mask, and eyewear to avoid contacting potentially infectious splatter. To protect patients, the dental assistant disinfects a fresh amount of pumice to create a slurry with a 1:10 mixture of chlorine bleach and water, or other recommended disinfectant.

Some practices find it helpful to use inexpensive, disposable fast-food containers or grocery store Styrofoam trays. The dental assistant writes the patient's name on the pan and places a brush wheel or rag wheel in each pan for one-time use with each patient's lab case.

Brush Wheels and Rag Wheels

Following each use, the dental assistant washes reusable rag wheels, then places them into a canister to be sterilized by steam under pressure. The canister tops should be loose to allow a free flow of the sterilant. Rag wheels may also be washed, rinsed, bagged, and cycled through the autoclave.

Rag wheels should not be cycled through a chemical vapor sterilizer because this process may burn the cloth portion.

A fresh wheel should be used for polishing each prosthesis or appliance. Disposable buffing wheels are a suggested alternative to reusable rag wheels. Brush wheels should be disinfected at least daily.

DISPOSAL OF LABORATORY WASTE MATERIALS

Proper disposal of laboratory waste materials is also the responsibility of the dental assistant. Solid laboratory waste products visibly contaminated with blood or other body fluids are placed in sealed, sturdy, impervious bags to prevent leakage of the waste materials. The dental assistant disposes of the bag, following regulations established by local or state environmental agencies.

SKILLS MASTERY ASSESSMENT: POSTTEST

Directions: Select the response that best answers each of the following questions. Only one response is correct.

1. Controlling cross-contamination in the lab area is _____ containing disease in the treatment rooms.
   a. more important than
   b. less important than
   c. equally as important as
   d. It is of unknown importance.

2. Laboratory supplies, materials, and appliances must be thoroughly and carefully cleaned because:
   a. this is a CDC guideline requirement.
   b. blood and saliva from the mouth contain contaminants.
   c. commercial laboratories do not generally clean or disinfect prostheses or appliances before returning them to the dental office.
   d. a and b only

3. When working in the dental lab area, the dental assistant must wear PPE because this
   a. aids in prevention of disease transmission.
   b. is a requirement under CDC guidelines.
   c. provides additional protection from harmful substances or injuries.
   d. keeps all dental staff color-coordinated in similar clinical wear.
   e. a, b, and c

4. Ideally, one dental assistant should be responsible for maintaining the dental lab case tracking system in the office.
   a. True   b. False

5. Prior to sending out a lab case, the dental assistant should complete all of the following steps EXCEPT
   a. carefully disinfect, dry, wrap, and mark the impression or prosthesis for shipment or pickup.
   b. complete a separate lab bill for the patient.
   c. check to ensure the patient's name or patient number is included with the case.
   d. enter all necessary information into the office's lab case tracking system.
   e. check to ensure the laboratory prescription is completed with instructions for the lab technician.

6. To save money on packaging costs, the dental assistant should save, recycle, and reuse lab packaging materials.
   a. True   b. False

7. All of the following can be used to safely disinfect plastic or porcelain full dentures EXCEPT
   a. glutaraldehydes.   c. sodium hypochlorite.
   b. iodophors.

8. Which of the following impression materials can be disinfected using glutaraldehydes with phenolic buffer?
   a. Alginates and polysulfides
   b. Polyethers
   c. Reversible hydrocolloids
   d. Compound

9. When disinfecting wax rims and wax bites, the dental assistant should allow the device to remain wet with disinfectant for the time recommended to attain
   a. saturation.
   b. disinfection.
   c. sterilization.
   d. tuberculocidal disinfection

10. When properly disposing of laboratory waste materials, the dental assistant should
   a. use waste receptacles in the treatment room.
   b. wash and reuse solid waste containers.
   c. follow regulations established by local or state environmental agencies.
   d. use the fastest and least expensive method.

CHAPTER

11

Infection Control in Dental Radiography

LEARNING OBJECTIVES

Upon completion of this chapter, the student should be able to:

1. Describe the need for awareness of office protocols for infection control with regard to dental radiography procedures.

2. List the steps necessary to ensure asepsis in radiographic procedures prior to, during, and following film exposure.

3. Describe infection control concerns regarding the use of a daylight loader on the automatic film processor.

4. Discuss disinfection of film packets.

5. Recall advantages and disadvantages of various infection control methods for exposing dental radiographs.

INFECTION CONTROL AWARENESS IN DENTAL RADIOGRAPHY

Until the release of OSHA's Bloodborne Pathogens Standard, little thought was given to dental radiographic procedures with regard to containment of infectious diseases. Today, the dental assistant is much more aware of the need for better infection control procedures in all areas of clinical dentistry, including during radiographic exposing, transport, and processing procedures.

This is true because many bloodborne pathogens, including hepatitis B, HIV disease, and full-blown AIDS, may be transmitted in the dental office, primarily through salivary contamination, which may occur when film packets are placed into the patient's oral cavity.

PRIOR TO EXPOSING RADIOGRAPHS

As with any procedure that invades the oral cavity, the dental assistant's hands must be washed with an antimicrobial soap with residual action and thoroughly dried at the beginning of each day and prior to gloving. The dental assistant must take universal precautions by wearing gloves, a mask, eyewear, and protective clothing at all times when exposing radiographs to prevent skin contact with the patient's blood, saliva, or mucous membranes.

The dental assistant must avoid touching any areas or surfaces such as doorknobs, unexposed film packets, or clinical records while wearing contaminated gloves. The assistant must take care to avoid touching anything that is nonessential to the radiographic procedure. Surfaces must also be decontaminated using the spray-wipe-spray technique between patients (see *Chapter 9: Environmental Surface and Equipment Asepsis* for further information).

Protective Barriers in the Radiographic Area

To prevent the spread of infectious diseases, the dental assistant must ensure that appropriate disposable barriers are placed to protect splash surfaces likely to be contaminated during the course of patient treatment, especially those difficult to disinfect.

Protective barriers consist of plastic sleeves over dental tubings and covers on dental light handles, light switches, patients' chairs, and x-ray machine tubeheads (Figure 11–1). These must be discarded after the patient has been dismissed and replaced before seating the next patient (see *Chapter 9: Environmental Surface and Equipment Asepsis* for further information).

As long as the barrier stays intact, the contaminated covering can simply be removed and replaced. At the end of the clinic day or following any contact between the surface and exposure to blood or other potentially infectious materials (OPIM), the dental assistant must apply appropriate precleaning and disinfection procedures.

Note

Some bite blocks and intraoral film holders, panoramic bite blocks, and beam aligning devices can be sterilized by autoclaving. Head positioners, chin rests, and ear rods, for which sterilization is not practical, can be disinfected with an EPA-registered, ADA-approved surface disinfectant.

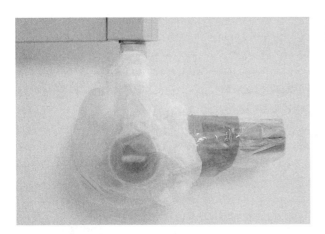

FIGURE 11–1
X-ray tubehead with protective barriers in place.

ADA INFECTION CONTROL RECOMMENDATIONS FOR X-RAY EQUIPMENT AND FILMS

The dental assistant should follow these steps, recommended by the ADA regarding infection control protocols for x-ray equipment and films.

Use protective coverings (Box 11–1) or disinfectants to prevent microbial contamination of position-indicating devices (Box 11–2). Handle intraorally

---

BOX 11–1

Procedure Into Practice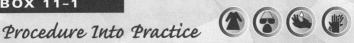

Placing and Removing Protective Surface Barriers in the Radiographic Operatory

The dental assistant should take the following steps to place and remove protective barriers in the radiography operatory:

1. Apply appropriate surface covers before environmental surfaces become contaminated with patients' bioburden. If the treatment surface to be covered has already been contaminated, preclean and disinfect the surface, remove gloves, and wash hands before applying the surface cover.

2. Place each surface barrier in a manner such that it protects the entire surface and does not dislodge when touched.

3. Wear gloves when removing contaminated surface barriers following patient care.

4. Remove contaminated barriers from touch-transfer surfaces, using care to avoid touching the underlying surface. If a surface is touched during removal of a barrier, reclean and disinfect the surface.

5. Discard used covers in regular office trash unless local laws or regulations classify these items as regulated waste, in which case they must be disposed of as per local regulations.

6. Remove and discard contaminated gloves, wash hands, and apply fresh barriers prior to seating the next patient.

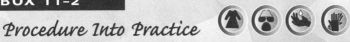

BOX 11-2

Procedure Into Practice

Infection Control Procedures for the Radiography Operatory

Following are recommended infection control procedures for the dental assistant to implement in the radiography operatory:

1. Surfaces likely to become contaminated must be covered with a protective barrier material such as plastic wrap or aluminum foil.

2. Surfaces not covered must be cleaned and disinfected using an EPA-registered, ADA-approved surface disinfectant.

3. Prepare and place necessary supplies, including film packets, film holding devices, paper cups, and towels.

4. Seat and drape the patient; use a lead apron with *thyroid* collar (Figure 11–2).

5. Wash the hands using an antimicrobial skin cleaner with *residual* action, meaning the bacteriostatic property continues after rinsing and drying.

6. Don gloves.

7. Expose the required number of films.

8. Blot film packets dry; deposit them into a film container (disposable paper cup or barrier-lined lead box) placed outside the operatory.

FIGURE 11–2 Barriers on a dental x-ray unit and a lead apron with thyroid collar placed on a patient.

9. Dismiss the patient, unless other dental procedures are necessary at this appointment.

10. Dispose of all contaminated supplies and barriers in an appropriate manner.

11. Clean and disinfect all touch and splash surfaces that may have become contaminated.

12. Remove gloves.

13. Carry container of exposed films to the darkroom.

contaminated film packets in a manner to prevent cross-contamination. Open contaminated packets in the darkroom while wearing disposable gloves.

The assistant should drop the individual films out of their respective packets without touching the films. Accumulate the contaminated packets in a disposable paper towel.

After all packets have been opened, discard them and remove gloves. Process the films without contaminating darkroom equipment with microorganisms from the patient.

Alternatively, place protective pouches over film packets before exposure. Drop the uncontaminated packets out of the pouches before processing.

HANDLING THE X-RAY FILM PACKET

The dental assistant must handle each film packet carefully to prevent cross-contamination. Because the outer film packet is coated with saliva when it is removed from the oral cavity, it should always be treated as though it were contaminated with blood. Note that the film packet has heat-sensitive emulsion and cannot be disinfected or sterilized per se. Thus, the dental assistant should protect the packet by keeping it in the factory-sealed package or dispenser until ready for use.

After exposing the film packets, the dental assistant wipes and dries them and carries them to the darkroom in a disposable container such as a paper cup or towel. The dental assistant must wear PPE while handling contaminated film packets and also to routinely disinfect all darkroom surfaces that could become contaminated.

There are two methods to prevent the transmission of microorganisms via the film packet: the *handling technique* and the *barrier protection technique*.

Handling Technique

The dental assistant places exposed film packets into a container, usually a paper cup or towel placed outside the radiography area. After all the exposures have been made, the assistant carries the container to the darkroom.

Under darkroom safelight conditions, the dental assistant opens the film packets. In doing so, the assistant takes care to avoid touching the films as they drop onto a separate paper towel or clean, disinfected surface. The assistant then removes and discards contaminated gloves and processes the films as usual.

Barrier Protection Technique

The alternative technique is to use barrier envelopes commercially available for film sizes #0, #1, and #2, which may be purchased from the supplier with film packets factory sealed (Figure 11–3).

After exposing the film packets in the barrier envelopes, the dental assistant takes the films to the darkroom (Box 11–3). The assistant opens each *barrier envelope*, allowing the film packet to drop onto a clean surface. Then, wearing gloves, the assistant opens the film packets and processes them as usual.

Automatic x-ray processor surfaces, the daylight loader (Box 11-4), the inlet rollers, the outlet port, and even the air around the processor may became contaminated during processing. Bacterial contamination is also on the inside of paper packets after contact with oral fluids.

> **Note**
>
> If the dental assistant must leave the radiography room for any reason during the procedure, gloves must be removed and disposed of. Upon return, the dental assistant must rewash the hands and don a fresh pair of gloves prior to resuming radiographic exposures.

> **Note**
>
> Some infection control authorities discourage the use of daylight loaders because cross-contamination is difficult to prevent.

DISINFECTION OF INTRAORAL FILM PACKETS

Dental infection control experts recommend treating intraoral film packets as an environmental surface and thus using surface disinfectants to prevent

FIGURE 11–3

Dental x-ray film supplied in protective barrier packet (Clin-Asept) provides sound infection control. *(Reprinted courtesy of Eastman-Kodak Company, Rochester, NY)*

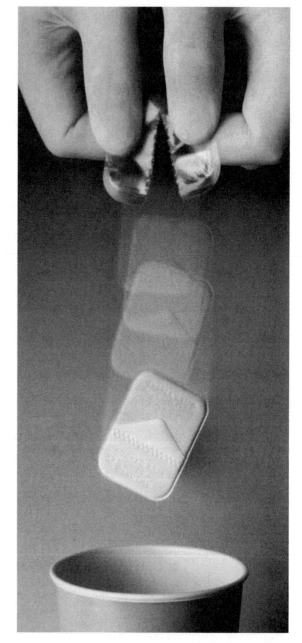

> **Note**
>
> All contaminated radiographic supplies that cannot be disinfected or sterilized for reuse must be disposed of properly, following local, state, or regional regulations. This is to minimize health hazards to patients and dental team members.

cross-contamination. Eastman-Kodak advises that polycoat films can be immersed for up to 15 minutes without damage to the film; however, immersion specifically is not recommended by Kodak.

Immersion of polycoat film packets in a 5.25 percent solution of sodium hypochlorite for 30 seconds is a suitable disinfection procedure for routine use.

BOX 11-3

Procedure Into Practice

Infection Control Procedures for the Darkroom

Following are recommended infection control procedures the dental assistant uses in the darkroom:

1. Don fresh gloves.

2. Maintain darkroom conditions, sealing out all visible light and using an approved safelight.

3. Remove films from film packets by letting them drop onto a clean, disinfected surface or paper towel. Avoid touching the film with the gloved hands because the gloves become contaminated as soon as they touch the film packets.

4. Dispose of the film packet wrappers and film container (paper cup or paper towel).

5. Remove and dispose of contaminated gloves.

6. Process uncontaminated films manually or with an automatic processor.

7. Mount radiographs. Note: It is not necessary to wear gloves while mounting radiographs.

BOX 11-4

Procedure Into Practice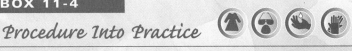

Infection Control Procedures While Using a Daylight Loader

Following are recommended infection control procedures to be implemented by the dental assistant when using a daylight loader. Daylight loaders require special infection control considerations. There are two suggested methods:

1. Barrier bags:
   a. Remove film packets from barrier bags.
   b. Use the daylight loader.

2. Nonuse of barrier bags:

a. Remove gloves and wash hands before using the daylight loader.

b. Place gloves and contaminated film packets inside the loader through the removable cover.

c. Put hands into the daylight loader cuffs and don fresh gloves.

d. Unwrap the film packets.

e. Remove the gloves before withdrawing the hands.

ADVANTAGES AND DISADVANTAGES OF VARIOUS INFECTION CONTROL METHODS FOR EXPOSING DENTAL RADIOGRAPHS

The corresponding charts (Table 11–1, Table 11–2, and Table 11–3) present advantages and disadvantages of various infection control methods to consider when exposing dental radiographs. As with all products and devices, the dental assistant is advised to make procedural decisions based on current guidelines and recommendations, as per the dentist's directions. Further, the assistant should keep a written copy of infection control protocols, including those on radiographic area infection control, on file and accessible at all times.

TABLE 11–1

ADVANTAGES AND DISADVANTAGES OF INFECTION CONTROL METHODS: DENTAL ASSISTANT'S EQUIPMENT

Assistant's Equipment	Advantages	Disadvantages	Comments
Barriers	• No chemical sprays used • No "wait time" to place new barriers	• Breakdown time • Environmental concerns • May be costly	• PPE and disposable or autoclavable products should be used • PPE may be considered during radiographic procedures as no aerosols are generated • Barriers may not be practical during some processing procedures
Plastic wrap	• Clear	• May affect voltage meter reading on control box	
Aluminum foil	• Inexpensive	• Blocks reading on control box	
Surface disinfection	• Inexpensive	• May discolor or corrode some surfaces • Moisture may damage electronic equipment in	• PPE must be worn while using these chemicals

Assistant's Equipment	Advantages	Disadvantages	Comments
		control panels • Cannot be used on cloth surfaces, lead shield, dental chair or cuffs or daylight loader • "Wait time" for disinfectant to dry	
Overgloves	• Less waste	• Awkward to put on and take off gloves numerous times	• Techniques may be difficult to teach and monitor for compliance

TABLE 11–2

ADVANTAGES AND DISADVANTAGES OF INFECTION CONTROL METHODS: ASSISTANT'S TRANSPORT OF CONTAMINATED FILMS

Transport of Contaminated Film	Advantages	Disadvantages	Comments
Paper cup	• Inexpensive	• None	• Contaminated films should be contained during transport
Paper towel or patient bib	• Inexpensive	• Name	• Contaminated films should be contained during transport

TABLE 11-3

ADVANTAGES AND DISADVANTAGES OF INFECTION CONTROL METHODS: RADIOGRAPHIC FILM

Radiographic Film	Advantages	Disadvantages	Comments
Barriers	• Time-saving	• Cost	• Person processing the film must be trained to open barriers utilizing the "no touch" method to avoid contamination

(continues)

TABLE 11-3 *(continued)*

Radiographic Film	Advantages	Disadvantages	Comments
barrier envelope	• Packets prepared by manufacturer—no staff time	• Relatively expensive • Adds "bulk" to film and difficulty in film placement	• Person processing the film must be trained to open barriers utilizing the "no touch" method to avoid contamination
Plastic heat-sealed envelope		• Adds bulk to film and difficulty in film placement • Time required to prepare packets	• Person processing the film must be trained to open barriers utilizing the "no touch" method to avoid contamination
Finger cot	• Inexpensive	• Time required to prepare packets	• Person processing the film must be trained to open barriers utilizing the "no touch" method to avoid contamination
"No touch" opening method	• May be used either with barrier envelopes or with regular film packets	• May be difficult to accomplish without contaminating edges of film	
Surface disinfection	• Inexpensive	• Not recommended by Kodak • Product or technique used must be sufficient to destroy all contaminants	• Research shows no leakage of polycoat film packets • An immersion or a "two wipe" method may be most effective

WASTE MANAGEMENT OF RADIOGRAPHIC CHEMISTRY

Liquid waste radiographic chemistry (developer and fixer) should be carefully poured into a drain connected to a sanitary sewer system. The dental assistant should take care to ensure compliance with applicable local waste regulations. Drains should be flushed or purged at the close of each clinical business day to reduce bacterial accumulation and growth.

SKILLS MASTERY ASSESSMENT: POSTTEST

Directions: Select the response that best answers each of the following questions. Only one response is correct.

1. The dentist on duty (whether the owner of the practice or an employee) is legally responsible for unsanitary conditions or lack of maintaining infection control protocols or procedures.
   a. True   b. False

2. Surfaces in the radiographic operatory likely to become contaminated must be covered with a protective barrier material such as plastic wrap or aluminum foil.
   a. True   b. False

3. Bloodborne pathogens, including _____, may be transmitted in the dental office, primarily through salivary contamination.
   a. hepatitis B   d. b and c only
   b. HIV disease   e. All of the above
   c. full-blown AIDS

4. A daylight loader is the film processing technique of choice because cross-contamination is easier to prevent than when processing films manually.
   a. True   b. False

5. Barriers in the dental radiography area
   a. save time.
   b. help eliminate the presence of strong odors associated with chemicals used for disinfection.
   c. need to be changed only once daily for maximum cost-effectiveness.
   d. a and b only
   e. All of the above

6. When processing dental radiographs the dental assistant should do all of the following EXCEPT
   a. remove films from film packets by letting them drop onto a clean, disinfected surface or paper towel.
   b. avoid touching the film with gloved hands.
   c. don a fresh pair of gloves when processing each film individually.
   d. dispose of the film packet wrappers and film container.

7. The dental assistant must wear gloves while mounting radiographs.
   a. True   b. False

8. Advantages of using barriers in the dental radiography operatory include which of the following?
   a. No chemical sprays are used.
   b. There is no "wait time."
   c. There is no chemical odor.
   d. All of the above

9. The dental assistant should discard protective barriers after the patient has been dismissed and must replace them before seating the next patient.

a. True   b. False

10. According to ADA recommendations, the dental assistant should

a. place protective coverings or use disinfectants to prevent microbial contamination of position-indicating devices.

b. handle intraorally contaminated film packets in such a manner as to prevent cross-contamination.

c. open contaminated packets in the darkroom while wearing disposable gloves.

d. accumulate contaminated packets in a disposable paper towel or cup.

e. All of the above

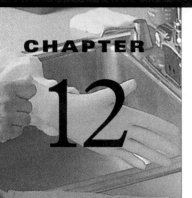

12

Hazard Communication

KEY TERMS

biohazard warning labels

engineering controls

exposure-control plan

exposure incident

hazard communication program

medical waste

work practice controls

LEARNING OBJECTIVES

Upon completion of this chapter, the student should be able to:

1. Describe the importance of maintaining a hazard communication program and the necessary components.

2. Describe physical, chemical, and biological hazards in the dental office.

3. List ways to reduce hazards inherent in the dental office.

4. Describe the necessary procedures for handling hazardous materials in the dental office.

5. List and describe the components of OSHA's Bloodborne Pathogens Standard and the responsibilities of the dental team to implement them.

6. Describe the necessary record keeping required by the government with regard to staff training.

7. Relate the changes reflected in OSHA's new compliance directive.

HAZARD COMMUNICATION PROGRAM

Every dental office that has 11 or more employees is required by OSHA to have a written **hazard communication program**.

To comply with the Hazard Communication Standard, the dentist must develop and implement a written compliance program. This must include an exposure-control plan (including the Bloodborne Pathogens Standard), a written hazard communication program, waste and sharps handling and management, and injury and illness prevention (Figure 12–1).

The dentist must designate a safety supervisor to provide staff training to new employees and once annually thereafter. The dentist must also maintain and update the written hazard communication program, develop ways to reduce hazards in the office, and provide a safe means for handling of hazardous materials.

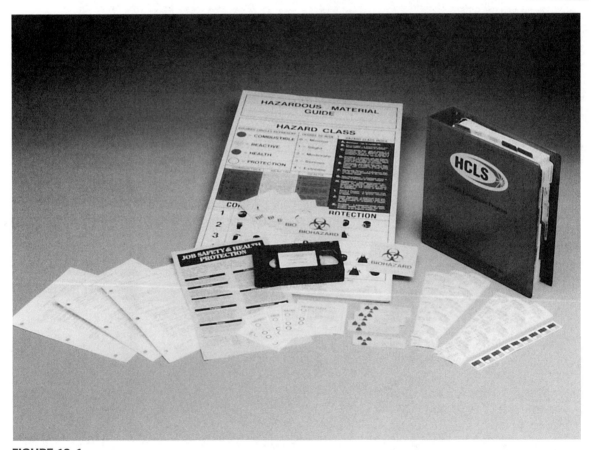

FIGURE 12–1
Each office must maintain an office manual with exposure control plans, training material, hazard communication and OSHA-required employee records. *(Reprinted courtesy of Medical Arts Press)*

PHYSICAL AND CHEMICAL HAZARDS IN THE DENTAL OFFICE

Physical hazards are evident in dental equipment, open flames, radiation, ultrasonic devices, sterilization units, and sharp instruments. Electricity is also a major source of physical hazard. All electrical equipment must be properly grounded, following the manufacturer's instructions and according to local electrical codes. All electrical cords and plugs must be kept in working order, with no frayed cords, exposed wires, or overloaded circuits. Extension cords should not be used except in an emergency.

Fire is another potential danger in the workplace, with fires occurring most often where open flames, such as Bunsen burners, are used. When using an open flame, such as for melting wax, the dental assistant must take care not to allow loose clothing or long hair to catch on fire. (For additional information on emergency fire evacuation and use of a fire extinguisher, refer to *Chapter 15: Office Emergency Procedures.*)

In other areas of the office, hot plates, automatic coffeemakers, and microwave ovens should be used, rather than open flames. The dental assistant should store flammable chemicals in a flameproof cabinet, away from heat sources and in a well-ventilated area.

The dental assistant must also take care when using pressurized sterilizers to prevent explosions and steam burns.

Chemicals present a variety of hazards in the dental office because they may be flammable, toxic, caustic, corrosive, carcinogenic, or mutagenic. The dental assistant or safety supervisor must make and maintain a hazardous chemical inventory of all products used in the office. These items must be appropriately labeled or tagged and have a corresponding Material Safety Data Sheet (MSDS) on file, accessible to all employees.

PRODUCT WARNING LABELS AND STICKERS

Hazardous chemicals used in the office must be properly labeled and other hazardous substances must have corresponding MSDSs. Under the revised hazard communication standard, all dental practices are required to communicate to their staff members the hazards of the chemicals they use in the practice. Labeling (Figure 12–2) is a key element of a sound and complete hazard communication program. Labels must provide a brief synopsis of the hazards of chemicals used in the practice.

Labels also help serve as a reminder to warn dental staff that the chemicals they contact require proper care, storage, and handling.

Chemical warning labels correspond to the information contained on MSDSs, identifying the contents of containers of hazardous chemicals and showing hazard warnings appropriate for staff protection, for example, "Gloves must be worn when handling certain chemicals." All chemicals used in the dental office must be labeled. In the majority of applications, the manufacturer's label is sufficient. However, if the chemical is transferred to

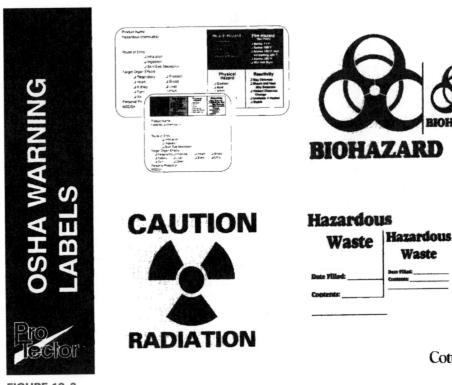

FIGURE 12–2

OSHA warning labels for hazardous products and devices, and biohazard labels for hazardous waste. *(Reprinted courtesy of Cottrell Ltd)*

a different container, a new label must be placed on that container if the material is not used up at the conclusion of an 8-hour work shift.

The label or sticker must contain appropriate warnings by hazard class, including routes of entry into the body and target organs of the body that may be affected. Product labels must contain the identity of the chemical, the appropriate hazard warnings, and the name and address of the manufacturer.

A container properly labeled when received from the manufacturer or supplier does not require an additional label. The exception for labeling is single-use or single-dispensing items or products.

All members of the dental team should familiarize themselves with the labels of hazardous substances and be aware of how to clean up spills or handle other emergencies that may arise when handling these products.

Fluorescent orange or red-orange **biohazard warning labels** contain the biohazard symbol. The word *biohazard* must be attached or affixed to containers of regulated waste and to refrigerators and freezers containing blood and OPIM, as well as to other containers used to store, transport, or ship blood or OPIM. Red bags or red containers may be substituted for labels as long as dental staff are trained to associate them with biohazardous contents.

Material Safety Data Sheets (MSDSs)

Manufacturers of chemicals are required by law to put hazard information on product labels and to provide corresponding MSDSs for every potentially hazardous chemical (Box 12–1). MSDSs (Figure 12–3) describe the physical and chemical properties of a product, physical and health hazards, route of exposure, precautions for safe handling and use, emergency and first-aid procedures, and control measures. It is the dental office's responsibility to ensure that these sheets are obtained and kept up to date.

The dental office must also maintain a hazardous materials log, which is a list, a file folder, or a binder of all hazardous materials or substances used in the office, as well as where each item is located in the office and the quantity on hand.

Staff Training

The dentist is required to provide staff training regarding potential hazards inherent in the practice, including hazardous chemicals. This training must be provided for new employees at the beginning of employment, for employees of record, whenever a new hazardous material is introduced into the office, and at least annually thereafter.

The dentist is legally responsible to provide this training, however he or she may delegate training responsibilities to the office manager, the safety coordinator, or other team member.

BOX 12-1

Material Safety Data Sheets

OSHA requires that each MSDS contain the following:

- Identification (chemical and common names)
- Hazardous ingredients
- Physical and chemical characteristics (boiling point, vapor pressure, and so on)
- Fire and explosion data
- Health hazard data
- Reactivity data
- Spill and disposal procedures
- Protection information
- Handling and storage precautions, including waste disposal
- Emergency and first-aid procedures
- Date of preparation of the MSDS
- Name and address of the manufacturer

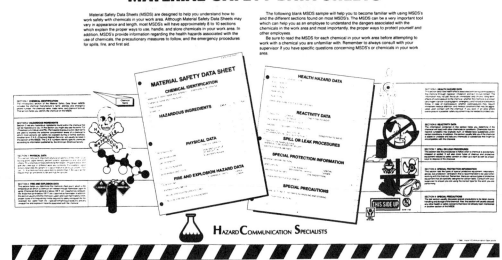

FIGURE 12–3

Material Safety Data Sheets (MSDSs) provide a wealth of product information. OSHA requires all dental personnel understand how to use MSDSs and where they are located in the office.

Training must include the following:

- Hazards of chemicals and proper handling
- Operation where hazardous chemicals are used
- Availability of MSDSs
- Explanation of the labeling of hazardous chemicals
- Explanation of OSHA regulations

OSHA also requires that hazard communication training include methods and observations that may be employed to detect the presence or release of a hazardous substance in the work area (for example, continuous radiation, nitrous oxide monitoring devices, or particular odors associated with chemicals).

Physical and health hazards of these chemicals used in the work area must be addressed (for example, avoidance of handling mercury with ungloved hands, or the potential for acid etch to burn skin or clothing).

Training must also include measures employees can take to protect themselves from hazardous materials using PPE, which must be supplied by the employer in appropriate sizes for all clinical staff members.

The dentist is responsible for explaining the details of the hazard communication program, including the labeling system, the use and nature of MSDSs, and how employees can obtain and use the appropriate hazard information for their safety.

Employee training may be conducted at staff meetings, using audiovisuals, lectures, and videotapes, or at continuing education courses offered through accredited providers. Training should be conducted in such a way that employees understand the information presented and their questions are answered; training must be conducted at no cost to employees, during standard working hours.

Training Record Keeping

Verification for training must be documented, indicating when and where the training took place and those present. Training records should be maintained for a minimum of 3 years and records must be available to employees upon request for review and copying Box 12–2.

In the event the practice is sold or transferred, employee records must be transferred to the new owner. If the practice is permanently closed due to death or retirement of the dentist, these records should be offered (in writing) to the National Institute for Occupational Safety and Health (NIOSH) 90 days prior to the anticipated close of the office.

BOX 12-2

Staff Training Record

Date: _____ To: _____ From: _____ Hours: _____

Title/topic: _____

Training summary: _____

_____

_____

Safety coordinator/trainer: _____

Staff members present   Job title

_____

_____

_____

_____

Reducing Hazards in the Dental Office

All members of the dental team are responsible for reducing hazards and the potential for hazards. This can be done by the following:

- Keeping the number of hazardous materials to a minimum
- Reading all product labels and following directions for use
- Storing hazardous chemicals in their original containers
- Keeping containers tightly closed or covered when not in use
- Avoiding the combination of two or more known hazardous chemicals—for example, mixing household chlorine bleach with ammonia may cause an explosion; inhaling the fumes may be fatal
- Wearing appropriate PPE when using hazardous chemicals or when there is potential for accidental exposure on contact with body fluids
- Washing and thoroughly drying hands before and after wearing gloves
- Keeping the office well ventilated and avoiding skin contact with known hazardous substances
- Keeping a functional fire extinguisher in the office
- Knowing proper cleanup procedures in the event of a chemical or hazardous chemical spill (Figure 12–4)
- Disposing of all hazardous chemicals and other substances in accordance with MSDS instructions or the product label

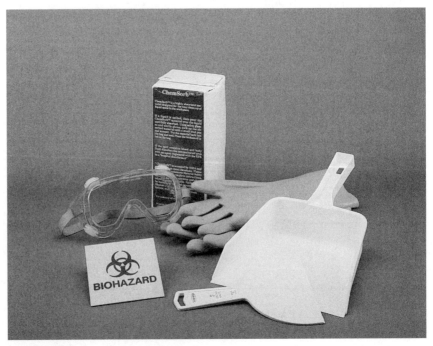

FIGURE 12–4
Emergency spill kit. *(Courtesy of SmartPractice, Phoenix, AZ)*

The Exposure Minimizing Form (Box 12–3) provides a guide to outline and define the primary tasks performed by each staff member who may, as part of the nature of the job, have potential or probable exposure to hazardous substances or OPIM.

The Tasks Assigned column should have general tasks, such as sterilizing instruments, sanitizing and setting up treatment rooms, and disinfecting and wrapping cases to send to outside dental lab.

The Engineering Controls column should include safety procedures used in the office to help minimize risks to employees. These may include scrubbing instruments with an ultrasonic cleaner, placing plastic barriers on treatment room equipment, or installing a protective shield on the model trimmer.

The Work Practice column should include measures taken by staff to eliminate or reduce exposure. These might include the following: avoid touching contaminated instruments directly, avoid inhaling glutaraldehyde fumes, or avoid using a model trimmer without a shield and face mask.

The PPE used for these procedures should be listed for each task, for example, gloves, eyewear, mask, and gowns.

Handling Hazardous Materials

Because contact with hazardous materials is inevitable when working in the dental office, there are measures the dentist and dental assistant can take to

---

BOX 12-3

Exposure Minimizing Form

Each dental staff member who has the potential to contact hazardous chemicals or products should have an Exposure Minimizing Form on file. When the job duties or description change, the form must be updated to reflect the changes or additions.

Name: _____ Job: _____ Date: _____

Tasks Assigned	Engineering Controls	Work Practice Controls	PPE Used

protect themselves. The most significant measure is using PPE, which is part of the universal precautions mandated by OSHA.

As part of the hazard communication program, the office must have a written procedure for handling and disposing of used or outdated materials that cannot be poured down the sanitary sewer or treated as routine or medical waste. These materials include, but are not limited to, outdated x-ray solutions, vapor sterilization fluid, lead foil from dental x-ray packets, scrap amalgam, and glutaraldehyde solution with a concentration higher than 2 percent.

Dental team members must be instructed how to handle spills and cleanup of hazardous substances and chemicals. In the event of an accidental spill, staff should follow the manufacturer's instructions (found on the label or on the MSDS) and wear appropriate PPE.

BIOLOGICAL HAZARDS IN THE DENTAL OFFICE

In addition to physical and chemical hazards, the dental assistant must be aware of biological hazards. Safety from biological hazards involves avoiding occupational contact with bloodborne illnesses such as hepatitis B and HIV/AIDS.

Prior to the Bloodborne Pathogens Standard, OSHA had developed laws for workers' protection that primarily involved protection from hazards such as falls, electrical shock, and chemical exposure.

Hepatitis B Vaccination

The dentist must make the hepatitis B vaccine and vaccination series available to all staff at risk for occupational exposure. Further, the vaccine is to be offered at no charge to staff members after they have received the OSHA-required training and within 10 days of employment. Boosters must also be made available free of charge to the employee if and when recommended by the United States Public Health Service.

Vaccination is not required to be offered to employees who have already received the complete series or for whom antibody testing has disclosed immunity.

Dental staff members who decline the vaccine are required to read and sign a declination statement as a waiver. Employees who sign the waiver and then decide to undergo vaccination must have it made available to them by the dentist free of charge.

For documentation compliance purposes, the dentist must obtain a written opinion from the physician responsible for administering the vaccine as to whether the series is indicated and whether the employee has received the series. The dentist is also required to retain this written record and also to provide a copy to the employee.

BLOODBORNE PATHOGENS STANDARD

OSHA's Bloodborne Pathogens Standard is the most significant OSHA regulation affecting healthcare practices. It is designed to protect dental office employees by limiting occupational exposure to blood, saliva, and OPIM, which otherwise could result in transmission of bloodborne pathogens to healthcare workers.

Although the standard was finalized in 1992, OSHA issued a new compliance directive in 1999, Enforcement Procedures for the Occupational Exposure to Bloodborne Pathogens (CPL 2-2.44D), that updates the previous Bloodborne Pathogens Standard. Updates appear in Box 12-5 and are discussed later in the chapter.

Exposure-Control Plan

Every dental office must have a written **exposure-control plan**, a plan designed to identify tasks, procedures, and job classifications where occupational exposure takes place. The exposure-control plan must include the following:

- Copies of all government regulations with an understandable explanation of the contents
- A general explanation of the nature and symptoms of bloodborne diseases, including but not limited to AIDS and hepatitis
- An explanation of the ways bloodborne pathogens are transmitted
- An explanation of how to recognize tasks and other activities that may involve exposure to blood, saliva, and OPIM
- An explanation of how to use measures known to prevent or reduce occupational exposure, specifically appropriate **engineering controls**, which are specific equipment or devices that facilitate prevention of accidental exposure; **work practice controls** changing the way procedures are currently performed to ensure a higher degree of safety or protection from accidental exposure; and PPE
- Information on the types of PPE available, including proper use, location, removal, handling, decontamination, and disposal
- An explanation of the criteria for selecting PPE
- Information on the hepatitis B vaccine, including its efficacy, safety, method of administration, and the benefits of vaccination; also that the vaccine will be offered by the employer at no charge to all full-time employees.
- Instructions on what to do if an accidental **exposure incident** (for example, an accidental needlestick) occurs, including how to report it and the necessary medical follow-up
- Information on the postexposure evaluation and follow-up, which the employer must provide at no charge, following an exposure incident

- An understandable explanation of the signs, labels, and color coding required for OPIM and other potentially harmful substances in the dental office

The practice compliance checklist may be helpful to the practice in complying with infection control and hazard communication requirements.

Engineering and Work Practice Controls

OSHA requires that engineering controls such as appropriate handwashing facilities be available and accessible to all staff members. Contaminated sharps, especially needles, must be handled appropriately and disposed of to prevent accidental exposure (Figure 12–5). A minimum of one eyewash station must be immediately available to all personnel. Other engineering controls applicable to dentistry include high-volume evacuation and use of dental dam.

OSHA guidelines also require work practice controls that prohibit eating, drinking, smoking, application of cosmetics or lip balm, and handling of contact lenses in areas of the office where there is a reasonable potential for occupational exposure. All food and beverages should be stored separately from areas where OPIM are present. Work practice controls also include proper handwashing and handling of sharps and proper containment of regulated waste.

Specimens of blood, saliva, or OPIM must be placed in containers that prevent leakage during collection, handling, processing, storage, or shipping; specimen containers must be closed and color-coded or carry the biohazard symbol. If the primary container's surface is contaminated, a second container must be used.

Any equipment in the dental office that requires servicing or shipping must be decontaminated (if it has become contaminated with blood, saliva, or OPIM prior to servicing), unless it can be demonstrated that decontamination is not feasible; equipment or portions thereof that remain contami-

FIGURE 12–5
Sharps disposal containers.

nated are to be identified with a biohazard symbol; identification and labeling information must be conveyed to all affected employees, as well as to the service representative prior to handling, servicing, or shipping.

Universal Precautions

Following universal precautions means treating each and every patient as though that patient were potentially carrying an infectious disease. Therefore, the same standards of personal protection must be observed when treating all patients.

Universal precautions emphasize employing engineering and work practice controls to reduce the level of contamination that may be involved during an accidental exposure.

Personal Protective Equipment

Personal protective equipment consists of a minimum of four items, which must be worn by chairside personnel who have a reasonable potential to come into contact with infectious diseases. PPE, including laundering and disposal, is addressed in *Chapter 7: Personal Safety and Barrier Protection.*

Housekeeping Schedule

The dentist is required to develop and implement a written cleaning schedule for all of the following:

1. Decontaminating and cleaning of all equipment, as well as environmental and work surfaces, that may have been contaminated with blood or OPIM
2. Removing and replacing all protective barriers when contaminated
3. Decontaminating and inspecting reusable receptacles such as pails, bins, and cans
4. Implementing a mechanical procedure to properly pick up broken glass
5. Sorting or processing reusable sharps in a safe and efficient manner
6. Placing regulated waste in reclosable, properly labeled, or color-coded containers
7. Routinely replacing sharps containers, not allowing them to be overfilled, keeping them upright and within reasonably easy access to personnel who use them, and keeping them closed during transit
8. Discarding regulated waste according to local, state, and/or federal regulations
9. Using appropriate PPE when handling contaminated laundry

Waste Management

Regulated **medical waste** (Box 12–4) refers to liquid or semiliquid body fluid, including any items in the dental office that release bioburden when compressed; items caked with dried body fluid that have the potential to

---

BOX 12-4

Definitions of Medical Waste

Following are the most common types of medical waste and their definitions. It is essential that the dental assistant include them in the practice's infection control or hazard communication manual.

- *Infectious waste* is waste capable of causing an infectious disease.
- *Contaminated waste* is items that have had contact with blood or other body secretions.
- *Hazardous waste* is waste posing a risk or peril to humans or the environment.
- *Toxic waste* is waste capable of having a poisonous effect.
- *Medical waste* is any waste (including discarded solid, liquid, semi-solid, or contained gaseous materials) generated in the diagnosis, treatment, or immunization of humans or animals in research, or in the production or testing of biologicals; the term does not apply to any hazardous or household waste.
- *Hospital, household, and/or dental office waste* is the total discarded solid waste generated by all sources within the specified location. Only a portion of the waste generated in the dental office is classified by the EPA as regulated waste, that is, infectious waste that requires special handling, neutralization, and disposal.

---

release bioburden during handling; contaminated sharps; and pathological and microbial wastes containing body fluid.

Any type of disposable sharps, that is, any item capable of puncturing the skin (needles, scalpels, burs, orthodontic wires), must be disposed of in puncture-resistant, color-coded or labeled, red, closable, leakproof containers. Sharps disposal containers must be located as close as possible to where sharps are used in the office. They must also be kept upright and must be closed during transport.

Needles must not be recapped by hand, nor may they be broken or sheared by hand prior to disposal. Instead, the dental assistant should use either a one-handed "scoop" technique or a mechanical device designed to hold the needle sheath. For procedures involving multiple injections using a single needle, the unsheathed needle should be placed in a location where it will not become contaminated or contribute to unintentional percutaneous (through the skin) needlesticks between injections (Figure 12–6).

OSHA requires that full sharps containers must be removed from the office within 7 days of reaching the "fill line" on the container.

Other regulated waste products, including those items saturated or visibly caked with blood or saliva, must be disposed of in closable, leakproof bags or covered containers. The containers must either be red or have a bio-

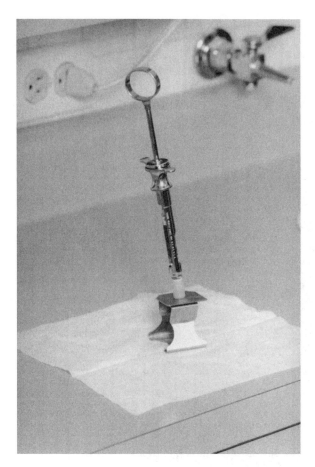

FIGURE 12–6
Needles must be recapped using a one-handed scooping method or a mechanical device.

hazard warning label, which is a label or tag affixed to hazardous waste items; it must be readable from a distance of 5 feet (Figure 12–7).

Contaminated refuse must be kept covered at all times. Receptacles must have a properly fitting lid, preferably one that can be opened using a foot pedal.

Waste receptacles should be kept closed to prevent air movement and the spread of contaminants. They should be lined with sturdy plastic bags; the assistant must wear PPE when changing waste receptacle bags. Double-bagging is recommended because it offers a second layer of protection if the bag breaks, is punctured, or tears.

Most states have enacted their own infectious waste disposal legislation, including proper waste transporting and tracking. Dental assistants should check with the local regulatory agency in their area for additional regulations. As a general requirement, medical waste must be disposed of within 30 days in offices that generate less than 20 pounds of medical waste per month.

FIGURE 12–7
Medical waste must be labeled and properly disposed of. *(Courtesy of Smart-Practice, Phoenix, AZ)*

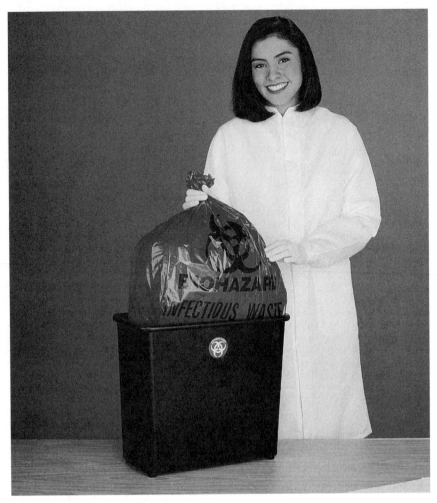

The following guidelines satisfy most regulatory requirements:

- In preparing regulated waste for shipment to the disposal site, log the weight and package containers so they remain rigid, leakproof, sealed, and impervious to moisture. Label as medical waste, as infectious waste, or with the universal biohazard symbol. Chemical hazardous waste requires a specific label that contains state-required information, including the length of storage, hazardous waste code, and generator EPA identification.
- Store containers in a protected area to maintain their integrity and prevent odor until disposal. (Some containers may require refrigeration.)
- Indicate the name, address, and permit number of the generator (the name of the dentist or the practice name) in permanent ink on the inner containers. Alternatively, containers can be identified with a water-resistant tag.

- Follow shipping instructions of the disposal service. Usually, the outer container should contain, in permanent ink, the generator's name, address, or permit number; the transporter's name, address, or permit identification number; and identification of contents as medical waste.

When using a transporter for medical waste, the dental assistant or safety supervisor should maintain a log containing the name, address, and identification number of the agent; the quantity of medical waste, categorized as treated or untreated; the date of shipment; and the signature of the transporter's representative. With permission of the disposal agent, small-quantity generators (those that produce less than 50 pounds of infectious waste per month, which generally includes the average dental office) can use their own vehicles to transport waste to the disposal site. If the generator transports the waste, the dental assistant should record the name and address of the disposal facility, the quantity of medical waste, the date of shipment, and other relevant information. Disposal logs should be maintained for 3 years.

Exposure Incidents

If a member of the dental team sustains an exposure incident directly related to the nature of employment, the dentist is required by OSHA to follow specific steps. For further information, refer to *Chapter 7: Personal Safety and Barrier Protection*.

Employee Medical Records

Medical records of staff must be kept confidential and must be retained by the dentist for the duration of employment plus 30 years. They should include the names and Social Security numbers of all employees; copies of all employees' hepatitis B vaccination records and any other medical records pertinent to the employees' ability to receive the vaccination; circumstances surrounding any exposure incidents; and documentation of all follow-up procedures, including the treating physician's written opinion.

Medical records are confidential and are not to be disclosed except to the employee, to anyone with written consent of the employee to review them, to representatives of the secretary of labor, or as permitted or required by state or federal law.

NEW OSHA COMPLIANCE DIRECTIVE

Following the 1991 OSHA final regulation regarding bloodborne pathogens and healthcare settings, OSHA issued a new compliance directive in 1999, Enforcement Procedures for the Occupational Exposure to Bloodborne Pathogens (CPL 2-2.44D), that updates the previous Bloodborne Pathogens Standard, which is still in effect.

The intent of the new directive is to guide compliance officers in enforcing OSHA standards consistently. It emphasizes the seriousness of health risks associated with blood and OPIM. The initial development of the new directive includes recommendations for improved methods to protect workers from needlestick and sharps injuries.

The new directive includes seven key points (Box 12–5). In addition to including engineering controls, the new directive emphasizes the importance of an annual review of the entire bloodborne pathogens program in the office, including exposure-control plans, training and education, and vaccination against hepatitis B. The directive also details inspection guidelines for compliance officers.

Exposure-Control Plan (Update)

In addition to developing an exposure-control plan that identifies employees, tasks, and procedures that may have occupational exposure potential, it is necessary to review and update this plan annually. The plan may be part of an overall health and safety plan, or it may be a stand-alone plan for bloodborne pathogens. Regardless of how the plan is structured, it must include all policies in place in the dental office to protect employees and must be readily accessible to them.

When reviewing and updating the exposure-control plan, the dentist must consider appropriate commercially available and effective engineering controls designed to eliminate or minimize occupational exposure. An example of this would be reviewing and incorporating resheathing or retracting needles designed to protect workers from accidental sticks.

OSHA compliance officers (inspectors) must review the plan to ensure that annual reviews and updates take place. All employees must have job classifications when the potential for occupational exposure exists. The use of PPE is a hazard abatement measure put in place to reduce exposure.

BOX 12-5

OSHA's New Compliance Directive

The seven key points of OSHA's new compliance directive include the following:

1. Annual review of exposure control plan
2. Engineering controls and work practices
3. FDA device approval evidence
4. Multiemployer work sites
5. CDC guidelines on vaccinations and postexposure management
6. Effective training and education
7. Replacement and update of appendices from the previous directive

This new directive does not replace or negate any of the obligations set forth in the original *Bloodborne Pathogens Standard* of 1991.

Engineering and Work Practice Controls (Update)

The exposure-control plan must show the use of engineering and work practice controls, specifically the use of safer medical devices, as a primary method of eliminating employee occupational exposure. OSHA encourages the dentist to involve staff in the evaluation and selection of safety devices but does not advocate the use of one product over another.

The OSHA inspector would look for patterns of injuries and whether safe devices and engineering or work practices were in use in the office. The officer would also look for documentation of the use of alternative devices, engineering controls, or work practice controls in the areas where exposure incidents had occurred.

FDA Device Approval (Update)

When the dental practice considers which medical devices to use, OSHA cautions that while the FDA is responsible for clearing engineering control devices for sale, clearance alone is insufficient to guarantee the device will work effectively in the dental office.

OSHA outlines four characteristics of medical devices that may assist the office in selection and evaluation of new safety products:

- The safety feature is fixed, provides a barrier between the hands and the needle following use, and requires the dentist's and dental assistant's hands to remain behind the needle.
- The safety feature is part of the device, rather than an accessory.
- The safety feature is in effect before disassembly and stays in effect following disposal.
- The safety feature is simple and requires little or no training to use appropriately.

Multiemployer Work Sites (Update)

This section of the directive is important to the dental assistant who works for or through temporary employment agencies and for dental practices that hire temporary staff members. The determination of responsibility is linked to the primary payer of the dental assistant.

An employment agency refers job applicants to prospective employers but does not put these workers on the payroll; the employment agency is not the employer and is not liable.

A personnel services firm employs workers and assigns them to work sites. The personnel services firm may be cited for violations of the Bloodborne Pathogens Standard in any of the six following categories: hepatitis B vaccinations; postexposure evaluation and follow-up; record keeping; generic training; violations occurring at the healthcare facility about which the personnel services firm actually knew but failed to take reasonable steps to have the host employer (dentist) correct the violation; and pervasive serious violations occurring at the facility about which the personnel services firm could have known with the exercise of reasonable diligence.

Home healthcare services, physicians, and other healthcare professionals who have established an independent practice are determined by whether they are unincorporated sole proprietors or partners may be cited if they employ only one staff member. Independent contractors are responsible for complying with all provisions of the standard in accordance with the multiemployer worksite guidelines.

CDC Guidelines on Vaccination and Postexposure Management (Update)

Vaccination of employees against hepatitis B must be available to the newly hired dental assistant within 10 days of the start of employment, and all related costs must be absorbed by the dentist. The dental assistant may decline the hepatitis B vaccination but must sign and date a waiver to that effect. The dental assistant may also decline if he or she has already received the hepatitis B vaccination or if medical tests show immunity.

Testing for hepatitis B surface antigen is recommended 1 to 2 months after the completion of the three-dose series. If the dental assistant does not respond to the primary vaccination series, OSHA recommends a second series, followed by retesting.

In the event of an occupational exposure, the OSHA compliance officer would look for verification of an employee's awareness of CDC guidelines; the officer would determine whether CDC guidelines were followed and would review the medical records. The officer would evaluate the circumstances of the exposure to determine whether PPE had been used, whether there was a lack of training, and what specific procedures were involved.

The employer is required to obtain a written medical opinion and provide it to the employee within 15 working days.

Training and Education (Update)

Dental employee training is crucial to the safe use of any device; however, access to training materials does not guarantee prevention of occupational injury. All dental office employees must receive initial and annual training on hazards associated with blood/OPIM, protective measures to employ, and management of exposures. The training must be interactive; that is, the dental assistant must have the opportunity to ask questions during training sessions. Thus, watching a video is insufficient training. Watching a video and then having a discussion with a knowledgeable trainer is acceptable.

The person conducting the training must have knowledge of the subject matter and expertise in occupational exposure in the workplace. The OSHA compliance officer would examine the credentials of the trainer or safety supervisor.

Replaced and Updated Appendices (Update)

A number of appendices are included in the new OSHA compliance directive, including information, resources, and sample forms and templates to incorporate into an office exposure-control plan. These appendices may be helpful to the dental assistant or office safety supervisor when writing, updating, or amending a dental office exposure-control plan. Box 12–6, Box 12–7, and Box 12–8 offer some additional information and checklists.

BOX 12–6

Practice Compliance Checklist

This checklist may be helpful to the dental assistant or office safety supervisor in organizing the practice's OSHA compliance list:

✓ Appropriate licenses, registrations, certificates, and OSHA posters posted in plain view of all employees

✓ X-ray certification of dental assistants posted (if required in the specific state of employment)

✓ A record of hepatitis B vaccination and any other appropriate vaccines administered

✓ Infection control manual, hazard communication manuals, hazardous materials log, and MSDSs accessible and available for review

✓ Appropriate handwashing procedures

✓ Appropriate use of PPE, available in sizes to fit clinical staff members

✓ Appropriate use of barrier wraps and disposable coverings for treatment room and laboratory area

✓ Appropriate use, management, and disposal of single-use items

✓ Appropriate surface disinfection of all splash areas

✓ Appropriate aseptic technique followed by all office personnel

✓ Appropriate sterilization/disinfection of contaminated, reusable instruments

✓ Appropriate biological monitoring as recommended in the state of employment

✓ Appropriate instrument sterilization/instrument recycling area

✓ Nitrile gloves for presoaking, cleaning, and processing of instruments prior to sterilization

✓ Appropriate disposal and tracking of regulated waste and OPIM, including sharps

✓ Eyewash stations in each operatory

✓ Appropriate infection control precautions for radiographic procedures

✓ Appropriate cross-contamination prevention in the dental laboratory area

✓ Appropriate safety checks and inspections for fire extinguishers, smoke detectors, radiation, and nitrous oxide monitors

BOX 12-7

Common OSHA Citations

The following are what OSHA inspectors look for when visiting dental offices. These are some of the areas most often cited:

- ✓ No OSHA "Employees' Rights and Responsibilities" poster
- ✓ No log and summary of illnesses and injuries
- ✓ Deficiencies in emergency plans
- ✓ Leaky waste receptacles
- ✓ Faulty or dangerous handling of biologic specimens
- ✓ Lack of proper labeling of biohazard materials with tags, stickers, or signs
- ✓ No access to records of employee exposures
- ✓ Deficient hazard communication programs
- ✓ Failure to label containers with hazardous chemicals or fumes
- ✓ Employees not properly trained or apprised of their rights about personal protective equipment
- ✓ Hepatitis B vaccination not offered to staff (or waiver missing)
- ✓ MSDSs missing or incomplete

BOX 12-8

Office Safety Documents and Records

This is a list of pertinent safety documents and records mandated by OSHA. Dental assistants may obtain additional information from their state, regional, or the national OSHA office.

Regulatory Documents

- OSHA Bloodborne Pathogens Standard
- OSHA Hazard Communication Standard
- Updated OSHA Directive/Enforcement Procedures
- State, local, or other required regulatory documents, for example, waste disposal sterilization monitoring

Policy Documents

- OSHA written exposure-control plan for the practice
- OSHA written hazard communication for the practice
- Management for emergencies, for example, fire, earthquake
- Other policies not covered by OSHA standards, for example, state regulations

(continues)

BOX 12-8 *(continued)*

- OSHA poster (form 2203), Job Safety and Health Protection Records
- OSHA bloodborne pathogens and hazard communication training records
- OSHA written schedule for cleaning and disinfecting the office
- OSHA form 101 (or equivalent) for individual occupational injury or illness
- OSHA form 200 (or equivalent) for annual summary of injury and illness reports
- OSHA employee and medical records, including the following:
    - ✓ Hepatitis B vaccination refusal forms/waivers
    - ✓ Written opinion from physician on vaccination of employees
    - ✓ Exposure incident reports
    - ✓ Written opinion from physician on postexposure medical evaluation and follow-up
- Sterilizer spore-testing results
- Radiographic equipment certification
- Fire extinguisher certification
- Manifests from regulated medical waste haulers
- Verification of on-site treatment of regulated medical waste
- Material Safety Data Sheets
- Inventory of hazardous chemicals

SKILLS MASTERY ASSESSMENT: POSTTEST

Directions: Select the response that best answers each of the following questions. Only one response is correct.

1. Hazard communication training must include all of the following EXCEPT
   a. hazards of chemicals and proper handling of chemicals.
   b. the availability and access of MSDSs to all staff.
   c. waivers for hepatitis C vaccinations.
   d. an explanation of the labeling of hazardous chemicals.

2. A dental assistant transfers a small amount of a known potentially hazardous chemical into a smaller container for use on a patient at chairside. He or she must place a new label on that container if
   a. more material is required during the course of treating that patient.
   b. the chemical material is not used up at the conclusion of an 8-hour work shift.

c. the patient recently tested positive for HIV.

d. no MSDS can be found on file for that material.

3. OSHA requires employers, including those in the healthcare profession, to do all of the following EXCEPT

    a. establish and carry out procedures to protect employees.

    b. implement and maintain employee exposure-incident records for 1 year.

    c. provide PPE to protect staff from infectious diseases and OPIM.

    d. maintain a hazardous chemical inventory list.

4. Hazard communication training must be provided

    a. for new employees at the beginning of employment.

    b. any time a new hazardous material is introduced into the office.

    c. annually.

    d. a and c only

    e. All of the above

5. OSHA's Bloodborne Pathogens Standard covers all dental employees who could reasonably anticipate coming into contact with blood, saliva, and other potentially infectious materials during the course of employment.

    a. True   b. False

6. OSHA's Bloodborne Pathogens Standard is designed to help protect dental patients from occupational exposure to bloodborne illnesses.

    a. True   b. False

7. Warning labels or stickers must contain all of the following information EXCEPT

    a. hazard class, including routes of entry and target organs that may be affected.

    b. the identity of the chemical and the appropriate hazard warnings.

    c. the name and address of the manufacturer.

    d. the telephone and fax number of the manufacturer.

8. The office must maintain Material Safety Data Sheets on every product that has a potential hazard. MSDSs must

    a. provide written information about the content and potential hazard of a specific product.

    b. be provided by the manufacturer or supplier.

    c. be available and accessible to employees for review during regular office hours only.

    d. a and b only

9. The hazardous materials log must contain all of the following information EXCEPT

    a. the price of all hazardous materials in the office.

    b. a list of all hazardous materials in the office.

    c. the location of each item in the office.

    d. the quantity of each item on hand.

10. When recapping the needle sheath, the dental assistant should use any of the following techniques or methods EXCEPT
   a. a one-handed "scoop."
   b. a mechanical device specifically designed to hold the needle sheath for recapping.
   c. any safety feature that is fixed, provides a barrier between his or her hands and the needle following use, and allows the dental assistant's hands to remain behind the needle.
   d. a two-handed "scoop" for maximum control.

11. The dental assistant may reduce exposure to occupational hazards and their potential by
   a. reading all product labels and following directions for use.
   b. avoiding the combination of two or more known hazardous chemicals.
   c. wearing appropriate PPE when using hazardous chemicals or when there is potential for accidental exposure or contact with body fluids.
   d. a and b only
   e. All of the above

12. Hazard communication training records should be maintained for a minimum of _____ years, and records must be available to employees upon request for review and copying.
   a. 3   c. 10
   b. 4   d. 30

13. Following the 1991 OSHA regulation regarding bloodborne pathogens and healthcare settings, OSHA issued a new compliance directive in 1999, Enforcement Procedures for the Occupational Exposure to Bloodborne Pathogens (CPL 2-2.44D), that replaces but still includes the previous Bloodborne Pathogens Standard.
   a. True   b. False

14. The intent of the new directive is to guide compliance officers in enforcing OSHA standards consistently. It encompasses all of the following EXCEPT
   a. the seriousness of health risks associated with blood and OPIM.
   b. improved methods to protect workers from needlestick and sharps injuries.
   c. inspection guidelines for EPA compliance officers.
   d. the importance of an annual review of the entire bloodborne pathogens program in the office, including exposure-control plans, training and education, and vaccination against hepatitis B.

15. All of these statements are true of sharps disposal containers EXCEPT for which of the following?
   a. They must be located as close as possible to where sharps are used in the office.
   b. They must be kept upright and must be closed during transport.
   c. They must be puncture resistant and leakproof.
   d. They must be provided individually for each clinical employee, if requested.

16. Fluorescent orange or red labels containing the biohazard symbol and the word *biohazard* must be attached to containers of regulated waste.
a. True   b. False

17. The updated exposure-control plan must show the use of engineering and work practice controls as a primary method of eliminating employee occupational exposure. An example would be
a. using only products endorsed or recommended by OSHA compliance officers.
b. upgrading the office's computer hard drive.
c. wearing two pairs of gloves when treating HIV/AIDS patients.
d. using improved needle safety devices.

18. Under the revised update, the OSHA inspector would look for
a. patterns of injuries.
b. whether safe devices and engineering or work practices were in use in the office.
c. for documentation of the use of alternative devices, engineering controls, or work practice controls in the areas where exposure incidents had occurred.
d. a and b only
e. All of the above

19. An employment agency that refers job applicants to prospective employers but does not put these workers on their payroll is not liable.
a. True   b. False

20. Which of the following diseases is not covered under OSHA's Bloodborne Pathogens Standard?
a. Hepatitis B   c. Tuberculosis
b. HIV/AIDS   d. Tetanus (lockjaw)

CHAPTER

13

Waterline Biofilms

Upon completion of this chapter, the student should be able to:

1. Define the term *biofilm* and the types of contaminants biofilm most commonly comprises.

2. Describe current ADA, CDC, and OSAP recommendations on dental office waterline safety.

3. List and discuss the stages of waterline biofilm formation.

4. Describe current safe water levels determined by federal agencies and the American Dental Association.

5. Discuss methods the dental assistant and other team members can employ to reduce waterline biofilms in the dental office.

6. List and discuss emerging solutions currently being offered by dental manufacturers to control waterline biofilms.

7. Discuss the differences between independent water reservoirs and water filters and when using a combination of both might be advantageous.

8. Describe boil-water procedures to be used in the event of a government-mandated restriction on the public water supply.

WHAT ARE BIOFILMS?

Biofilms are microorganisms that accumulate on surfaces inside moist environments such as dental unit waterlines, allowing bacteria, fungi, and viruses to multiply; this can significantly increase a patient's susceptibility to transmissible diseases. Biofilms can be found virtually anywhere moisture and a suitable solid surface coexist. They are composed of millions of microorganisms that accumulate on surfaces in aqueous (watery) environments. These film-forming microbes excrete a gluelike substance that anchors them to metals, plastic, tissue, and soil particles.

Most common biofilms consist of bacterial cells that adhere to surfaces, often forming a protective slime layer. When these cells attach to surfaces, such as the small-bore plastic tubings used to keep handpieces cool and to supply air-water syringes, they create an ideal environment for growth of biofilm.

Mature biofilms are complex microbial communities that vary considerably in their architecture and in the types of organisms inhabiting them. Fungi, algae, protozoans, and nematodes may be found in fresh water aquatic biofilms, as well as *Pseudomonas aeruginosa, Escherichia coli, Legionella,* and the highly resistant protozoan *Cryptosporidium* (Table 13–1). These can make people ill and in some cases can be fatal. Thus, reduction of waterline biofilms is essential in implementing an infection control program in the dental office.

Dental waterlines also exhibit a phenomenon called *laminar flow,* which means the rate of water flow inside the tubing is greatest in the center and decreases down to nearly zero at the inner tubing surface. This results in a nearly stagnant condition of the tubing inner wall surface, including when water actively flows through the tubing.

As the inside diameter of the waterline decreases, the surface area available for biofilm growth increases geometrically in relation to a fixed volume of water. As a result of this vast increase in surface area, the number of bacteria, fungi, and viruses living inside dental units can become highly concentrated in contrast to water mains and pipes that deliver water to the dental unit.

CONDITIONS THAT FACILITATE BIOFILM FORMATION IN WATERLINES

The following characteristics promote the growth of biofilms in dental waterlines:

- Flowing water incorporates nutrients and new organisms that initiate and sustain biofilms. Low numbers of microbes continually enter the tubing.
- Water in dental lines is stagnant 99 percent of the time, allowing the release of microorganisms into water. Stagnant water in narrow-bore tubing allows biofilm bacteria to concentrate to levels 1,000 to 1 million times those deemed "safe" for drinking water.

TABLE 13–1

MICROBES DETECTED IN DENTAL UNIT WATER

Bacteria	Main Source	Disease Activity
Achromotobacter	Water	Low pathogenicity
Acinetobacter	Water	Opportunistic
Actinomyces	Mouth	Periodontal disease
Alcaligenes	Water	Opportunistic
Bacillus	Water	Low pathogenicity
Bacteroides	Mouth	Periodontal disease
Flavobacterium	Water	Low pathogenicity
Fuscobacterium	Mouth	Periodontal disease
Klebsiella	Water	Opportunistic
Lactobacillus	Mouth	Caries progression
Legionella	Water	Legionnaires' disease
Micrococcus	Water	Low pathogenicity
Norcardia	Mouth	Low pathogenicity
Ochromobacterium	Water	Low pathogenicity
Pasteurella	Water	Opportunistic
Peptostreptococcus	Mouth	Periodontal disease
Pseudomonas	Water	Opportunistic
Serratia	Water	Opportunistic
Staphylococcus	Mouth	Low pathogenicity
Streptococcus	Mouth	Caries, pulp infection
Xanthomonas	Water	Low pathogenicity

Fungi

Penicillium, Cladosporium, Alternaria, Scopulariopsis

Protozoa

Acanthamoeba

Note

The dental assistant should be aware that purchased bottled water, including distilled water, may contain significant numbers of pathogenic microorganisms. Handling and processing of self-contained water reservoir systems by dental personnel can inadvertently introduce pathogens that may proliferate if systems are not maintained properly.

- Bacteria incorporated in protective slime are up to 500,000 times more resistant to chemical removal and treatment than floating microorganisms.
- Some chemically treated biofilms are resistant to antibiotics.
- Many biofilm microbes are difficult to culture and are not always easily detected by standard in-office water quality tests.
- Water in the tubing is not under high pressure.
- The small diameter of the tubing creates a large surface-to-volume ratio.
- Biofilm continually sheds fragments into dental unit water. Biofilm sloughing occurs when the tubing is used or flushed.
- Sloughing of pieces of dislodged biofilm leads to gross downstream contamination.

Of additional concern is that retraction of pathogens from the oral cavity and tissues at the treatment site may allow pathogenic organisms to enter the tubing and exit later, mixed with reserved treatment water. This may occur through the high-speed handpiece and through some ultrasonic handpieces. Thus, it is critical that handpieces are sterilized between patients to prevent cross-contamination.

STAGES OF BIOFILM FORMATION IN WATERLINES

There are three stages of biofilm formation: initial attachment, accumulation, and release.

Initial Attachment

In the initial attachment stage, microbes enter the tubing from the incoming municipal water supply and, to a smaller degree, from the patient's mouth during treatment. These microbes have the ability to adhere to surfaces, including the inside walls of dental tubings, within a few hours after the tubing is used.

Accumulation

In the accumulation stage, these attached microbes begin to multiply and start to form a spreading film or layer on the tubing walls. Additional microbes from the incoming water continue to attach and multiply. The microbes coat the cells, forming a slime layer. Within a few weeks, if untreated, the biofilm covers most of the inner walls of the dental unit tubing.

Release

During the release stage, microbes are continuously released from the biofilm into the flowing water.

WHAT IS THE QUALITY OF DRINKING WATER?

Coolant and irrigating water used in the dental office become highly contaminated as clumps of bacterial and viral cells break off from the biofilm and are discharged through dental handpieces, air-water syringes, and ultrasonic scalers. This results in water used during dental procedures that is often many times more contaminated than tap water supplied from the faucet in the same operatory.

The quality of drinking water in the United States is usually monitored by measuring the number of *coliform bacteria*. The 2000 proposed Federal Safe Drinking Water Act would reestablish an upper (safe) limit of 500 cfu/ml (coliform bacteria units per milliliter) for noncoliform water bacteria. The American Public Health Association has also set a recommended upper limit of 500 cfu/ml for bacterial contamination in recreational waters (swimming pools, spas, and so on).

The American Dental Association (ADA) recommends that dental equipment consistently deliver no more than 200 cfu/ml of aerobic bacteria at any time.

The ADA also recommends water quality indicators be used that inexpensively test for a broad range of microbes at room temperature.

RECOMMENDATIONS FOR DENTAL UNIT WATERLINE BIOFILM REDUCTION

The CDC, the ADA, and the OSAP recommend that the dental assistant flush the dental unit waterlines for 30 seconds at the start of each day and between patients (Box 13–1 and Box 13–2).

BOX 13–1

Procedure Into Practice

Reduction of Waterline Biofilms

The ADA recommends these guidelines to improve the quality of water dental office unit lines to minimize disease transmission. This is what the dental assistant should do to comply:

1. At the start of each day, run and discharge water from the dental unit waterlines for several minutes.

2. Run high-speed handpieces for 20 to 30 seconds after each patient to release air and water.

3. Always follow the manufacturer's instructions for proper maintenance of handpieces and waterlines.

4. Consider other options to improve water quality such as special filters, chemical therapeutics, and separate water reservoirs.

BOX 13-2

Current Guidelines and Recommendations for Dental Office Waterline Quality

The Centers for Disease Control and Prevention recommends the following:

- Flush air/water through handpieces for 20 seconds between patients to help reduce patient-borne microbes that may have entered the handpiece and been sucked back down the dental unit waterline.
- Avoid using dental unit water for performing procedures involving bone cutting.

Further, both the ADA and the CDC recommend sterile saline or sterile water as a coolant or irrigant when performing surgical procedures that involve cutting bone.

As of August 1996, the California State Board of Dental Examiners officially mandated sterile coolants/irrigants to be used for surgical procedures involving soft tissue or bone. Further, sterile coolant/irrigants are considered sterile when delivered using a device or process that has an FDA marketing clearance for delivery of sterile/coolant irrigants to the patient.

SOLUTIONS TO REDUCE WATERLINE BIOFILMS

A number of strategies are currently being considered to improve dental unit water quality (Box 13–3). They include improving the quality of the

---

BOX 13-3

Methods of Water Treatment

- **Distillation:** A purification (rather than sterilization) process that may remove volatile chemicals, endotoxins, and some microorganisms from water
- **Reverse osmosis:** A purification (rather than sterilization) process that produces potable drinking water
- **UV radiation:** May not kill some organisms in drinking water, such as *Giardia* and *Cryptosporidium*
- **Chemical treatment:** Uses chlorine or sodium hypochlorite to treat drinking and recreational water; some organisms are resistant to these chemicals

incoming water, controlling biofilms in the tubing, and controlling the quality of the output water.

Improve the Quality of the Incoming Water

To improve the quality of incoming water, do the following:

- Use nonmunicipal incoming water.
- For irrigation, employ a separate reservoir or use a hand syringe filled with either sterile water, distilled water, or deionized water.
- Use municipal water that has been either boiled or filtered.
- Use no water; instead, cut oral tissue "dry."

Control Biofilms in the Tubing

Within the office waterlines, the goal is to control biofilms in the tubing by doing the following (Box 13–4):

- Routinely decontaminating the lines
- Replacing lines and routinely decontaminating them
- Air purging the lines and letting them dry overnight
- Using disposable lines with a sterile water supply
- Using sterilizable lines with a separate water supply

BOX 13-4

Procedure Into Practice

Steps for Weekly Waterline Asepsis

The following information is helpful to the dental assistant in maintaining high-quality dental unit waterline asepsis in an effort to reduce or eliminate biofilm growth.

Disinfectant Solution

Use a disinfectant solution of one part household bleach (5.25 percent sodium hypochlorite) plus nine parts treatment water. This 1:10 solution should be used in all bottle and waterline asepsis. Dental manufacturers have determined that 100 ml (about 3.3 oz or ⅓ cup) of the 1:10 disinfectant solution is sufficient to treat one system.

Bottle Disinfection

To disinfect a water bottle attached to the dental unit, the dental assistant should pour 100 ml (about ⅓ cup) of the 1:10 solution into the bottle, cap the bottle, and shake it for 5 seconds; allow it to stand for 10 minutes. Shake the bottle again. Empty the bottle and rinse twice with treatment water.

Weekly Procedures

The dental assistant should perform the following procedures a minimum of once weekly, preferably at the beginning of each clinic week, before the first patient. For infrequently used dental units, the dental assistant should follow steps 1 through 4 immediately before and after storing the unit. As with any disinfection procedure, the dental assistant should wear the proper PPE, including nitrile gloves, in accordance with OSHA guidelines.

(continues)

BOX 13-4 *(continued)*

The dental assistant should do the following:

1. Make certain the unit has been purged with air.

2. Fill and flush the unit with disinfectant.

   a. Make sure the unit is turned off. Remove the empty water bottle and set it aside for disinfection.

   b. Add 100 ml of 1:10 disinfectant solution to a disinfected bottle.

   c. Hold handpiece tubings and syringe over a basin or bucket. Turn the unit on, wait a few moments, then operate the unit flush valve, syringe, and foot control until a steady stream of disinfectant solution begins flowing through the tubing (15–20 seconds).

3. Allow disinfectant to remain in the unit for at least 10 minutes but never longer than 30 minutes.

4. Purge the unit with air.

   a. Hold handpiece tubings and syringe over a basin or bucket. Turn the unit on, wait a few moments, then operate the unit flush valve, syringe, and foot control until the disinfectant solution is purged from the system.

   b. Turn off the unit. When storing the unit, stop here, and do not proceed to step 5.

5. Fill with treatment water.

   a. Make sure the unit is off. Remove the empty disinfectant bottle. Install a disinfected bottle filled with treatment water.

   b. Hold handpiece tubings and syringe over a basin or bucket. Turn the unit on, wait a few moments, then operate the unit flush valve, syringe, and foot control until a steady stream of treatment water begins flowing throughout the tubing (about 20 to 30 seconds). Your dental unit is now ready for use.

Control Water Quality As It Leaves the Tubing

For output water, the goal is to control water quality as it leaves the tubing. Methods to do this include use of microbial filters and high-volume evacuation with all water sprays.

EQUIPMENT MANUFACTURERS MAKE MODIFICATIONS

A number of U.S. dental manufacturing companies have begun to provide solutions to the waterline problem by making modifications in their dental units. One solution is a water reservoir separate from the public water supply.

The CDC has recommended that sterile water or *saline* (salt water) be used as a coolant or an irrigant when chairside procedures require cutting of bone. Provided with a separate water reservoir, dental professionals may choose the water source and perform waterline asepsis.

Nonsterile Water Delivery Systems

Self-contained water systems featuring reservoirs can be retrofitted to control the source water, allowing access to dental unit tubing for chemical treatment and to introduce barriers (check valves and filters).

Sterile Water Delivery Systems

Only sterilizable water delivery systems can deliver water for use during surgical procedures requiring sterile water. These systems actually bypass the dental unit water tubing system, replacing it with an autoclavable reservoir or disposable pouch and autoclavable tubing and fittings.

One system provides an autoclavable pump, which works off dental unit air pressure. It has a peristaltic pump that does not contact the water directly; the tubing, handpieces, connectors, and water reservoirs must be autoclaved. This adapts to high-speed handpieces, sonic scalers, and irrigation tips. The handpieces must be sterilized; the dental assistant must use sterile water. The pumps must be sterilized after every use, unless FDA-cleared antiretraction check valves are used. Note that the system allows for the addition of solutions and other medicaments to the water.

Methods of Sterilizing Water for Reservoirs

If the practice uses sterilized water for reservoirs, it is the dental assistant's job to ensure sterility is achieved.

Autoclaving kills bacteria, viruses, fungi, molds, protozoa, and all viable organisms; however, endotoxins and some chemicals often remain.

Sterilization filtration has been an accepted technique for more than 30 years, especially as an option when heat processing would damage or change a liquid. Filters are considered "sterilizing" when they remove particles and microbes larger than 0.22 microns; however, smaller viruses, endotoxins, and chemicals can pass through filters.

Sterile water suitable for surgical procedures must pass FDA requirements. Water samples must pass specific tests for bacterial growth and contain acceptable levels of endotoxins and pathogens.

When purchasing sterile water, the dental assistant should look for "USP 23 Sterile" water on the label; it is classified as filter-sterilized water, purified water, water for injection, bacteriostatic water for injection, sterile water for injection, or sterile water for irrigation.

INDEPENDENT WATER RESERVOIRS VERSUS FILTERS

According to OSAP, independent water reservoirs may be fitted to most dental units. Older equipment can be retrofitted employing a wide variety of independent reservoir devices. The dental assistant should be cautioned,

Note

To deliver sterile irri-
gating solutions for
surgical procedures,
all components,
including tubing,
must be single-use
disposable or heat
sterilized following
each use.

however, that the water reservoir alone is insufficient to ensure the quality of dental treatment water.

To control the quality, waterlines must be chemically treated with disinfectants.

Another option is to filter water at the point of use; however, this will not completely eliminate the biofilms in the waterlines. Use of either method alone, or in combination, can produce water that meets or exceeds the ADA's recommendation that water used for nonsurgical dental treatment contain 200 or fewer cfu/ml of bacteria.

Although both methods can produce water of acceptable quality for nonsurgical procedures, the dental assistant should be cautioned that neither of these methods can consistently produce sterile water.

BOIL-WATER ADVISORY PROCEDURES

The Division of Oral Health, part of the National Center for Chronic Disease Prevention and Health Promotion at the Centers for Disease Control and Prevention (CDC), suggests the following procedures may be appropriate for dental offices during boil-water advisories. It is recommended that the dental assistant follow these procedures, in addition to any specific instructions issued by the state or local health department during these advisories.

While a Boil-Water Advisory Is in Effect

Water from your public water system should *not* be delivered to patients through dental units, handpieces, ultrasonic scalers, or other dental equipment that uses the public water system until the boil-water advisory is canceled.

Patients should not use water from the public water system for rinsing their mouths during or following dental procedures; instead, they should use water provided from alternative sources, such as bottled or distilled water.

Dental personnel should not use water from the public water supply for handwashing. Instead, antimicrobial products that do not require the use of water, such as alcohol-based hand rubs, should be used until the boil-water notice is canceled. Use only alternative handwashing products that have been reviewed and cleared for marketing by the FDA.

When the Boil-Water Advisory Is Canceled

First, flush incoming waterlines for 1 to 3 minutes. Turn on all faucets in the office for 30 minutes; this includes waterlines to dental equipment that uses the public water system.

After the incoming public water system waterlines are flushed, disinfect dental unit waterlines. Consult the manufacturer of your dental unit to determine the appropriate procedures to properly disinfect them.

Because water from the affected public system should not be delivered to patients during a boil-water advisory, many dental procedures cannot be performed. Alternative water sources, such as separate water reservoirs that have been cleared for marketing by the FDA, can be used. However, if the alternative water source were to flow through a dental unit previously connected to the affected public water supply, the dental unit waterlines should first be flushed and disinfected according to the manufacturer's instructions.

SKILLS MASTERY ASSESSMENT: POSTTEST

Directions: Select the response that best answers each of the following questions. Only one response is correct.

1. Bacteria found in dental office waterlines may include which of the following?
   a. *Pseudomonas aeruginosa*
   b. *Escherichia coli*
   c. *Legionella*
   d. *Cryptosporidium*
   e. All of the above

2. The CDC and the ADA recommend that the dental assistant flush the dental unit waterlines at the start of each day and between patients.
   a. True
   b. False
   c. Currently there are no recommendations about reducing waterline biofilms.

3. Aquatic biofilms may contain
   a. fungi.
   b. algae.
   c. protozoans.
   d. nematodes.
   e. All of the above

4. Biofilms are composed of millions of microorganisms that accumulate on surfaces in dry environments.
   a. True
   b. False

5. The rate of water flow inside the tubing is greatest
   a. at the tubing surface.
   b. in the center.
   c. in the treatment room faucet
   d. in the Cavitron.

6. The CDC recommends flushing waterlines at the beginning of the day for _____ seconds to temporarily reduce the level of microbes in the water.
   a. 30
   b. 60
   c. 90
   d. 120
   e. 190

7. During the accumulation stage, microbes are continuously released from the biofilm into the flowing water.
   a. True
   b. False

8. Independent sterile water systems allow for the addition of solutions and other medicaments to the water.
   a. True   b. False

9. Autoclaving kills bacteria, viruses, fungi, molds, protozoa, all viable organisms, and endotoxins.
   a. True   b. False

10. Purchased bottled water, including distilled water, may contain significant numbers of pathogenic microorganisms. Handling and processing of self-contained water reservoir systems can inadvertently introduce pathogens that may proliferate if systems are not maintained properly.
   a. True   b. False

11. Which of the following is a list of the stages of biofilm formation in the correct sequential order?
   a. Accumulation, initial attachment, and release
   b. Release, accumulation, and initial attachment
   c. Initial attachment, accumulation, and release
   d. Retention, initial attachment, and accumulation

12. The American Dental Association recommends that dental equipment consistently deliver no more than _____ cfu/ml of aerobic bacteria at any time.
   a. 100   c. 200
   b. 1,000   d. 2,000

13. To comply with ADA recommendations, the dental assistant should
   a. run and discharge water from the dental unit waterlines for several minutes at the start of each day.
   b. run high-speed handpieces to release air and water for 20 to 30 seconds after each patient.
   c. always follow the manufacturer's instructions for proper maintenance of handpieces and waterlines.
   d. consider other options to improve water quality such as special filters, chemical therapeutics, and separate water reservoirs.
   e. All of the above

14. Methods to improve dental unit water quality include
   a. improving the quality of the incoming water.
   b. controlling biofilms in the tubing.
   c. controlling water quality as it leaves the tubing.
   d. a and b only
   e. a, b, and c

15. Waterline biofilms can be controlled in dental unit tubing by
   a. routinely decontaminating the lines.
   b. replacing lines and routinely decontaminating them.
   c. air purging the lines and letting them dry overnight.
   d. a and b only
   e. All of the above

16. To deliver sterile irrigating solutions for surgical procedures, all components, including tubing, must be single-use disposable or heat sterilized following each use.

    a. True   b. False

17. To disinfect a water bottle attached to the dental unit, the dental assistant should

    a. pour about ⅓ cup of a 1:10 disinfectant solution into the bottle.
    b. cap and shake the bottle for 5 seconds.
    c. allow the bottle to stand for 10 minutes.
    d. shake the bottle again.
    e. All of the above steps are necessary in the order listed.

18. When disinfecting the waterlines in the unit, the dental assistant should allow disinfectant to remain in the unit for at least 10 minutes but never longer than 30 minutes.

    a. True
    b. False
    c. It is not necessary to disinfect waterlines in the dental unit.

19. When performing any disinfection procedure, the dental assistant must wear all of the following in accordance with OSHA guidelines EXCEPT

    a. nitrile gloves.   d. protective eyewear
    b. face mask.   e. protective clothing.
    c. hepafilter mask.

20. The recommended ratio of bleach to water in disinfectant solution is _____.

    a. 1:1   c. 1:100
    b. 1:10   d. 1:1,000

CHAPTER

14

Occupational Environmental Hazards

KEY TERMS

aeroallergens (AIR-o-AL-ur-gins)

bioaerosols (BI-o-AIR-ah-solz)

cutaneous (kew-TANE-e-ous)

dermatitis (durm-a-TITE-us)

ergonomics (urh-ga-NOM-iks)

paresthesia (pare-es-THEE-sha)

LEARNING OBJECTIVES

Upon completion of this chapter, the student should be able to:

1. Relate and describe potential work-related environmental hazards associated with employment in the dental office.

2. Relate and describe methods and measures to reduce the potential of occupational hazards associated with employment in the dental office.

3. Describe common health risks and preventive measures associated with working with radiation, caustic agents and chemicals, nitrous oxide, oxygen and ethylene oxide, airborne particles and contaminants, latex allergies, white visible light and dental lasers, and bonding materials and acrylics.

4. Describe common health risks and preventive measures associated with working with hazardous noise levels and ergonomic concerns related to employment in the dental office.

HEALTH HAZARDS OF CONCERN TO THE DENTAL ASSISTANT

There are many potential occupational health hazards associated with employment in the dental office. The dental assistant is not immune to these potential hazards and thus must take precautions and employ preventive measures to reduce personal health risks associated with these hazards.

Some health risks have long been known to the dental profession; others have only more recently been discovered as potential health risks.

MERCURY

Mercury, used in the trituration (mixing) of alloy to form amalgam restorations, has long been known to be a health hazard to those who ingest, contact, or inhale its vapors for prolonged periods. Excessive exposure to mercury has been associated with mental impairment, skin rashes, and spontaneous miscarriage.

Mercury, in the minimal amounts used in amalgam restorations, should not pose an occupational health risk to members of the dental team (Box 14–1). All members of the dental team should be trained in the proper handling and potential hazards of mercury vapor, as well as the necessity of observing sound mercury hygiene practices.

The American Dental Association states that mercury-containing amalgam is a safe, economical, and effective restorative material and that there is no scientific evidence that exposure to mercury from amalgam restorations poses a serious health risk in humans, except for the exceedingly small number of allergic reactions.

The FDA concludes there is no reason to routinely remove amalgam fillings for replacement with composite or gold restorations.

Burnishing of the amalgam restoration after the final carving removes most of the excess mercury from the patient's oral cavity. Scrap amalgam may be safely stored using a scrap mercury container with the contents kept covered to prevent the release of mercury fumes and the mercury submerged completely in photo processing or x-ray fixer solution, or a solution of bleach and water.

As with all hazardous substances, mercury should be handled carefully, which includes proper labeling, keeping an MSDS on file, and proper disposal.

In the event that a mercury spill occurs, the dental assistant should follow the recommended guidelines for cleaning up the spill (Box 14–2).

RADIATION

Radiation safety is of primary importance in protecting both dental team members and their patients. Because radiation is cumulative, that is, it builds up over time, repeated exposure may eventually cause harmful side

BOX 14-1

Procedure Into Practice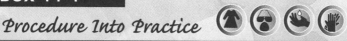

Guidelines for Handling Mercury

The assistant who selects, handles, mixes, manipulates, transfers, and disposes of silver amalgam material should consider the following guidelines for safe mercury management:

1. Work in well-ventilated operatories.

2. Avoid direct skin contact with mercury—always wear gloves during patient care.

3. Never inhale mercury vapors. If the dental assistant must handle mercury, do so over a tray, which will help contain an accidental spill.

4. Use predispensed capsules in an amalgamator with a cover that prevents mercury vapor from escaping during trituration (Figure 14–1). Always close the cover before and during trituration. Close capsule as soon as it is emptied.

5. Use high-volume evacuation when finishing or removing amalgam restorations. Evacuation systems should have traps or filters. Check and clean or replace disposable traps and filters periodically.

6. Store mercury in unbreakable, tightly sealed containers away from heat sources.

7. Salvage scrap amalgam by storing it under photographic or dental x-ray fixer solution or submerged in a solution of bleach and water in a tightly closed, unbreakable container. (Water alone is inadequate for this purpose.)

FIGURE 14–1 Amalgamator with cover closed to contain mercury vapors.

8. Clean up spilled mercury using appropriate procedures and equipment, such as a mercury spill kit; do *not* use bare hands or a household vacuum cleaner.

9. When feasible, recycle scrap amalgam and waste amalgam. Otherwise, dispose of amalgam scrap and waste amalgam in accordance with applicable local laws.

10. Place contaminated disposable mercury-containing materials in double-sealed, polyethylene bags for proper disposal.

11. Apply a biohazard sticker or label to the waste bag.

effects such as birth defects, spontaneous miscarriage, skin and eye damage, sterility, hormonal imbalances, blood changes, or cancer in susceptible individuals.

All individuals working with radiation, however small the dose, should be aware that it carries with it some risk. Thus all dental team members are urged to follow the "A-L-A-R-A" principle (*As Low As* it can be *Reasonably Achieved*), which recognizes that no matter how small the dose, there may be some risk effect.

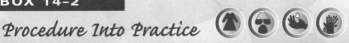

BOX 14–2

Procedure Into Practice

Recommended Guidelines for Cleaning Up a Mercury Spill

In the event of a mercury spill, the dental assistant should follow these guidelines:

1. If a spill occurs on a carpeted floor, do not use a vacuum cleaner or bare hands to collect it.

2. Pick up all visible droplets of spilled mercury with a narrow-bore tubing connected by a wash bottle trap to a low-volume aspirator on the dental unit. The trap bottle connections will keep the mercury in the bottle and prevent it from being sucked back into the dental unit.

3. Use adhesive tape to clean up small spills.

4. If the spilled mercury droplets are not easily within reach, dust them with sulfur powder, which will form a film coating on the top of the mercury droplets.

5. Keep a commercial mercury spill kit on hand. Follow the manufacturer's directions and document the circumstances of the accidental spill with the date and cleanup measures used.

When precautions are properly taken, radiation exposure should not pose a threat to the dental assistant.

Protection of the Operator and the Dental Assistant

Following are steps that operators or dental assistants should take to protect themselves from the cumulative effects of radiation.

1. Never attempt to hold a film in a patient's mouth during radiographic exposure.

2. Never stand in the direct path of the x-ray beam during exposure.

3. Always stand at a right angle to the x-ray tubehead and a minimum of 6 to 8 feet away from the patient or behind a lead-lined wall or lead shield during exposure. The minimum thickness of the lead lining required in most states is 1/32 of an inch.

4. Ensure that the x-ray machine is monitored by an independent examiner according to local or state laws, usually annually.

5. Always wear a monitoring dosimeter badge (Figure 14–2) on uniforms or scrubs and send it to an outside monitoring agency for monthly assessment. The resulting report provides legal documentation of radiation safety standards in the office.

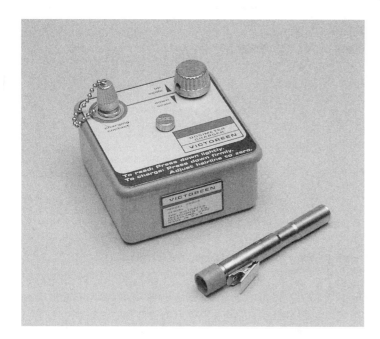

FIGURE 14–2
Dosimeter badges designed to clip onto the uniform or scrub suit pocket and monitor. The dosimeter records the amount of radiation received during the use period (usually 1 month). *(Courtesy of Nuclear Associates, Carie Place, NY)*

Protection of the Patient

Following are steps the operator or dental assistant may take to protect patients from radiation.

1. Place a protective lead apron with *thoracic* (pertaining to the throat and upper chest) collar high enough to protect the thyroid gland on all patients being exposed to radiation (Figure 14–3). When not in use, store the lead apron over a dowel or on a wooden hanger to prevent cracking of the apron. Never fold the lead apron or place it over a hook because this may result in cracking, puncturing, or tearing of the apron.
2. Take only the minimum number of films required by the dentist.
3. Use proper film positioning, exposure, and processing procedures to reduce the number of retakes.
4. Use the fastest (E-speed) film available to reduce the amount of radiation by 50 percent.
5. The use of digital intraoral imaging techniques requires only 40 percent of the radiation of E-speed films.
6. The use of rare-earth intensifying screens in extraoral radiographs is up to eight times more sensitive to x-rays than conventional screens.
7. The use of long-cone instead of short-cone exposure techniques reduces exposed tissue volume by 32 percent.
8. Leaded aprons and collars reduce the amount of scatter radiation to the patient's abdomen by 98 percent.

FIGURE 14–3
A lead apron with thoracic collar protects the patient from radiation.

Policy for Protecting Pregnant Patients

Another important aspect of exposing the patient to radiation is the possibility of pregnancy and the increased risk to the unborn child. Thus, it is essential that the office manager or chairside assistant take or update each patient's medical history at each recall visit. Many practices display a sign or print a notice on the health history form such as the following: "If you are pregnant or think you may be pregnant, please notify the doctor or a staff member."

Before exposing radiographs on a pregnant patient, the chairside assistant should alert the dentist, who may wish to consult the patient's obstetrician first. Only if x-rays are absolutely necessary should they be taken on a pregnant patient and then preferably during the second or third trimester when the developing fetus is less susceptible to the effects of radiation.

CAUSTIC AGENTS AND OTHER HAZARDOUS CHEMICALS

As when working with any caustic agent or chemical, the dental assistant should wear the required PPE.

Disinfectants and Cleaning Solutions

Disinfectants may be harmful if inhaled excessively or used in areas with inadequate ventilation. The dental assistant should always use disinfecting chemicals with great caution, taking care not to spill, splash, or inhale them. Skin and clothing contact with disinfectants should also be avoided because this may cause stinging, burning, or permanent discoloration of clothing.

Glutaraldehyde

Glutaraldehyde, a high-level disinfectant and an ingredient in x-ray developers, has been associated with skin, eye, and respiratory irritation, as well as allergic contact dermatitis, headaches, nausea, nosebleed, mucous membrane irritation, and asthmatic outbreaks. Glutaraldehyde can also aggravate preexisting asthma and inflammatory or fibrotic pulmonary disease. Sensitized individuals may experience asthmatic responses following exposure to minute quantities of glutaraldehyde, well below the legal exposure limits.

Exposure in the dental office most commonly occurs during manual scrubbing of instruments, during retrieval of instruments soaking in precleaning solution, during mixing and preparation of the activated solution, from evaporation of the solution out of open containers into the ambient air, from application of solution to touch and splash surfaces such as countertops, from x-ray processing procedures, and during disposal down the sanitary sewer.

The National Institute for Occupational Safety and Health (NIOSH) has established a recommended exposure limit of 0.2 ppm, which should not be exceeded during any part of a work shift. A mask should be worn by all dental staff who may be exposed above this limit or during emergency work-related procedures.

Thus, the dental assistant is advised to use glutaraldehyde products carefully when proper controls are in place (Box 14–3), following adequate training and using proper protection.

BOX 14-3

Procedure Into Practice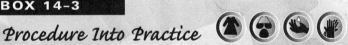

Guidelines for Protection When Working with Glutaraldehyde

If the dental assistant must work with glutaraldehyde, the following steps should be taken for adequate protection:

1. Use glutaraldehyde in a separately designated area that is properly ventilated. Ideally, a local exhaust system should be installed at the point of glutaraldehyde vapor release.

2. Keep containers of glutaraldehyde covered when they are not in use.

3. Wear eye protection such as goggles or a full face shield as well as a protective lab coat or apron.

4. Wear protective gloves made with polyethylene. (Note: Latex and neoprene gloves do *not* provide adequate protection from glutaraldehyde.)

5. Wear a mask if you are exposed to glutaraldehyde at levels above the NIOSH-established recommended exposure limits of 0.2 ppm (0.8 mg/ml) or during emergency procedures.

GASES: NITROUS OXIDE, OXYGEN, AND ETHYLENE OXIDE

While nitrous oxide (Figure 14–4), oxygen, and ethylene oxide may seem to be relatively harmless substances, they are dangerous if not monitored or handled properly (Box 14–4). For women of childbearing years, miscarriage is the most commonly cited side effect associated with nitrous oxide vapors leaking into operatory air. Tanks must be stored away from heat and flame and in well-ventilated areas.

The dental assistant must be vigilant at all times when nitrous oxide or oxygen is being delivered to a patient, as well as when ethylene oxide gas is being used for instrument and equipment disinfection and sterilization.

Adverse Effects of Nitrous Oxide

Adverse effects associated with occupational nitrous oxide exposure in dental personnel have been well documented. Members of the dental team who routinely work with nitrous oxide are exposed to a nitrous oxide concentration that is two to three times greater than the concentration to which hospital personnel are exposed. Chronic exposure to nitrous oxide may result in nausea, perspiration, and hallucinations. Other documented adverse effects of chronic nitrous oxide exposure include reproductive problems such as reduced fertility, spontaneous abortion, testicular changes, and decreased sperm count; neurological defects; hematological and immunological problems; liver problems; kidney problems; and cancer.

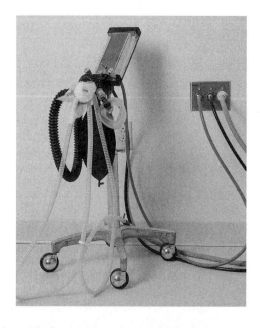

FIGURE 14–4
Portable nitrous oxide/oxygen unit.

BOX 14–4

Procedure Into Practice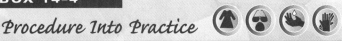

Guidelines to Reduce Exposure During Conscious Sedation Administration of Nitrous Oxide

The dental assistant should follow these guidelines to reduce exposure during conscious sedation administration:

1. Monitor anesthetic equipment when it is installed and every 3 months thereafter:

   ✓ Test equipment for leaks.

   ✓ Monitor air in the dental employees' personal breathing zones.

   ✓ Monitor the environment (treatment room air).

2. Prevent leakage from the delivery system with proper maintenance and inspection of equipment. Eliminate or replace the following:

   ✓ Loose-fitting connections

   ✓ Loosely assembled or deformed slip joints and threaded connections

   ✓ Defective or worn seals, gaskets, breathing bags, and hoses

3. Control waste nitrous oxide with a well-designed scavenging system that includes the following:

   ✓ Securely fitting masks (Masks are available for your smallest to largest patients and their respective noses)

   ✓ Sufficient flow rates (45 liters per minute) for the exhaust system

   ✓ Properly vented vacuum pumps

4. Ensure that the treatment room ventilation effectively removes waste nitrous oxide. If concentrations of nitrous are above 25 ppm, do the following:

   ✓ Increase the airflow into the treatment room.

   ✓ Use supplemental local ventilation to capture nitrous at the source.

   ✓ Institute an education program that describes nitrous oxide hazards and defines prevention measures.

5. Minimize patient conversation during use of nitrous oxide.

6. Use dental dam, where applicable, for procedures involving administration of nitrous oxide.

Methods of Reducing Health Hazards Associated with Nitrous Oxide

NIOSH recommends that dental practices control nitrous exposure by inspecting and maintaining the delivery system to prevent leaks in hoses, connections, and fittings. All necessary repairs should be made immediately.

Dental practices should also use a scavenging system to maintain ventilation of the gas from the patient's mask at an airflow rate of 45 liters per minute, measured by a calibrated flow device. The system should be vented outside, not into the treatment room ventilation system.

Scavenging masks should be of proper size to fit patients. Nitrous oxide should be used prudently when providing patients with conscious sedation. The dental assistant should monitor the air concentration of nitrous to ensure the controls are effective in achieving low levels during dental procedures.

General Guidelines for Safe Use of Oxygen

The dental assistant or safety supervisor should check the oxygen tanks weekly for faulty regulators, which can fail, or for leaking tanks. Consequences of neglect to check oxygen tanks can be disastrous. Extra oxygen in the atmosphere may cause objects to burn or explode (by itself, however, oxygen is not explosive).

Every dental office or clinic should have a minimum of two Series E oxygen tanks, which can be held upright in a portable carriage. The oxygen used in the office in conjunction with nitrous oxide in each treatment room is insufficient to deliver emergency oxygen in the reception area, hallway, or elevator. Thus, a backup oxygen tank is essential because one tank may not last until emergency personnel arrive on the scene of an emergency.

Instructions for Oxygen Tank Operation

The dental assistant should follow these instructions regarding oxygen tank operation.

1. To turn on the tanks, attach oxygen delivery system to the tank.
2. Turn the key on the top of the tank in a counterclockwise direction to open the flow of oxygen.
3. Read the low flow regulator knob; turn in the direction the arrow indicates to increase or open. (Many regulators are opposite of sink faucets and open clockwise instead of counterclockwise.)
4. Attach the oxygen delivery system to the person requiring it.

To turn off the oxygen, the dental assistant should do the following:

1. Remove the oxygen delivery system from the person using it.
2. Turn the key on the top of the tank in a clockwise direction to shut off the flow of oxygen.
3. Turn the low flow regulator knob to the open position to bleed oxygen from the system.
4. After bleeding the system, gently close the low flow regulator knob.

The dental assistant should always follow safety precautions when working with oxygen (Box 14–5).

Precautions for Ethylene Oxide Use

Ethylene oxide is a gaseous sterilant used in larger dental offices and clinics to disinfect and sterilize instruments and equipment. Ethylene oxide has

---

BOX 14-5

Procedure Into Practice

Safety Precautions for Oxygen Use

The dental assistant should follow these safety guidelines for oxygen use:

1. Never use combustibles or flammables in the presence of oxygen, including petroleum products and nail polish remover.

2. Never smoke or light matches near a source of oxygen.

3. Do not store oxygen in temperatures exceeding 120°F.

4. Never adjust the regulator with your body positioned directly over the tank.

5. Connect the tubing to the tank and adjust the regulator before placing the delivery system (oxygen mask) on the patient's face.

6. Do not deliver high concentrations of oxygen to those with chronic obstructive pulmonary disease because this may reduce their hypoxic drive.

7. Post "Oxygen in Use" signs in treatment rooms where oxygen is routinely used.

8. Avoid use of electrical appliances near oxygen because they may cause sparks, which can, in turn, cause an explosion.

9. If oxygen tanks are used, they must be secured in a base or chained to a carrier or the wall.

---

been shown to cause mutations (changes), chromosomal aberrations (deviations from the norm), and fetal abnormalities. Ethylene oxide may also cause cancer.

Ethylene oxide is associated with an increase in spontaneous miscarriages and preterm and post-term births in female dental assistants with occupational exposure.

A dental office that uses ethylene oxide must provide adequate ventilation and proper protective equipment to staff who may contact this substance.

BIOAEROSOLS

Bioaerosols are living microbes that travel via a mist and may contain bacteria, viruses, molds, fungi, or yeast. These airborne microorganisms can be found in most buildings as well as in air conditioners, humidifiers, carpets, plants, wall hangings, aerosolized sprays and chemicals, and coverings.

Because bioaerosols are generally invisible, most individuals are unaware of their presence. The dental assistant can take steps to reduce or eliminate unhealthful bioaerosols (Box 14–6), which, if uncontained, may cause illness.

Another airborne substance the dental assistant should avoid inhaling is alginate powder because it may lead to bronchial irritation. When preparing

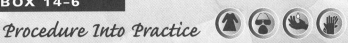

BOX 14–6

Procedure Into Practice

Reducing Bioaerosols in the Dental Office

The dental assistant can help reduce the presence of bioaerosols in the office by following these steps:

1. Clean office furnishings and the compressed air filtration system frequently.

2. Use oral evacuation techniques during procedures involving production of aerosols.

3. Use dental dam to minimize exposure to oral fluids.

4. Always wear appropriate PPE.

5. Avoid hand scrubbing of instruments—use an ultrasonic cleaner, instead.

6. Minimize the use of latex-containing products, especially gloves and dental dams.

7. Wear powder-free gloves.

8. Keep all containers of chemicals tightly covered.

9. Avoid excessive spraying of chemicals—pour them, instead, whenever possible.

10. Use a vacuum system during dust-producing lab procedures.

11. Flush all dental unit waterlines into the high-volume evacuator (HVE).

to open a can of alginate powder, the dental assistant should take great care in fluffing the material; the dental assistant should then stand back when opening the cover to breathe in as little of the rising powder as possible. Some manufacturers make a dust-free alginate, which is an acceptable option for many dental practices.

LATEX ALLERGIES

Mandates that all clinical dental personnel wear gloves when treating patients have brought about an unexpected problem for members of the dental team—sensitivity to natural rubber latex (NRL), the substance from which most examination gloves are made. Ironically, a mandate designed to protect healthcare personnel has created another health problem for as many as 150,000 healthcare workers in the United States.

Latex sensitivity may affect patients as well as the dental personnel who treat them. For information on preventing and reducing latex sensitivity reactions in patients, refer to *Chapter 3: Patient Assessment.*

Contact dermatitis and sensitization to latex following prolonged exposure are the two most common latex allergy reactions in dental healthcare workers. Symptoms can range from itchiness and redness to respiratory distress and occasionally fatal anaphylaxis.

Approximately one-third of all healthcare workers who regularly use latex gloves report some type of **dermatitis** (skin irritation) (Table 14–1).

TABLE 14-1

COMMON DERMATITIS PROBLEMS AFFECTING DENTAL ASSISTANTS	
Problem	**Recommended Solution**
Irritant dermatitis	Reestablish skin integrity
Latex allergy	Vinyl gloves; other nonlatex gloves
Handwashing allergy	Change antimicrobial agent; use liquid soap
Dermatomycosis	Prolonged topical antifungal therapy

Between 10 percent and 15 percent of those individuals occupationally exposed to latex will eventually develop some form of latex allergy.

Latex allergy exposure develops from three sources:

1. Gloves worn by dental healthcare workers
2. Air breathed by dental healthcare workers
3. Direct tissue exposure

The cause of NRL allergy begins with a protein harvested from the rubber tree; this protein provides the essential stretch to many products used in the dental profession—including latex gloves. The latex allergy originates in the manufacturing process during which ammonia is added to the latex sap. The ammonia causes an estimated 240 proteins to change and degrade, creating protein allergens.

Cornstarch powder is the most common glove lubricant and is associated with reactions due to the adsorption of antigens to the cornstarch particles, producing aerosolized latex antigen. Powder-free gloves are preferred by some sensitive dental assistants; however, the powder is not the cause of latex allergy.

Types of Allergic Reactions to Latex

There are three distinct reactions directly attributed to NRL products:

1. Immediate hypersensitivity (type I)
2. Delayed hypersensitivity (type IV)
3. Irritant dermatitis (ID)

Type I (Immediate Hypersensitivity)

Immediate hypersensitivity (type I) is a **cutaneous** (pertaining to the skin) reaction, which results in an immediate "wheal and flare" reaction that develops within minutes of contacting the user, either by direct contact or carried airborne by powdering agents contained in some NRL products. Type I hypersensitivity is potentially the most severe and may be life threatening;

type I reactions may involve the skin, respiratory tract, gastrointestinal tract, or the cardiovascular system. Those who develop immediate type I allergy symptoms may also experience eye watering, nasal congestion, sneezing, coughing, wheezing, shortness of breath, decreased blood pressure, or dizziness within minutes of being exposed to latex. Severity can range from mild itching, irritation, and allergic conjunctivitis, to a brief period of difficulty in breathing, to life-threatening anaphylaxis.

Type I reactions may result from latex **aeroallergens** (airborne substances that carry or cause allergic reactions), often carried through ventilation air exchange systems or by settling on clothing and equipment. These aeroallergens remain present in high quantities from frequent donning and discarding of powdered latex gloves.

Affected dental assistants often find that their hands begin to burn and itch soon after donning latex gloves; after removing the gloves, they may also notice rapid appearance of hives and localized edema, usually within 20 minutes after exposure to the protein antigens.

Type IV (Delayed Hypersensitivity)

Type IV hypersensitivity is most commonly caused by the residual processing chemicals found in NRL products. Dental assistants suffering with type IV hypersensitivity develop lesions slowly with a several-hour delay in the onset of symptoms, reaching maximal appearance in 24 to 48 hours.

Type IV latex hypersensitivity is the most common NRL allergy. Symptoms include diffuse or patchy eczema on the contact area often accompanied by itching, redness and vesicles, and later by dry skin, fissures, and sores, often confined to the contact area. A classic example is that of glove dermatitis showing a sharp delineation where the latex glove cuff ends.

Irritant Dermatitis (ID)

Irritant dermatitis may be caused by numerous irritants commonly present in the dental office (acrylates, soaps, disinfectants, metals, lotions, improper hand drying, excessive scrubbing of the hands, solvents, vapors, and so on) as well as by surgical and examination gloves.

When associated with glove use, the ID reaction is most often caused by the residual processing chemicals, donning lubricants, or the assistant's hand perspiration inside of the glove.

Some chemicals such as acrylates, disinfectants, and resins have the ability to penetrate NRL and other glove materials, causing hand eczema or **paresthesia** (loss of sensation). ID reactions are often attributed to the gloves rather than to the actual offending agents. If clinically mismanaged or left untreated, ID may cause permanent skin damage.

Treatment for Latex-Sensitive Dental Assistants

The dental assistant suffering with chronic eczema should avoid NRL if at all possible. Premedication with corticosteroids or antihistamines may help; cotton glove liners or barrier creams may also be helpful for some assistants.

A number of alternatives to latex gloves are currently available, including vinyl and decreased allergenicity gloves, which have helped alleviate the symptoms; gloves labeled *hypoallergenic* may not always prevent adverse reactions.

The dental assistant can take a number of precautions to help combat allergic response to NRL. Some authorities on latex sensitivity recommend rinsing the hands with cool water, which helps close the pores of the skin.

WHITE VISIBLE LIGHT AND DENTAL LASERS

Recent technological advances have brought dramatic treatment options and results that have made delivery of dental services faster and easier, for both patients and dental team members. The alert dental assistant must be aware that certain products involving visible white light (associated with some bonding procedures) and dental lasers may cause permanent retinal damage and other health risks associated with long-term use.

When using these products, the dental assistant must be an educated consumer, always reviewing manufacturers' instructions for use and cautions or warnings.

When working with visible light-cured materials, the dental assistant must take the precaution of never looking directly at or into the light when applying it to the surface of the teeth. Also, the dental assistant must check to ensure the curing unit is supplied with a protective shield (Figure 14–5), which should be used when the light is turned on.

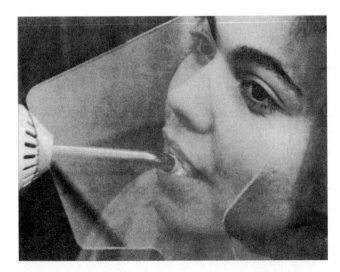

FIGURE 14–5

A special shield protects the dental assistant's eyes when using a curing light. *(Courtesy of Premier Dental Products Co, King of Prussia, PA)*

Some manufacturers either include or recommend specific tinted shields or dark glasses to be worn when exposing lasers to soft or hard oral tissues. Under some circumstances, according to the manufacturer's recommendations, dark glasses should also be provided to the patient for protection when exposing a laser beam.

The smoke plume arising from vaporization of oral tissues with a laser may present an occupational health hazard. The energy resulting from the laser beam is very intense, such that the resultant smoke from oral tissue vaporization may contain cellular material or intact cells explosively disrupted near the focal point of the laser beam. Malignant (cancerous) cells, bacteria, and viruses have been detected in laser smoke and may pose an occupational health threat if inhaled by the dental assistant. Infectious human immunodeficiency virus (HIV) has been detected in laser smoke resulting from laser tissue cultured from HIV-infected individuals.

A mechanical smoke evacuator system adjacent to the operative site, in conjunction with a mask, may significantly reduce the occupational health risk to the dentist and dental assistant.

BONDING MATERIALS AND ACRYLICS

Bonding materials are used in the placement of restorations, pit and fissure sealants, and orthodontic brackets. To make the bonding material adhere to the tooth surface, an etching solution or gel is used. The etchant contains one or a variety of phosphoric or orthophosphoric acids, which may cause burning of unprotected skin, the eyes, or clothing.

The dental assistant may avoid personal damage from the acid contained in bonding etchant by following a number of precautions (Box 14–7).

Dental products that contain acrylic, including methyl methacrylate, include removable dental prostheses, custom impression trays, orthodontic devices, occlusal splints, temporary and permanent crowns and bridges, and composite resins.

The dental assistant must be especially careful when working with self-curing acrylics because of the rapid onset of an exothermic (heat-releasing) chemical action that occurs as the material polymerizes (hardens). The dental assistant may easily be burned if he or she is handling acrylic materials without proper protection of gloves or in the lab with Vaseline-coated hands.

Acrylics may also cause anaphylactic reactions in sensitive individuals, requiring immediate administration of oxygen and transport to the hospital for further monitoring.

HAZARDOUS NOISE LEVELS

Noises generated in the dental office may be hazardous to the dental assistant's hearing. Disagreeable or unpleasant noises or sounds may eventually cause unwanted masking of sounds, interference with speech and communication, pain and injury, and temporary or permanent loss of hearing.

BOX 14–7

Procedure Into Practice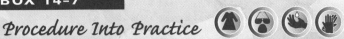

Guidelines for Preventing Injury Caused by Acid Etch Materials

The dental assistant should follow these precautions when handling acid etchant materials:

1. Handle any acid etchant-soaked materials using forceps and always wear gloves.

2. Clean up acid etchant spills using a commercial acid spill kit.

3. Never allow acid etchant material to contact bare skin or the oral mucosa.

4. In the event of skin or eye contact, rinse the affected area using copious amount of running water. If necessary, after rinsing the affected eye, place an eye patch and obtain medical attention immediately.

Loud noises may also physiologically cause an elevation in blood pressure, an increased pulse rate, and constriction of the blood vessels.

Sources of potentially dangerous noises associated with working in the dental office include the high-speed handpiece, lab engines, the HVE aspirator, the x-ray buzzer, the ultrasonic scaler, mixing devices for stone and amalgam, and music. The degree of risk depends upon a number of factors, including the intensity of the noise, frequency spectrum of the noise, the daily duration of exposure, the distance from the source, and the dental assistant's age and general health.

The maximum permissible noise level is 85 decibels; high-speed turbine handpieces generate a higher noise level than low-speed handpieces.

Noise-induced hearing loss (NIHL) is generally not a treatable condition; it can only be partly alleviated by rehabilitative means. There are steps the dental assistant can take to prevent occupational NIHL (Box 14–8).

BOX 14–8

Procedure Into Practice

Precautions for Preventing Occupational NIHL

Preventive measures the dental assistant can take to avoid NIHL include:

1. Reduction of exposure time to the offending noise source.

2. Maintenance of equipment and early repair or replacement of defective items.

3. Use of personal protection with ear muffs or ear plugs when working in a high noise level environment.

4. Periodically undergoing routine otologic and audiometric examination to determine current hearing status.

REPETITIVE MOTION INJURY AND CARPAL TUNNEL SYNDROME

Ergonomics, the study of motion economy, can help all members of the dental team, including the dental assistant, save time and motion using correct posture and correct finger, hand, arm, and body movements. Improper posture and continually repeated motions such as gripping, turning, or applying pressure may result in physical ailments. If left untreated, these symptoms may lead to a potentially disabling condition, carpal tunnel syndrome (CTS). If CTS goes untreated for prolonged periods, atrophy of the thenar muscle at the base of the thumb may result.

CTS is a nerve compression disorder that affects the median nerve as it passes through the carpal tunnel of the wrist. It results in inflammation of the tendons in the wrist, aggravated by overuse. This nerve supplies sensation to parts of the thumb, index, middle, and ring fingers. The carpal tunnel is surrounded on three sides by the eight carpal bones. It is covered on the palmar aspect by the transverse carpal ligament, which protects the median nerve. Repetitive, forceful exertions of the fingers, especially with the wrist in a deviated position, may result in thickening of synovium surrounding the tendons. Because there is little room for expansion inside the tunnel, compression neuropathy of the median nerve may result. Most common symptoms reported include pain, burning, tingling, and numbness.

Dental professionals with CTS commonly complain of their hands "going to sleep"; shaking the affected hand often relieves the symptoms. Sometimes pain and burning are present and may extend up the forearm, even as high as the shoulder in some cases. Clumsiness and weakness may also be reported. In more extreme cases, a decreased sensitivity to touch also occurs.

A Simple Self-Test for CTS

The dental assistant may take a simple self-test for CTS (Box 14–9) by doing the following: Tap the fingers along the inside of the opposite wrist. If a "pins and needles" sensation is felt, this may be indicative of CTS. This test brings on symptoms in almost 50 percent of patients who suffer from CTS but only in about 6 percent of people who do not have it.

Methods to Prevent Hand Injuries and CTS

The dental assistant can employ a number of ergonomic methods to prevent or reduce the potential for hand injuries and CTS:

- Limit use of digital motions; make every effort to maintain the wrist in a normal, neutral position.
- The wrist motion should not exceed the functional optimum of 10° flexion to 35° extension.
- Keep hand instruments sharp.
- Alternate "pinch" patterns, when possible.
- Use greater leverage, which requires less force.

BOX 14–9

Predisposing Factors Associated with CTS

Factors that may predispose the dental assistant to cumulative wrist trauma and CTS include the following:

- Pregnancy
- Initiation of oral contraceptive therapy
- Premenstrual syndrome
- Middle age

  Contributory etiologic factors to CTS include the following:

- Constant flexion and extension motions of the wrist
- A strong relationship between wrist positioning during work and the onset of cumulative trauma injury
- Movements in which the wrist is caused to digress from the neutral, straight position
- Working for too long without resting the wrist

  Additional factors include the following:

- Frequent repetitive wrist and forearm motion
- Sustained "pinch" positioning of the hand (involving the thumb, index, and middle fingers together)
- Use of the wrist and hand in awkward positions
- Mechanical stresses to digital nerves from sustained grasps or serrated handles and contact with the handle on the radial aspect of the index finger
- Vibratory instruments and pulling motions
- Temperature extremes
- Poor operator posture
- Wearing of ambidextrous or ill-fitting gloves that causes the thumb to constantly tug at the glove

---

- Use lighter instruments. Switch to instruments with large, round diameters (#4 handles) and contra-angled shanks.
- Anti-inflammatory drugs may be prescribed; also, volar splinting, tendon gliding exercises, and/or steroid injections may relieve symptoms.
- Slow down! (A 10 percent increase in speed at which a person works causes a 32 percent increase in the pinch force necessary to maintain control.)
- Switch to left-right fitted gloves.
- Take frequent rest breaks.

The symptoms of CTS can often be managed effectively without the necessity of surgical intervention. Prevention and education are key.

SKILLS MASTERY ASSESSMENT: POSTTEST

Directions: Select the response that best answers each of the following questions. Only one response is correct.

1. The oxygen used in the office in conjunction with nitrous oxide in each treatment room is insufficient to deliver emergency oxygen throughout the office.
   a. True
   b. False

2. Powder and cornstarch are the most common causes of latex allergy associated with glove use in the dental office.
   a. True
   b. False

3. The distinct reactions directly attributed to NRL products include all of the following EXCEPT
   a. immediate hypersensitivity (type I).
   b. delayed hypersensitivity (type IV).
   c. intermediate hypersensitivity (type III).
   d. irritant dermatitis (ID).

4. Soon after donning required PPE, a dental assistant notices the following symptoms: watering eyes, nasal congestion, sneezing, coughing, wheezing, shortness of breath, and dizziness. This dental assistant may be experiencing which type of reaction?
   a. Immediate hypersensitivity (type I)
   b. Delayed hypersensitivity (type IV)
   c. Intermediate hypersensitivity (type III)
   d. Irritant dermatitis (ID)

5. After several weeks of employment in a new office, a dental assistant notices diffuse or patchy eczema on his or her hands, accompanied by itching, redness, and vesicles. Use of hand creams do not seem to improve the condition. Eventually, the skin on the assistant's hands becomes dry, with fissures and sores appearing. He or she also notices a sharp delineation where the latex glove cuff ends. This dental assistant is suffering from which type of latex allergy?
   a. Immediate hypersensitivity (type I)
   b. Delayed hypersensitivity (type IV)
   c. Intermediate hypersensitivity (type III)
   d. Irritant dermatitis (ID)

6. The maximum permissible noise level is _____ decibels.
   a. 55
   b. 65
   c. 75
   d. 85

7. Preventive measures the dental assistant can take to avoid NIHL associated with occupational exposure include all of the following EXCEPT
   a. reducing exposure time to the offending noise source.
   b. using earmuffs or earplugs when working in a noisy office.
   c. ordering a hearing aid to prevent further hearing loss.
   d. undergoing routine hearing tests.

8. The dental assistant may employ all of the following techniques to reduce the amount of radiation exposure to patients EXCEPT
   a. use D-speed film.
   b. use E-speed film.
   c. use long-cone technique.
   d. use digital intraoral imaging techniques.

9. Excessive exposure to mercury has been associated with
   a. eczema of the skin, coughing, and wheezing.
   b. mental impairment, skin rashes, and spontaneous miscarriage.
   c. anaphylaxis.
   d. asthmalike symptoms with wheal and flare reactions.

10. If the spilled mercury droplets are not easily within reach, the dental assistant should dust them with _____, which will form a film coating on the top of the mercury droplets.
    a. talc
    b. cornstarch
    c. sulfur powder
    d. ethylene oxide

11. When working with glutaraldehyde, the dental assistant should wear protective gloves made with _____.
    a. latex
    b. neoprene
    c. vinyl
    d. polyethylene

12. Ethylene oxide is associated with an increase in spontaneous miscarriages and preterm and post-term births in female dental assistants with occupational exposure.
    a. True
    b. False

13. All of the following may be a potential health risk for dental assistants who are exposed to smoke plumes resulting from laser-vaporized oral tissues EXCEPT
    a. cancerous cells.
    b. bacteria.
    c. asthma.
    d. HIV.

14. The dental assistant may easily be burned if handling acrylic materials without proper protection of gloves or Vaseline-coated hands.
    a. True
    b. False

15. Factors that may predispose the dental assistant to cumulative wrist trauma and CTS include all of the following EXCEPT
   a. pregnancy.
   b. advanced age.
   c. initiation of oral contraceptive therapy.
   d. premenstrual syndrome.

16. Switching to instruments with large, round diameters and contra-angled shanks may _____ the symptoms associated with CTS.
   a. help reduce
   b. exacerbate
   c. have little effect upon
   d. have no effect upon

CHAPTER 15

Office Emergency Procedures

LEARNING OBJECTIVES

Upon completion of this chapter, the student should be able to:

1. Describe fire safety and office evacuation procedures.
2. List the ABCs of fire extinguishers, how to use a fire extinguisher, and how to follow an emergency evacuation plan.
3. List procedures for natural disaster emergencies, including tornado safety, hurricane emergencies, and earthquakes.
4. List procedures for handling bomb threats, handguns and other concealed weapons, and violence in the workplace.
5. Describe common signage requirements.
6. Discuss the contents of a basic first-aid and emergency kit and their uses and know how to administer emergency oxygen.

GENERAL OFFICE SAFETY

Office safety is something most people take for granted. The wise dental assistant, however, must be prepared for a variety of emergencies, including fire, natural disasters, bomb threats, concealed handguns and other weapons, workplace violence, and medical emergencies that may occur without warning.

The office may be held liable if patients or other people on the premises are injured in a variety of emergency situations.

FIRE SAFETY AND EMERGENCY EVACUATION

The office should have a written fire safety protocol and emergency evacuation plan. Copies of the nearest emergency exit routes with instructions should be posted at all entrances to the office and should be checked periodically by the office safety supervisor or other staff member in charge.

The fire evacuation plan (Figure 15–1) usually states that all patients and office personnel in immediate danger should be moved from the area.

An example of instructions posted with the emergency evacuation map might be as follows: *"You are at the northeast entrance to the building.* (This position is keyed in relation to the office plan and highlighted with a marker or colored pen.) *In the event of fire, do not use the elevator. Proceed to the hall, turn right, and take the stairs to the parking lot. Wait for further instructions."*

FIGURE 15–1
All dental personnel should familiarize themselves with the fire evacuation plan.

In the event of a fire, the alarm should be activated as quickly as possible. If possible, the dental assistant should close all doors and windows to prevent drafts, which cause a fire to spread more rapidly. The dental assistant should shut off all electrical equipment, oxygen, and nitrous tanks. Above all, the dental assistant should remain calm and focus on helping prevent loss of life or serious injury to others during a fire.

How a Fire Starts

Three elements are required to start a fire: oxygen (or air), fuel (any material that will burn), and heat (sparks, matches, or flames).

The most common causes of fire are carelessness in smoking and carelessness with matches. Other common causes include misuse of electricity (worn or frayed wires and overloaded electrical outlets), defects in heating systems, spontaneous ignition, improper handling of waste materials, and arson.

If the dental assistant becomes trapped in a smoke-filled office, he or she should stay as close to the floor as possible. The dental assistant should crawl to an exit, covering the mouth and staying on hands and knees.

Before entering a room, the dental assistant should touch the door with the back of the hand. If it is hot to the touch, do not open it. If you become trapped in a room and the door is very hot to the touch, stay in the room and put wet blankets or towels under the door to keep the smoke out. The dental assistant should stay low to the floor because the bottom of the room has the most available oxygen and because smoke rises. Wait for rescue personnel to arrive.

The ABCs of Fire Extinguishers

Fire extinguishers are classified according to the type of fire they are intended to extinguish. The dental assistant should check the fire extinguisher(s) in the office to determine the type (Figure 15–2).

Following are the most common types. It is the job of the office safety supervisor to routinely inspect fire extinguishers (and smoke detectors) to ensure they are in proper working order. All personnel in the dental office should be familiar with the parts of a fire extinguisher and should be trained how to use the extinguisher to put out a fire (Box 15–1)

- *Class A* fire extinguishers contain pressurized water. They are used on fire involving combustibles such as paper, cloth, and wood.
- *Class B* fire extinguishers contain carbon dioxide. They are used on gasoline, oil, paint, liquid, and cooking fat fires. These types of fires spread when water is used to put them out. Carbon dioxide is used in Class B extinguishers because it smothers these types of flammables. Class B extinguishers leave a powdery, snowflakelike residue, which may irritate the skin and eyes. The residue should not be inhaled.

FIGURE 15–2
Check the type of extinguisher(s) in your office.

- *Class C* fire extinguishers contain potassium bicarbonate or potassium chloride, which are dry chemicals. These chemicals are nonconducting and are used on electrical fires; they may also be used on burning liquids to create a smothering action.
- *Class ABC,* or *combination,* fire extinguishers contain a graphite-type chemical, which is multipurpose. These may be used on all types of fires; they also leave a residue that may be irritating to the eyes and skin.

NATURAL DISASTER PREPAREDNESS

Other types of disasters, usually generalized as natural disasters, may occur, depending upon the area of the country in which the office is located. The office should include natural disaster preparedness in its hazard communication manual, with instructions on what to do in the event of a natural disaster. Following are general guidelines for natural disaster preparedness.

Tornado Safety

Tornados cannot always be predicted well in advance. Although more common in some parts of the country than others, a tornado can occur any-

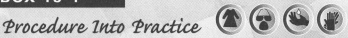

BOX 15-1

Procedure Into Practice

How to Use a Fire Extinguisher

The "PASS" system is an aid in remembering how to use a fire extinguisher (Figure 15–3). To activate a fire extinguisher, the dental assistant should do the following:

Pull the pin out of the upper extinguisher handle.
Aim the fire extinguisher at the base of the fire.
Squeeze the handle to discharge the contents of the fire extinguisher.
Sweep the fire extinguisher from side to side, keeping it aimed at the base of the fire.

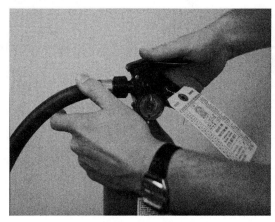

FIGURE 15–3 Release the pin, aim the nozzle at the base of the fire, and push the handle to discharge the extinguisher.

where. The area will be placed under a tornado watch if conditions are favorable for a tornado to develop. A tornado warning is issued when a tornado is actually in the area.

During a tornado warning, the dental assistant may be required to help with evacuation of patients from the office or clinic. This means that all patients will be moved to the basement if the facility has one. Often, patients are moved to a strong area in the center of the building. Patients should be kept away from windows because of the potential for injury from breaking glass. They should be covered with blankets to provide protection from debris and broken glass. The dental assistant should close room doors, fire doors, windows, and curtains facing the direction of the oncoming tornado. The dental assistant should open the doors, windows, and curtains on the opposite side of the building or room.

Hurricane Emergencies

Coastal areas are at risk for hurricanes. Unlike tornados, hurricanes can be predicted in advance and thus there is usually sufficient time to evacuate before the hurricane strikes. If there is insufficient time to evacuate the office or clinic, the dental assistant should move patients into interior rooms or hallways. Patients should be protected from flying glass and other debris. The dental assistant should close doors to treatment rooms and offices and fire doors. Emergency exits should not be blocked.

Earthquakes

The ground shakes during an earthquake. Earthquakes may cause building destruction and fire. Windows often break and debris and other objects may fly around. Earthquakes occur suddenly and without warning. The dental assistant should remain calm during an earthquake, covering or protecting his or her head from flying debris. Taking cover under a large, heavy object is the best protection from an earthquake.

Following an earthquake, the dental assistant should check patients for injuries sustained. The dental assistant should not attempt to move injured patients unless they are in imminent danger. The dental assistant should clean spills on the floor to prevent falls or cuts. There should be no smoking, use of matches, or open flames during cleanup from an earthquake. Earthquakes can rupture gas lines, creating a fire hazard.

The dental assistant should be prepared for aftershocks. If the lights are out, a flashlight may be necessary. The dental assistant should not try to use electrical appliances. A battery-operated radio may be helpful in obtaining earthquake emergency information.

BOMB THREATS AND VIOLENCE IN THE WORKPLACE

Any bomb threat should be taken very seriously. When such an occurrence takes place, the building should be evacuated immediately. Law enforcement and fire officials should be alerted and will search the office or clinic for the bomb; they may also assist with and direct the evacuation.

If the dental assistant answers the telephone and is informed that a bomb is in the building, the dental assistant should keep the caller on the line for as long as possible to obtain as much information as possible. The assistant should ask the caller where the bomb is located and at what time it is set to explode.

The dental assistant should also make mental notes regarding the caller's gender, approximate age, and any other identifying factors such as an accent, speech impediment, or grammatical style.

The assistant should also listen for background noises such as music, church or campus chimes, or specific types of machinery.

This information may be of significant help to the authorities later in trying to apprehend the caller. Law enforcement authorities will advise all occupants of the building when it is safe to return.

Preventing Violence in the Workplace

Violence in the workplace continues to receive media attention. Healthcare facilities are not exempt from workplace violence. The office or clinic should have a written violence prevention program with training that details procedures to be followed in the event of an attack.

The goal of this training is to reduce or eliminate occupational exposure to a situation that can lead to personal injury or attack. OSHA has developed guidelines to prevent violence in the healthcare facility; many employers use these guidelines to implement safety programs to train and protect their employees.

Concealed Handguns and Other Weapons

Carrying concealed handguns and other weapons is illegal in many states. In other states, it is permissible. Even in states where carrying concealed weapons is legal, guns may not be carried into any healthcare facility.

If a visitor or patient is known to be carrying a concealed handgun into the office or clinic, he or she must be requested to leave the weapon in his or her car prior to entering the facility. If the dental assistant notices anyone carrying a handgun or other potentially harmful weapon, he or she must inform the dentist immediately.

SIGNAGE REQUIREMENTS

OSHA requires dental offices to post appropriate warning signs, tags, or labels in specific areas of the office, including office exits and potential exposure hazards such as x-rays machines, ultrasonic machines, and microwaves. Exit signs must be illuminated and be a minimum of 5 inches high. Doors to other rooms should also be appropriately marked with such signs as *Storage, Private,* and *Not an Exit.*

OSHA is concerned with safety and requires specific signage to alert people to potentially harmful equipment, fumes, or machinery that may be in use in the office. For example, ultrasonic cleaners and some microwave ovens may be harmful to pacemaker patients.

The office should post a sign in a prominent area that states, "Ultrasonic devices and microwave ovens are used in this office. Ultrasonics and microwaves may be harmful to patients with implanted devices such as pacemakers. Please inform us if you have a pacemaker." Another example is to post "Warning, radiation in use" signs in areas where radiation is used in the office.

FIRST-AID AND EMERGENCY KITS

All offices should have a basic first-aid kit, which contains bandages, scissors, over-the-counter ointments and analgesics, and wound disinfectants.

Offices should also have a medical emergency kit (Figure 15–4) that contains a variety of controlled substances, scalpels, syringes, portable oxygen, and masks.

Many dentists prefer to have an emergency kit made up by the local pharmacist to their specifications. Other offices purchase a drug manufacturer's preassembled kit with automatic refills sent to the office to replace

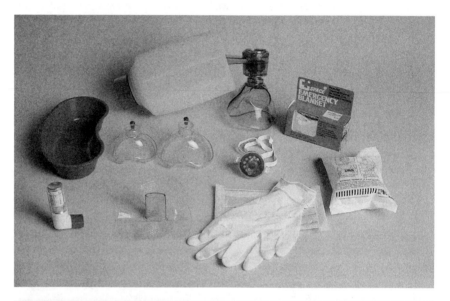

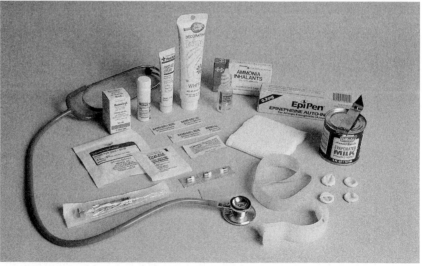

FIGURE 15–4
Contents of a medical emergency kit.

medications as they become outdated. A medical emergency kit in a dental office should contain the following items:

- Sterile syringes, tourniquets, tracheotomy needle, barrier devices for delivery of CPR, and several oral airway devices
- Oxygen inhalation equipment (if the office does not have any other form of oxygen or nitrous oxide delivery)
- Stimulant drugs, including ammonia ampules for the treatment of syncope
- Vasodilators to increase oxygenated blood supply to the heart, including nitroglycerin, translingual nitroglycerine, or amyl-nitrite inhalants
- Antihistamines for treatment of asthmatic and anaphylactic reactions
- Vasopressors to increase blood pressure
- Analgesics for pain
- Depressants for convulsions related to epilepsy
- Vagal blockers to increase the pulse rate

The first-aid and emergency kits should be labeled and stored in an area of the office easily accessible to the dentist and staff but not readily noticeable to patients. The dental assistant or office safety supervisor should check the contents of both kits monthly to determine that they are in place and within the expiration date and should also check for leakage or any unusual appearance. If drugs or other shelf-life items have expired, the dentist must be alerted to this and appropriate action taken to replace these items.

Emergency Oxygen

Emergency oxygen must also be available in the event of heart attack or a closed or blocked airway (Box 15–2). Dental assistants should enroll in

---

BOX 15–2

Procedure Into Practice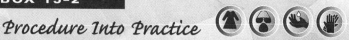

Emergency Administration of Oxygen

The dental assistant may be required to administer emergency oxygen to a patient, the dentist, or a fellow team member in a medical emergency. The dental assistant should perform the following steps:

1. Place the patient comfortably in a supine or Trendelenburg position.
2. Explain to the victim what is going to happen and reassure him or her that this will help him or her breathe more easily.
3. Gently place the oxygen mask over the victim's nose and drape the tubing on either side of his or her face. The mask may require adjustment to fit securely over the nose.
4. Start the oxygen flow immediately at between 2 and 4 liters per minute.
5. Instruct the victim to breathe through his or her nose and keep the lips closed.
6. Calm the patient by speaking in reassuring tones until help arrives.

either an American Heart Association or American Red Cross CPR training course and keep their CPR cards current.

The office should also have a written emergency policy and plan in place in case a medical incident occurs in the office. Emergency numbers should be posted at each telephone, and everyone in the office should have a designated responsibility, including alerting the EMS, attending to the patient, monitoring vital signs, reassuring other patients who may be in the waiting room, and directing EMS personnel to the patient.

Annual training sessions should include both CPR updates and instruction on the handling of other routine medical emergencies.

SKILLS MASTERY ASSESSMENT: POSTTEST

Directions: Select the response that best answers each of the following questions. Only one response is correct.

1. Common causes of fires include all of the following EXCEPT
   a. carelessness in smoking and carelessness with matches.
   b. worn or frayed wires and overloaded electrical outlets.
   c. larceny.
   d. arson.

2. During a fire, the dental assistant should stay low to the floor because the bottom of the room has the least available oxygen and because smoke rises.
   a. True   b. False

3. _____ fire extinguishers contain carbon dioxide and are used on gasoline, oil, paint, liquid, and cooking fat fires. These types of fires spread when water is used to put them out. Carbon dioxide is used in Class B extinguishers because it smothers these types of flammables. Class B extinguishers leave a powdery, snowflakelike residue, which may irritate the skin and eyes. The residue should not be inhaled.
   a. Class A   c. Class C
   b. Class B   d. Class ABC or combination

4. Which class of fire extinguishers leaves a residue that is irritating to the eyes and skin and should not be inhaled?
   a. Class A only   c. Class C only
   b. Class B only   d. Class B or combination

5. The dental assistant should open room doors, fire doors, windows, and curtains facing the direction of the oncoming tornado.
   a. True   b. False

6. The dental office or clinic should have a written violence prevention program with training that details procedures to be followed in the event of an attack.
   a. True   b. False

7. The goal of violence prevention training is to
   a. reduce the number of sick days out of the office.
   b. teach members of the dental team techniques in personal self-defense.
   c. find ways to prevent arson fires in the office.
   d. reduce or eliminate occupational exposure to a situation that can lead to personal injury or attack.

8. If a visitor or patient is known to be carrying a concealed handgun or other weapon into the office or clinic, the dental assistant should
   a. ask the person to leave the weapon in his or her car prior to entering the office.
   b. inform the dentist immediately.
   c. call the police and/or 911 immediately.
   d. a and/or b

9. OSHA requires specific signage to alert people to potentially harmful equipment, fumes, or machinery that may be in use in the dental office.
   a. True   b. False

10. The contents of office first-aid and emergency kits should be checked _____ by the dental assistant or office safety supervisor for expiration dates, leakage, or unusual appearance.
   a. daily   c. monthly
   b. weekly   d. annually

CHAPTER 16   *Marketing Infection Control*

16

Marketing Infection Control

KEY TERMS

chairside marketing

marketing

statement stuffers

web site

LEARNING OBJECTIVES

Upon completion of this chapter, the student should be able to:

1. Describe the need to market infection control to patients and the role of the dental assistant in providing this service.

2. List and describe various methods the dental assistant may employ to market infection control to patients, including office brochures, signage, statement stuffers, letters, web sites, and tours of the instrument recirculation area.

3. List ten facts that the dental assistant can use to educate patients about HIV/AIDS.

4. Describe the importance of having an AIDS treatment policy in the practice.

5. Describe effective chairside marketing techniques the dental assistant may employ to help educate patients about infection control.

THE NEED TO MARKET INFECTION CONTROL

The emphasis on infection control, the prevention of cross-contamination of communicable diseases, and increasing government regulation have brought about a need for **marketing** of infection control. Marketing means creating the need or demand for, or awareness of, a product or service the consumer may have been unaware was available, or that he may have been unaware that he desired.

Marketing infection control means creating an awareness, to patients and potential patients, of infection control techniques or procedures employed in the dental office to help minimize or eliminate the risk of disease transmission.

In a broader sense, dental practices may ethically promote their services through a variety of internal and external marketing strategies. Internal marketing refers to strategies and techniques used within the practice to educate and inform patients of the disease-containment measures used to protect them. External marketing refers to strategies used to educate the general public, including those who may become potential patients of the practice, about infection control and the measures dentistry takes to protect the public in the dental office.

Role of the Dental Assistant in Marketing Infection Control

Because the dental assistant is one of the initial and most frequent contacts with patients (Figure 16–1), both in the front office and in clinical aspects of the practice, he or she is in a prime position to relate to patients and

FIGURE 16–1
The dental assistant is often the first contact with patients.

prospective patients the measures the practice takes to meet or exceed government regulations and guidelines to protect their health.

Because the dental assistant, as a rule, spends more time with patients, he or she has the opportunity to explain infection control procedures employed by the practice and also to answer patients' questions about disease containment.

FRONT OFFICE MARKETING

Infection control marketing begins in the front office, which is the hub of communications between the practice and its patients. The receptionist or office manager has the first and pivotal contact with patients. Patients who call or physically enter the office meet this staff member first; thus, the opportunity exists to set up a dialog about office services, including sound infection control procedures, that benefit patients; these measures also help to allay anxiety and put patients at ease who may have concerns about cross-contamination of infectious disease in the dental office.

The Need to Explain Infection Control Procedures to Patients

While some dental team members are outgoing and gregarious, others may be more shy about interacting with patients, especially about potentially serious, sometimes intimidating topics, such as communicable or sexually transmitted diseases.

Regardless of personality style, the following marketing adjuncts are helpful to the dental assistant in explaining procedures and alleviating patients' fears.

It is advisable that the dental assistant remember to act professionally at all times because he or she is the "public information officer" of the office.

Infection Control Brochures

Infection control can be marketed using a variety of brochures that explain various infection control measures used throughout the practice. Whether prepared and printed by professional marketing companies, dental organizations, or the practice, the intent and end result are the same: to educate patients about infection control measures used in the practice, to allay patients' apprehensions about communicable diseases, and to open the dialog between patients and the practice and encourage patients to ask questions about procedures and preventive measures.

Signs, Plaques, and Posters

Signs, plaques, and posters act as "silent communicators" to patients and should be positioned so that patients can easily read them. Many offices choose quality materials, including finished hardwood or a high-tech acrylic look to complement the office decor.

Signs, plaques, and posters should communicate in a way that is positive and beneficial to the patient. For example, "Don't forget to pay your bill" is negative and may be considered offensive to patients. A more positive way to communicate the same message is, "Payment is appreciated at the time services are rendered."

With regard to infection control policies, the practice may wish to place signs, plaques, or posters about infection control that communicate a message that says, "To protect your health, this office meets or exceeds all government regulations regarding infection control." Another popular signage message is, "To protect you and your family, all dental handpieces are sterilized between patients in this practice."

Statement Stuffers

Statement stuffers, which are usually single sheets of paper printed with a message or promotional theme sent to patients as a form of marketing, are so called because they are inserted along with each monthly statement sent out from the practice. An infection control statement stuffer may contain brief checkpoint information on measures the practice employs to protect patients' health and the health of their families while in the office (Box 16–1).

Letters and Newsletters

Some practices send out letters to patients or publish newsletters that convey specific information about practice policies, procedures, and announcements.

A letter to patients, written by the doctor, may address a specific new product, procedure, or technique used in the practice. For example, a letter about infection control may inform patients that the doctor and staff have been inoculated against hepatitis B, that a new sterilizer or technique has been added, or that the doctor and staff just completed a course in infectious disease containment.

A question-and-answer column in the practice newsletter may include a message from the dentist addressing patients' concerns about emerging diseases such as hepatitis C; the sterilization of handpieces; or why he or she and the staff all wear masks, gloves, and protective eyewear when treating patients.

Web Sites

The World Wide Web has recently become an accepted means of electronic communication. A **web site** is a specific form of electronic information available to computer users who log in and go on-line to a specific topical area and is a new form of electronic marketing. The dentist may post his or her web site on the Internet, sometimes called a web page. Interested

---

BOX 16-1

Sample Inspection Control Statement Stuffer

The following information may be contained in an infection control statement stuffer. Information is presented succinctly and in bulleted or check-marked bits of information.

To Protect You and Your Family

In our practice, we take the following measures, recommended by the Centers for Disease Control and Prevention (CDC) and required by the government (OSHA) to ensure a safe and healthy practice. This helps protect you and your family and provides a clean, safe environment for all our patients. To support your continued health, we do the following:

✓ Employ the latest proven sterilization and disinfection techniques on all instruments, handpieces, and other items used in your mouth

✓ Wear disposable gloves, masks, and eyewear when treating each patient

✓ Wash our hands with an EPA-approved bacteriostatic soap before and after treating all patients

✓ Carefully clean, sanitize, and disinfect treatment room chairs, countertops, and other "touch" surfaces to prevent cross-contamination

✓ Use disposable products whenever possible to reduce or eliminate the risk of cross-infection

✓ Carefully handle all disposable materials as recommended by federal government guidelines and state and local regulatory agencies

If you have questions regarding any of our infection control techniques, please feel free to ask us at your next dental visit.

---

patients or potential patients may surf the Internet looking for sources of information on specific topics or for a dentist.

A web site is an individually designed and controlled electronic information device, upon which the dentist can post information about the practice or services offered. The web site provides the dentist the opportunity to make the latest infection control information available to any interested party. Many web sites are programmed to capture information about the inquiring party to provide additional information upon request.

Office Tours of Instrument Recirculation Area

Some practices make it a matter of policy to give all new patients a tour of the office, introducing them to all team members. The benefits to the patient include increased familiarity, a sense of being treated as a partner in the healthcare decision-making process, increased understanding of the routine procedures of the office, and opportunities to ask questions about sterilization procedures.

Office managers and dental assistants who conduct introductory tours find that patients enjoy meeting staff members and learning more about the infection control methods used for their dental care. Touring the inner workings of areas they seldom see gives patients a sense of feeling welcomed as a friend and better informed.

Patients concerned about highly publicized instances of alleged disease transmission via dental equipment can see firsthand and ask questions about the practice's compliance with government-mandated guidelines for infection control management.

EDUCATING PATIENTS ABOUT INFECTIOUS DISEASES

Often the role of patient education falls to the dental assistant. This occurs because patients may often be reluctant to asks the dentist questions they fear may seem too silly. Also, because the dental assistant spends more chairside time with patients, patients may feel more comfortable asking the assistant specific questions while waiting for anesthesia or while the dentist is out of the treatment room with another patient.

When patients ask questions about infectious diseases, this presents an opportunity for the dental assistant to provide education in a nonthreatening, one-on-one manner.

Ten Facts Used to Educate Patients about HIV/AIDS

Patients are often curious about the HIV virus, which causes AIDS. They may feel especially reluctant to ask questions about possible dental office transmission of disease.

The following paragraphs contain 10 facts about HIV/AIDS that the dental assistant can use to educate patients.

AIDS Is a Worldwide Problem. Although death rates from AIDS have declined in the United States, many people infected with AIDS live longer and healthier lives as a result of new treatment options. The CDC estimates that 650,000 to 900,000 Americans live with HIV and at least 40,000 new infections occur annually.

HIV Causes AIDS. AIDS is the most serious outcome of HIV infection; a positive HIV test result does not mean a patient has AIDS. Today, there are medical treatments that can slow down the rate at which HIV affects the immune system.

It is estimated that approximately one-half of all patients with HIV develop full-blown AIDS within 10 years of becoming infected.

HIV Is Transmitted through Intimate Contact with Infectious Body Fluids. HIV transmission may occur when blood, semen, vaginal fluid, or breast milk from an infected person enters the body of an uninfected person. HIV can enter the body not only through a vein or other opening but also through other mucous membranes, including the eyes, nose, or mouth.

The three most common ways HIV is transmitted are by (1) having sexual intercourse with an HIV-infected person; (2) sharing needles or injection equipment with an injection drug user who is infected with HIV; (3) an HIV-infected woman passing the virus to her baby during pregnancy, delivery, or breast-feeding.

HIV Is Not Transmitted through Casual Contact. HIV is not casually transmitted. Even if the other person has the virus, healthy, intact skin provides a good barrier. There are no documented cases of HIV being transmitted from ordinary social contact as dry kisses, hugs, or handshakes. A person cannot become infected from a toilet seat, a drinking fountain, a doorknob, eating or drinking utensils, food, or pets. HIV is not an airborne, waterborne, or foodborne virus and does not survive long outside the body.

There Are Many Myths about HIV Transmission. *Kissing:* Although open-mouth kissing is considered a very low-risk activity, if prolonged, it could damage the mouth or lips and allow the virus to pass from an infected person to a partner, entering through cuts or sores in the oral cavity.

Insect bites: Blood-sucking insects do not transmit HIV because the virus does not reproduce or survive in insects. In addition, insects do not inject their own or a previously bitten individual's blood into the next person bitten. It is the saliva of specific species of mosquitoes that transmits diseases such as yellow fever and malaria.

HIV Testing Is Recommended Six Months after the Last Possible Exposure to HIV. The average time between infection and the development of detectable antibodies is 25 days, but it may take up to 6 months, or even 1 year in rare cases. The standard screening test is the enzyme immunoassay (EIA), which requires the drawing of blood and waiting for laboratory results. A negative result means the individual is not infected with HIV. However, a positive result requires further testing—additional EIAs and supplemental antibody tests—to prove an accurate HIV diagnosis. There is also a more rapid test that produces results in 5 to 30 minutes. It is equally accurate but costs more.

Pregnant Women Should Be Tested. It is important for a woman who is pregnant to be tested not only for her own health but for the health of her baby. Medical therapy is available to lower the risk that an HIV-infected pregnant woman will pass HIV to her infant before, during, or after birth. ZDV (zidovudine, also known as AZT) is the only drug that has been clinically tested and shown to reduce this risk.

Patients in a Physician's or Dentist's Office Are at Very Low Risk of Becoming Infected with HIV. Although HIV transmission is possible in a healthcare setting, it is extremely rare.

The U.S. Blood Supply Is Considered Safe. The U.S. blood supply is about the safest in the world. Nearly all people infected with HIV through blood transfusions received those transfusions prior to 1986, the year HIV testing began for all donated blood. Even though an estimated 1 in 450,000 to 1 in 660,000 donations per year is positive for HIV but not detected by current antibody screening tests, additional screening and processing methods were implemented in 1995 to further reduce the risk of infection.

Information and Education Are Important and Accessible. The CDC has many resources available to learn more about HIV, how to prevent transmission, how to treat infection, where to get tested, and how to help reduce the spread of HIV through education.

THE IMPORTANCE OF AN AIDS TREATMENT POLICY

HIV/AIDS has significantly affected the healthcare profession. Legally, a practice may not refuse to treat patients who are infected. The Americans with Disability Act of 1990 requires that all businesses, including dental practices, make *reasonable accommodation* to treat patients with all forms of disabilities, and AIDS falls under this act. The key term is *reasonable.*

There are exceptions, however, if the patient requires special procedures not available in the practice, such as intravenous sedation or general anesthesia.

Practices should have some form of written policy statement regarding treatment of patients who present with any infectious disease (Box 16–2). (For additional information, see *Chapter 4: Legal and Ethical Considerations of Infection Control.*)

CHAIRSIDE MARKETING

Chairside marketing encompasses any and all education and information provided to patients at chairside by the dental assistant or other clinical members of the dental team. It is useful and effective when used by clinical personnel. Because chairside assistants typically spend more time with the patient, they have an opportunity to open a dialog with the patient about infection control measures used by the entire clinical staff to protect patients and themselves from communicable diseases.

BOX 16-2

Sample HIV/AIDS Status Written Policy

An example of a written policy might state the following:

We are dedicated to serving the health and wellness of all patients in our practice and to helping each patient attain the highest level of oral healthcare possible.

In compliance with the Americans with Disabilities Act of 1990, our practice makes every effort to accommodate all patients, regardless of HIV/AIDS status.

Therefore, we request that all questions regarding infectious disease, including HIV/AIDS status, be completed on your medical health history form accurately and honestly. All health status information regarding our patients is kept strictly confidential.

If you or a family member has questions about HIV/AIDS disease, please request to speak privately with the dentist.

Sincerely,

Dr. John Williams and staff

Rationale for Protecting Patients

The dental assistant as educator and infection control marketer can explain and describe the techniques used to protect patients, including universal precautions.

A common reaction from patients who see PPE for the first time is one of alarm, often followed by, "But I don't have any infectious diseases."

When made aware that all patients are treated using the same high standards of barrier protection, patients are all assured the same level of protection.

Rationale for Personal Protective Equipment

The chairside assistant may explain to patients that PPE provides a barrier form of protection that keeps potential splash and splatter as well as inhalants, chemicals, and flying objects from harming the doctor and staff.

Rationale for Opening Sterile Instrument Packs in Front of the Patient

After admitting, seating, and draping the patient, the dental assistant washes his or her hands and dons PPE. Only then does the dental assistant retrieve the sterile instrument tray, cassette, or pack and place it on the tray in front of the patient. The dental assistant can use this as an opportunity to explain the sterilization system used in the office and to provide assurance that all instruments used in the patient's mouth undergo the same scrupulous cleaning, sanitizing, disinfecting, and sterilization techniques.

SKILLS MASTERY ASSESSMENT: POSTTEST

Directions: Select the response that best answers each of the following questions. Only one response is correct.

1. The emphasis on infection control, the focus on prevention of cross-contamination of communicable diseases, and increasing government involvement have brought about a/an _____ need for marketing of infection control in the dental office.
   a. increased
   b. decreased
   c. undetermined
   d. overestimated

2. Marketing infection control means _____
   a. increasing the number of sterilizers in the office.
   b. creating an awareness of infection control techniques used in the office.
   c. employing universal precautions.
   d. "selling" more services.

3. The _____ most often has the first and pivotal contact with patients.
   a. dentist
   b. dental hygienist
   c. receptionist or office manager
   d. chairside dental assistant

4. Marketing infection control helps put patients at ease and allays their fears about cross-contamination of infectious diseases.
   a. True
   b. False

5. Patient education brochures on infection control
   a. are available only from private hospitals.
   b. are most often a single sheet of paper stuffed inside a monthly statement.
   c. replace the need for the staff to discuss with patients infection control measures employed by the practice.
   d. open the dialog between patients and the practice and encourage patients to ask questions about preventive measures employed.

6. Signs, plaques, and posters should communicate in a way that is _____ to the patient.
   a. positive and beneficial
   b. forthright and ADA approved
   c. negative and demanding
   d. highly technical

7. A web site is an individually designed and controlled electronic information device, upon which the dentist can post information about the practice or services offered. Any interested party can access the information.
   a. True   b. False

8. A positive HIV test result means a patient has AIDS.
   a. True   b. False

9. Approximately one-half of all patients with HIV develop full-blown AIDS within 10 years of becoming infected.
   a. True   b. False

10. The risk of an HIV-infected pregnant woman transmitting the disease to her baby during pregnancy, delivery, or breast-feeding is
   a. undocumented and has never occurred.
   b. fairly low and not very common.
   c. moderately high and fairly common.
   d. very high and one of the three most common ways the disease is spread.

Bibliography

ADA Council on Scientific Affairs and ADA Council on Dental Practice. (1996, May). Infection control recommendations for the dental office and the dental laboratory. *The Dental Assistant: Journal of the American Dental Association, 127,* 672–680.

ADA Council on Scientific Affairs. (1999, July). Dental mercury hygiene recommendations. *Journal of the American Dental Association, 130.*

American Dental Association. (1992, February). *OSHA's Bloodborne Pathogens Standard: Questions and answers.* Chicago: Author.

American Dental Hygienists' Association. (n.d.). Ten things you need to know about HIV/AIDS [Fact sheet]. Chicago: Author.

Anderson, P., & Burkart, M. (2001). *The dental assistant* (7th ed.). Albany, NY: Delmar.

Andrews, N. (1996, July/August). Management of biofilm and water quality in dental devices. *Practical Hygiene.*

Arizona State Board of Dental Examiners. (1997, January). *Infectious disease control in the dental office.* Phoenix, AZ: Author.

Bednarsh, H. (1996, November/December [Part 1]; 1997, January/February [Part 2]). Check your dental unit water IQ. *The Dental Assistant: Journal of the American Dental Assistants Association.*

Bednarsh, H., & Ekland, K. (1997, March/April). Universal precautions reconsidered. *The Dental Assistant: Journal of the American Dental Assistants Association.*

Bednarsh, H., & Ekland, K. (2000, March). OSHA issues new compliance directive. *ACCESS.*

Biron, C. R. (2000, August). Have you checked your oxygen tanks lately? *RDH Magazine.*

Brayer, C. (1999, October). Viewing conditions affect x-ray quality. *RDH Magazine.*

Cal/OSHA requires safety needle covers. (2000, July). *The Explorer.* (Available from the National Association of Dental Assistants, 900 S. Washington Street, Suite G-13, Falls Church, VA 22049)

Caution: Handle sharps with "kid gloves." (1999, October). *The Explorer.* (Available from the National Association of Dental Assistants, 900 S. Washington Street, Suite G-13, Falls Church, VA 22049)

Centers for Disease Control and Prevention: Recommended infection control practices for dentistry. (1997, November/December). *The Dental Assistant: Journal of the American Dental Assistants Association.*

Christensen, G. (1995, April). Highspeed handpieces, sterilizability, documentation. *Clinical Research Associates Newsletter, 19*(4).

Christensen, G. (1997, March). Dental unit waterline contamination. *Clinical Research Associates Newsletter, 21*(3).

Combs, R. (1997, Summer). Dentistry battles waterline microorganisms. *Dental Economics: Dental Equipment and Supplies Supplement.*

Cottone, J. A., Terezhalmy, G. T., & Molinari, James A., et al. (1996). *Practical infection control in dentistry* (2nd ed., p. 80). Philadelphia: Williams & Wilkins.

Cuny, E., Fredekind, R., & Budenz, A. (1999, July). Safety needles: New requirements of the OSHA bloodborne pathogens rule. *CDA Journal, 27*(7).

Dental Assisting National Board. (1996). *DANB infection control task analysis* (ICE requirements, pp. 16–18). Chicago: Author.

The dental infection control program: OSAP offers an office "tune-up." (1998). *OSAP Monthly Focus, 2.* (Available from the Organization for Safety and Asepsis Procedures, P.O. Box 5297, Annapolis, MD 21401)

Dietz, E. (1989). *Infection Control: Stay on the safe side.* Phoenix, AZ: Semantodonics.

Dietz, E. (1996, October). Spray-wipe-spray: Simple as 1-2-3! *The Explorer.* (Available from the National Association of Dental Assistants, 900 S. Washington Street, Suite G-13, Falls Church, VA 22049)

Dietz, E. (1997, February). Caution: Handle mercury with care! *The Explorer.* (Available from the National Association of Dental Assistants, 900 S. Washington Street, Suite G-13, Falls Church, VA 22049)

Dietz, E. (1997, May). Does your practice screen patients for latex allergy? *The Explorer.* (Available from the National Association of Dental Assistants, 900 S. Washington Street, Suite G-13, Falls Church, VA 22049)

Dietz, E. (1997, June). New source offers alternative to those with latex allergies. *The Explorer.* (Available from the National Association of Dental Assistants, 900 S. Washington Street, Suite G-13, Falls Church, VA 22049)

Dietz, E. (1997, September). Day-to-day operations: Latex allergies in healthcare. What's under your skin? *M.D. News Magazine.*

Dietz, E. (1997). *Career enrichment: Expand the skills you have to create the job you want.* Falls Church, VA: National Association of Dental Assistants.

Dietz, E. (1997). *Managing latex allergies in the healthcare setting.* GSC Home Study Course. Published by GSC: 2335 American River Drive, Suite 406, Sacramento, CA.

Dietz, E. (1998, January). Glutaraldehyde linked to respiratory and other effects. *The Explorer.* (Available from the National Association of Dental Assistants, 900 S. Washington Street, Suite G-13, Falls Church, VA 22049)

Dietz, E. (1998, March). *Personal protective equipment for the dental assistant.* One-credit accredited Continuing Dental Education Home Study Program sponsored by the National Association of Dental Assistants, 900 S. Washington Street, Suite G-13, Falls Church, VA 22049.

Dietz, E. (1998, May). Cleaning up a mercury spill: Would you know what to do? *The Explorer.* (Available from the National Association of Dental Assistants, 900 S. Washington Street, Suite G-13, Falls Church, VA 22049)

Dietz, E. (1998). *Controlling waterline biofilms in dental units.* GSC Home Study Course. Published by GSC: 2335 American River Drive, Suite 406, Sacramento, CA.

Dietz, E. (1998). *The role of the dental assistant in patient screening and assessment.* One-credit continuing education course sponsored by the National Association of Dental Assistants, 900 S. Washington Street, Suite G-13, Falls Church, VA 22094.

Dietz, E. (1998, October). *What the dental assistant needs to know about viral hepatitis* [One-hour accredited Continuing Dental Education Home Study Program]. Falls Church, VA: National Association of Dental Assistants.

Dietz, E. (1999, January). Dental noise levels hazardous to your hearing. *The Explorer.* (Available from the National Association of Dental Assistants, 900 S. Washington Street, Suite G-13, Falls Church, VA 22049)

Dietz, E. (2000, March). Is fungus lurking in the pumice? *The Explorer.* (Available from the National Association of Dental Assistants, 900 S. Washington Street, Suite G-13, Falls Church, VA 22049)

Dietz, E. (2000). *Infection control techniques for today's dental assistant.* Falls Church, VA: National Association of Dental Assistants.

Dietz, E. (2000, April). Bioaerosols management in the dental office. *The Explorer.* (Available from the National Association of Dental Assistants, 900 S. Washington Street, Suite G-13, Falls Church, VA 22049).

Dietz, E. (2000, June). Your doctor could be subject to vicarious liability. *The Explorer.* (Available from the National Association of Dental Assistants, 900 S. Washington Street, Suite G-13, Falls Church, VA 22049)

Dietz, E. (2000). *Dental office management.* Albany, NY: Delmar.

Dietz, E. (2000). *Infection control in dental radiology.* GSC Home Study Course. Published by GSC: 2335 American River Drive, Suite 406, Sacramento, CA 95825.

Dietz, E. (n.d.). Proper handling and disposal of "sharps" products and biohazard materials in the dental office. *The Dental Assistant: Journal of the American Dental Assistants Association.*

Dofka, C. (1996). *Competency skills for the dental assistant*. Albany, NY: Delmar.

Eleazer, P. (1997, May). A chemical treatment regimen to reduce bacterial contamination in dental waterlines. *Journal of the American Dental Association, 128*.

Estride, B. H., Reynolds, A. P., & Walters, N. J. (2000). *Basic medical laboratory techniques* (4th ed.). Albany, NY: Delmar.

Farran, H. (1996, April). ADA concludes three-year study of water quality. *The Farran Report*.

FDA requires labeling of exam gloves. (1998, June). *The Explorer*. (Available from the National Association of Dental Assistants, 900 S. Washington Street, Suite G-13, Falls Church, VA 22049)

Finkbeiner, B. L., & Johnson, C. S. (1995). *Mosby's comprehensive dental assisting: A clinical approach*. St. Louis, MO: Mosby.

Gamolka, K. (1996, September). Improving dental unit water quality. Infection control report. *Dental Products Report*.

Gamolka, K. (1997, January). Emerging and existing disease challenges: HIV, tuberculosis and hepatitis. *Dental Products Report*.

Gooch, B. (1996, January/February). Risk and prevention of occupational exposures to blood in dentistry. *The Dental Assistant: Journal of the American Dental Assistants Association*.

Hand asepsis. (1998). *OSAP Monthly Focus, 3*. (Available from the Organization for Safety and Asepsis Procedures, P.O. Box 5297, Annapolis, MD 21401)

Handpiece operation and maintenance guidelines by Athena Technology Inc. (1997, May). *Dental Products Report*.

Helms, V. S. (n.d.). *Radiology asepsis protocol* [Handout]. Albuquerque, NM: Data Auxiliary Academy.

Jajosky, R. A., & Jennison, E. (n.d.). *Glutaraldehyde: Guidelines for safe use and handling in health care facilities*. A New Jersey SENSOR fact sheet.

Kauffman, M., & Cushyner, K. (1997, March/April). Recommendations for routine immunizations of oral health care providers. *The Dental Assistant: Journal of the American Dental Assistants Association*.

Labeling on examination gloves. (1998, February). *ACCESS, 12*(2).

Latex-associated allergies and conditions. *OSAP Monthly Focus, 4*. (Available from the Organization for Safety and Asepsis Procedures, P.O. Box 6297, Annapolis, MD 21401)

Lindh, W. Q., Pooler, M. S., Tamparo, C. D., & Cerrato, J. U. (1998). *Delmar's clinical medical assisting*. Albany, NY: Delmar.

Marx, J. F. (1998, July). Understanding the varieties of viral hepatitis. *Nursing*.

Massachusetts Department of Public Health, Occupational Surveillance Program. (1998, March/April). Respiratory effects of glutaraldehyde exposure. *The Dental Assistant: Journal of the American Dental Assistants Association, 67*(2).

Merchant, V. (1996). Infection control in the dental laboratory environment. In J. Cottone, G. Terezhalmy, & J. Molinari (Eds.), *Practical infection control in dentistry* (2nd ed.). Baltimore: Williams & Wilkins.

Miller, C. H. (1997, June). Safety coordinator's duties go beyond casual organization of safety plans. *RDH Magazine*.

Miller, C. H. (1998, February). Review of Bloodborne Pathogens Standard clarifies OSHA's expectations of dental offices. *RDH Magazine*.

Miller, C. H. (1999, October). Answers about what the year 2000 will bring. *RDH Magazine*.

Miller, C. H. (2000, April). Chemical indicators help assure instruments are safe to use. *RDH Magazine*.

Miller, C. H., & Palenik, C. (1998). *Infection control and management of hazardous materials for the dental team* (2nd ed.). St. Louis, MO: Mosby.

Mills, S. (1996, May/June). Dental waterlines and biofilms: Implications for clinical practice. *Dental Teamwork Magazine*.

Molinari, J. (1996, July/August). Dermatitis in dental professionals: Causes, treatment and prevention. *Journal of Practical Hygiene*.

Molinari, J. (1996, August 23). *Practical infection control for the 1990s*. Arizona State Dental Hygienists Association Annual Scientific Session, Phoenix, AZ.

Molinari, J. (1997, January). *Emerging issues in infection control and dental unit waterline contamination*. Meeting of the Albuquerque District Dental Society, Albuquerque, NM.

Molinari, J. (2000, April 6). Emerging infection control challenges: Science vs. perception. Phoenix, AZ: Arizona Dental Association.

Murdock-Kinch, C. (1997, September). Comparison of dental water quality management procedures. *Journal of the American Dental Association, 128*.

Occupational exposure to bloodborne pathogens: Final rule. (1991, December 6). *Federal Register, 29* CFR 1910.1030.

Organization for Safety and Asepsis Procedures. (1995, June). *Infection control in dentistry guidelines.* Annapolis, MD: Author.

Organization for Safety and Asepsis Procedures. (1997, September). *Infection control in dentistry guidelines.* Annapolis, MD: Author

Organization for Safety and Asepsis Procedures. (1997, Third quarter). *OSAP Report, 10*(2). (Available from the Organization for Safety and Asepsis Procedures, P.O. Box 6297, Annapolis, MD 21401; e-mail: osap@clark.net)

Organization for Safety and Asepsis Procedures (1999). *OSAP dental infection control and office safety resource guide* (Vol. II). Annapolis, MD: Author.

OSAP Research Foundation. (1996). *Dental unit waterline update: Know what the regulations are for treatment devices.* Annapolis, MD: Author.

OSAP Research Foundation. (1997). *Dental unit waterlines* [Position paper]. Annapolis, MD: Author.

OSHA Instruction CPL2-2, 44C, Enforcement for the Occupational Exposure to Bloodborne Pathogens Standard. (1992, March 6). *Federal Register, 29* CFR 1910.1030.

OSHA general requirements. (1995, June 28). OSHA CD-ROM.

OSHA training requirements for dental and other healthcare workers. (1997, March). *OSAP Monthly Focus.* (Available from the Organization for Safety and Asepsis Procedures, P.O. Box 5297, Annapolis, MD 21401)

Ostrem, C. (1996, March/April). Carpal tunnel syndrome: A look at causes, symptoms, remedies. *Dental Teamwork Magazine.*

Otis, L., & Cottone, J. A. (n.d.). *The use and abuse of gloves in dentistry.*

Owner's guide: Self-contained water system. (1996). Newberg, OR: A-dec.

Personal protective equipment for protection against exposure to bloodborne organisms. (1997). *OSAP Monthly Focus, 8.* (Available from the Organization for Safety and Asepsis Procedures, P.O. Box 5297, Annapolis, MD 21401)

Phinney, D. J., & Halstead, J. H. (2000). *Delmar's dental assisting: A comprehensive approach.* Albany, NY: Delmar.

Pollack-Simon, R. (1998, February 27). *Staying current and in compliance with OSHA and infection control.* Seminar sponsored by the Arizona State Dental Association, Phoenix, Arizona.

Pre-procedural mouthrinses. (1999). *OSAP Monthly Focus, 8.* (Available from the Organization for Safety and Asepsis Procedures, P. O. Box 5297, Annapolis, MD 21401.

Recommended vaccines for dental healthcare workers. (1998, September). *The Explorer.* (Available from the National Association of Dental Assistants, 900 S. Washington Street, Suite G-13, Falls Church, VA 22049)

Respiratory effects of glutaraldehyde exposure. (1997, September/October). *ACCESS, 11*(8).

Shearer, B. (1996, February). Biofilm and the dental office. *Journal of the American Dental Association, 127.*

Simmers, L. (2001). *Diversified health occupations* (5th ed.). Albany, NY: Delmar.

Stone, G. E., & Durley, C. (2000). *Preparing for the Certified Dental Assistant Examination: The official study guide and practice examination of the Dental Assisting National Board, Inc.* Chicago: Dental Assisting National Board.

Ten leading nationally notifiable infectious diseases. (1996, October 18). *Morbidity and Mortality Weekly Report, 45*(41), 883.

Terezhalmy, G. (1996). *Immunizations for oral healthcare providers. Practical infection control in dentistry* (p. 129). Philadelphia: Williams & Wilkins.

Torres, H., & Ehrlich, A. (1999). *Modern dental assisting* (6th ed.). Philadelphia: W. B. Saunders.

U.S. Department of Health and Human Services and Centers for Disease Control and Prevention. (1996, July/August). Backflow prevention and the dental unit. *The Dental Assistant: Journal of the American Dental Assistants Association.*

U.S. Department of Health and Human Services and Centers for Disease Control and Prevention. (1999, February). *ACCESS.*

U.S. Department of Labor. (1992). *Controlling occupational exposure to bloodborne pathogens in dentistry* (OSHA Document 3129). Washington, DC: Author.

Vaccinations update. (1997). *OSAP Monthly Focus, 12.* (Available from the Organization for Safety and Asepsis Procedures, P.O. Box 5297, Annapolis, MD 21401)

Williams, H. (1997, February). *Lab Management Today,* 737–739.

Wolfe, F. D. (1998). Latex gloves: Protection or punishment? *RDH Magazine.*

Resources

The following organizations cited in this chapter may be contacted for further information:

American Dental Association (ADA): 800-621-8099

Association of Dental Assistants of America (ADAA): 800-733-2322

Dental Assisting National Board, Inc. (DANB): 800-367-3262

National Association of Dental Assistants (NADA): 800-237-8616

Organization for Safety and Asepsis Procedures (OSAP): 800-298-6727

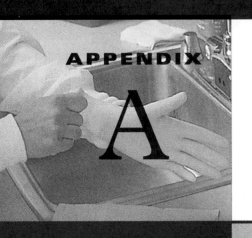

DANB Infection Control Task Analysis (ICE) Requirements Cross-Referenced by Chapter

Dental assistant certification may be earned in one of several areas. Upon successful completion of the requirements set forth by the Dental Assisting National Board, Inc. (DANB), the dental assistant, office manager, or chairside assistant may use the credential Certified Dental Assistant (CDA) following his or her name and may wear the DANB pin.

DANB has established respective designations of certification, which include Certified Dental Assistant, Certified Orthodontic Assistant, Certified Oral and Maxillofacial Surgery Assistant, and Certified Dental Practice Management Administrator. Certification may be earned through a variety of eligibility pathways established by DANB for each. Regardless of the pathway selected or the type of certification sought, each pathway requires proof of current cardiopulmonary resuscitation (CPR) certification from either the American Heart Association or the American Red Cross.

To assist faculty and students, DANB periodically publishes and updates a *Task Analysis* booklet (available for a minimal fee) to facilitate dental assisting programs in developing and designing curricula and learning experiences to prepare students to sit for one or all of the national certification examinations for dental assistants. Instructors and students should be aware that the items in the *Task Analysis* are periodically reviewed, revised, and updated as deemed necessary by the Dental Assisting National Board; test bank questions are reviewed and updated annually by members of the Test Construction Committee.

The Infection Control Exam (ICE) may be taken by individuals without prerequisites, and DANB does not set eligibility requirements for it, although the *Task Analysis* provides competency prerequisites. Students should be aware that some states may require various eligibility standards because successful completion of these tests may complete that state's requirements for certification. The ICE and Dental Radiation Health and Safety Exam (RHS) comprise two-thirds of the general (chairside) CDA examination.

The following grids are designed as a cross-reference between book chapters and DANB ICE criteria.

SAFETY STANDARDS AND INFECTION CONTROL FOR DENTAL ASSISTANTS TO DANB ICE CRITERIA

Book Chapter Number and Title	ICE Criteria Section Number
1 Introduction to Microbiology	II.A, III.A, III.B
2 Disease Prevention in the Dental Office	II.B, II.C, III.A, III.B, III.C, III.D, III.E
3 Patient Assessment	I.A, I.B
4 Legal and Ethical Considerations of Infection Control	I.C, II.A, II.B, II.C
5 Regulatory Government Agencies and National Associations	IV.A, IV.B
6 The Dental Office Safety Supervisor	I.C, II.A, II.B
7 Personal Safety and Barrier Protection	II.C, III.A, III.B, IV.B
8 Instrument Recirculation	III.C, III.D, III.E
9 Environmental Surface and Equipment Asepsis	III.A, III.E
10 Dental Laboratory Asepsis	III.A, III.B, III.C, III.E
11 Infection Control in Dental Radiography	I.C, III.A, III.B, III.C, III.D, III.E
12 Hazard Communication	I.C, III.A, III.B, IV.A, IV.B
13 Waterline Biofilms	I.C, II.A, II.B, III.A, III.B, III.C, III.D, III.E, IV.A, IV.B
14 Occupational Environmental Hazards	IV.B
15 Office Emergency Procedures	IV.A, IV.B
16 Marketing Infection Control	II.A, II.B

DANB Infection Control Task Analysis (ICE), 1999, Chicago.

Note

Neither the author nor Delmar Thomson Learning holds responsibility for content or changes in the DANB *Task Analysis*. Test applicants and program instructors are encouraged to periodically contact DANB to request updates. All attempts were made as of the publication date of this text to include interpretation of the latest requirements. To obtain a copy of the current *Task Analysis*, contact DANB at 800-FOR-DANB.

DANB ICE CRITERIA TO SAFETY STANDARDS AND INFECTION CONTROL FOR DENTAL ASSISTANTS

ICE Criteria Section Number	Book Chapter Number and Title
I.A	3 Patient Assessment
I.B	3 Patient Assessment
I.C	4 Legal and Ethical Considerations of Infection Control
	6 The Dental Office Safety Supervisor
	11 Infection Control in Dental Radiography
	12 Hazard Communication
	13 Waterline Biofilms
II.A	1 Introduction to Microbiology
	4 Legal and Ethical Considerations of Infection Control
	6 The Dental Office Safety Supervisor
	13 Waterline Biofilms
	16 Marketing Infection Control
II.B	2 Disease Prevention in the Dental Office
	4 Legal and Ethical Considerations of Infection Control
	6 The Dental Office Safety Supervisor
	13 Waterline Biofilms
	16 Marketing Infection Control
II.C	2 Disease Prevention in the Dental Office
	4 Legal and Ethical Considerations of Infection Control
	7 Personal Safety and Barrier Protection

(continues)

Note

Neither the author nor Delmar Thomson Learning holds responsibility for content or changes in the DANB *Task Analysis*. Test applicants and program instructors are encouraged to periodically contact DANB to request updates. All attempts were made as of the publication date of this text to include interpretation of the latest requirements. To obtain a copy of the current *Task Analysis*, contact DANB at 800-FOR-DANB.

DANB ICE CRITERIA *(continued)*

III.A	
	1 Introduction to Microbiology
	2 Disease Prevention in the Dental Office
	7 Personal Safety and Barrier Protection
	9 Environmental Surface and Equipment Asepsis
	10 Dental Laboratory Asepsis
	11 Infection Control in Dental Radiography
	12 Hazard Communication
	13 Waterline Biofilms
III.B	
	1 Introduction to Microbiology
	2 Disease Prevention in the Dental Office
	7 Personal Safety and Barrier Protection
	10 Dental Laboratory Asepsis
	11 Infection Control in Dental Radiography
	12 Hazard Communication
	13 Waterline Biofilms
III.C	
	2 Disease Prevention in the Dental Office
	8 Instrument Recirculation
	10 Dental Laboratory Asepsis
	11 Infection Control in Dental Radiography
	13 Waterline Biofilms
III.D	
	2 Disease Prevention in the Dental Office
	8 Instrument Recirculation

(continues)

Note

Neither the author nor Delmar Thomson Learning holds responsibility for content or changes in the DANB *Task Analysis.* Test applicants and program instructors are encouraged to periodically contact DANB to request updates. All attempts were made as of the publication date of this text to include interpretation of the latest requirements. To obtain a copy of the current *Task Analysis,* contact DANB at 800-FOR-DANB.

DANB ICE CRITERIA *(continued)*

	11 Infection Control in Dental Radiography
	13 Waterline Biofilms
III.E	2 Disease Prevention in the Dental Office
	8 Instrument Recirculation
	9 Environmental Surface and Equipment Asepsis
	10 Dental Laboratory Asepsis
	11 Infection Control in Dental Radiography
	13 Waterline Biofilms
IV.A	5 Regulatory Government Agencies and National Associations
	12 Hazard Communication
	13 Waterline Biofilms
	15 Office Emergency Procedures
IV.B	5 Regulatory Government Agencies and National Associations
	7 Personal Safety and Barrier Protection
	12 Hazard Communication
	13 Waterline Biofilms
	14 Occupational Environmental Hazards
	15 Office Emergency Procedures

DANB Infection Control Task Analysis (ICE), 1999, Chicago.

Note

Neither the author nor Delmar Thomson Learning holds responsibility for content or changes in the DANB *Task Analysis*. Test applicants and program instructors are encouraged to periodically contact DANB to request updates. All attempts were made as of the publication date of this text to include interpretation of the latest requirements. To obtain a copy of the current *Task Analysis*, contact DANB at 800-FOR-DANB.

References

Certified Press. (2000, Spring). Number 35, Volume 1. Chicago: IL.

Dental Assisting National Board. (n.d.). *Certified dental assistant examination fact sheets.* Chicago: Author.

Dental Assisting National Board. (1996). *DANB infection control task analysis.* Chicago: Author.

Dietz, E. (2000). *Dental office management.* Albany, NY: Delmar.

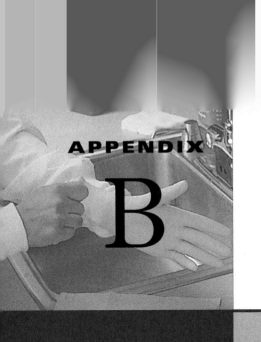

Summary of OSHA's Bloodborne/ Hazardous Materials Standard

Scope and Application

- The Standard applies to all occupational exposure to blood and other potentially infectious materials (OPIM) and includes part-time employees, designated first aiders, and mental health workers, as well as exposed medical personnel.
- OPIM includes saliva in dental procedures, cerebrospinal fluid, unfixed tissue, semen, vaginal secretions, and body fluids visibly contaminated with blood.

Methods of Compliance

- General—Standard precautions.
- Engineering and work practice controls.
- Personal protective equipment.
- Housekeeping.

Standard Precautions

- *All* human blood and OPIM are considered to be infectious.
- The *same* precautions must be taken with all blood and OPIM.

Engineering Controls

- Whenever feasible, engineering controls must be the primary method used to control exposure.
- Examples include needleless IVs, self-sheathing needles, sharps disposal containers, covered centrifuge buckets, aerosol-free tubes, and leakproof containers.

- Engineering controls must be evaluated and documented on a regular basis.

Sharps Containers

- Readily accessible and as close as practical to work area.
- Puncture resistant.
- Labeled or color coded.
- Leakproof.
- Closable.
- *Routinely replaced* so there is no overflow.

Work Practice Controls

- Handwashing following glove removal.
- No recapping, breaking, or bending of needles.
- No eating, drinking, smoking, and so on, in work area.
- No storage of food or drink where blood or OPIM are stored.
- Minimize splashing, splattering of blood, and OPIM.
- No mouth pipetting.
- Specimens must be transported in leakproof, labeled containers. They must be placed in a secondary container if outside contamination of primary container occurs.
- Equipment must be decontaminated prior to servicing or shipping. Areas that cannot be decontaminated must be labeled.

Personal Protective Equipment (PPE)

- Includes eye protection, gloves, protective clothing, and resuscitation equipment.
- Must be readily accessible and employers must require their use.
- Must be stored at work site.

Eye Protection

- Is required whenever there is potential for splashing, spraying, or splattering to the eyes or mucous membranes.
- If necessary, use eye protection in conjunction with a mask or use a chin-length face shield.
- Prescription glasses may be fitted with solid side shields.
- Decontamination procedures must be developed.

Gloves

- Must be worn whenever hand contact with blood, OPIM, mucous membranes, nonintact skin, or contaminated surfaces/items or when performing vascular access procedures (phlebotomy).

- Type required—Vinyl or latex for general use.
  - —Alternatives must be available if employee has allergic reactions (e.g., powderless).
  - —Utility gloves for surface disinfection.
  - —Puncture resistant when handling sharps (e.g., Central Supply).

Protective Clothing

- Must be worn whenever splashing or splattering to skin or clothing may occur.
- Type required depends on exposure. Prevention of contamination of skin and clothes is the key.
- Examples—Low-level-exposure lab coats.
  - —Moderate-level-exposure, fluid-resistant gown.
  - —High-level-exposure, fluid-proof apron, head and foot covering.
- *Note:* If PPE is considered protective clothing, then the *employer must* launder it.

Housekeeping

- There must be a written schedule for cleaning and disinfection.
- Contaminated equipment and surfaces must be cleaned as soon as feasible for obvious contamination or at end of work shift if no contamination has occurred.
- Protective coverings may be used over equipment.

Regulated Waste Containers (Nonsharp)

- Closable.
- Leakproof.
- Labeled or color coded.
- Placed in secondary container if outside of container is contaminated.

Laundry

- Handled as little as possible.
- Bagged at location of use.
- Labeled or color coded.
- Transported in bags that prevent soak-through or leakage.

Laundry Facility

- Two options:
  1. Standard precautions for all laundry (alternative color coding allowed if recognized).

2. Precautions only for contaminated laundry (must be red bags or biohazard labels).
- Laundry personnel must use PPE and have a sharps container accessible.

Hepatitis B Vaccination

- Made available within 10 days to all employees with occupational exposure.
- At no cost to employees.
- May be required for student to be admitted to college health program as well as for externship.
- Given in accordance with United States Public Health Service guidelines.
- Employee must first be evaluated by healthcare professional.
- Healthcare professional gives a written opinion.
- If the vaccine is refused, the employee signs a declination form.
- Vaccine must be available at a future date if initially refused.

Postexposure Follow-Up

- Document exposure incident.
- Identify source individual (if possible).
- Attempt to test source if consent obtained.
- Provide results to exposed employee.

Labels

- Biohazard symbol and word *Biohazard* must be visible.
- Fluorescent orange/orange-red with contrasting letters may also be used.
- Red bags/containers may be substituted for labels.
- Labels required on—Regulated waste.
    —Refrigerators/freezers with blood or OPIM.
    —Transport/storage containers.
    —Contaminated equipment.

Information and Training

- Required for all employees with occupational exposure.
- Training required initially, annually, and if there are new procedures.
- Training material must be appropriate for literacy and education level of employee.
- Training must be interactive and allow for questions and answers.

Training Components

- Explanation of bloodborne standard.
- Epidemiology and symptoms of bloodborne disease.

- Modes of HIV/HBV transmission.
- Explanation of exposure-control plan.
- Explanation of engineering, work practice controls.
- How to select the proper PPE.
- How to decontaminate equipment, surfaces, and so on.
- Information about hepatitis B vaccine.
- Postexposure follow-up procedures.
- Label/color-code system.

Medical Records

Records must be kept for each employee with occupational exposure and include:

- A copy of employee's vaccination status and date.
- A copy of postexposure follow-up evaluation procedures.
- Healthcare professional's written opinions.
- Confidentiality must be maintained.
- Records must be maintained for 30 years plus the duration of employment.

Training Records

Records are kept for 3 years from date of training and include:

- Date of training.
- Summary of contents of training program.
- Name and qualifications of trainer.
- Names and job titles of all persons attending.

Exposure-Control Plan Components

- A written plan for each workplace with occupational exposure.
- Written policies/procedures for complying with the standard.
- A cohesive document or a guiding document referencing existing policies/procedures.

Exposure-Control Plan

- A list of job classifications where occupational exposure control occurs (e.g., medical assistant, clinical laboratory scientist, dental hygienist).
- A list of tasks where exposure occurs (e.g., medical assistant who performs venipuncture).
- Methods/policies/procedures for compliance.
- Procedures for sharps disposal.
- Disinfection policies/procedures.
- Procedures for selection of PPE.
- Regulated waste disposal procedures.
- Laundry procedures.

- Hepatitis B vaccination procedures.
- Postexposure follow-up procedures.
- Training procedures.
- Plan must be accessible to employees and be updated annually.

Employee Responsibilities

- Go through training and cooperate.
- Obey policies.
- Use universal precaution techniques.
- Use PPE.
- Use safe work practices.
- Use engineering controls.
- Report unsafe work conditions to employer.
- Maintain clean work areas.

Cooperation between employer and employees regarding the Bloodborne Pathogens Standard will facilitate understanding of the law, thereby benefiting all persons who are exposed to HIV, HBV, and OPIM by minimizing the risk of exposure to the pathogens.

Meeting the OSHA standard is not optional, and failure to comply can result in a fine that may total $10,000 for each employee.

Glossary

A

abandonment—Failure to provide necessary dental treatment.

accidental exposure—Contact with blood or other potentially infectious materials (OPIM) that directly results from the performance of an employee's duties directly related to the nature of the employment. Specific exposures may occur to the eye, mouth, or other mucous membranes; nonintact skin; or parenterally.

acute stage—When a disease reaches its peak; the patient's symptoms are fully developed and can often be readily differentiated from other specific symptoms.

aeroallergens—Airborne substances that may cause allergic reactions in sensitive individuals.

American Dental Assistants Association (ADAA)—A national organization for dental assistants; its purpose is to promote the profession of dental assisting.

American Dental Association (ADA)—A national organization of licensed dentists; the ADA prints a variety of publications to educate patients, establish protocols, and inform dentists about pertinent issues in dental practice.

Americans with Disabilities Act—Requires facilities to be accessible to handicapped (physically or mentally compromised) patients, including those with infectious diseases.

aseptic technique—Employs all forms of washing, sanitizing, disinfecting, and sterilizing of items that come into contact with patients to reduce the likelihood of infection with a contaminant or disease.

autoclave—A sterilization instrument that uses time, temperature, and pressure to kill all forms of microbial life, including spores.

B

bioaerosols—Living microbes that travel via a mist.

biofilms—Microorganisms that accumulate on surfaces inside moist environments such as dental unit waterlines, allowing bacteria, fungi, and viruses to multiply; this can significantly increase a patient's susceptibility to transmissible diseases.

biohazard warning labels—Labels or tags affixed to hazardous waste items; they must be readable from a distance of 5 feet.

biological monitor—Commercially prepared device that provides confirmation that sterilization has taken place.

Bloodborne Pathogens Standard—An OSHA regulation that covers all dental employees who could *reasonably anticipate* coming into contact with blood, saliva, and other potentially infectious materials (OPIM) during the course of employment.

burden of proof—The patient seeking to impose liability against the dentist must supply the more convincing evidence that the dentist's action caused resulting harm or injury.

C

Centers for Disease Control and Prevention (CDC)—A federal agency that sets guidelines for healthcare practitioners; the CDC's guidelines are enforced by OSHA.

chairside marketing—Encompasses any and all education and information provided by the dental assistant (or other clinical members of the dental team) conducted at chairside with patients.

chemical treatment—Uses chlorine or sodium hypochlorite to treat drinking and recreational water; some organisms are resistant to these chemicals.

chemical vapor sterilization—Uses a combination of heat, water, chemicals, and pressure to kill all forms of microbial life on contaminated instruments.

convalescent stage—When recovery and recuperation from the effects of a specific infectious disease occur; the individual regains strength and stamina and returns to his or her overall original state of health.

critical items—Those instruments and related items used to perform invasive procedures and that come into direct contact with soft tissues or bone of the oral cavity.

cutaneous—Pertaining to the skin.

cycle time—The amount of time required during instrument sterilization to attain the combination of proper temperature, time, and/or pressure to kill all forms of microbial life.

D

declining stage—Occurs when the patient's symptoms begin to subside; the infectious disease remains, although the patient demonstrates improving health.

Dental Assisting National Board, Inc. (DANB)—The national organization responsible for issuing the required task analyses for all national certification tests for dental assistants, including certification in infection control.

dermatitis—Skin irritation.

disabled—Having any neurologic or physical disabilities that impair function. Neurological handicaps may be motor, sensory, emotional, or intellectual in nature. Advanced age and obesity do *not* qualify as impairments under the Americans with Disabilities Act.

disinfection—The inhibition or killing of pathogens; spores are not killed during disinfection procedures.

distillation—A purification (rather than sterilization) process that may remove volatile chemicals, endotoxins, and some microorganisms from water.

dry heat sterilization—A form of sterilization that uses time and heat to kill all forms of microbial life, including microbial spores.

E

emerging diseases—Diseases of recent virulence or newly discovered diseases that are growing rapidly such as hepatitis C.

employee category—A method of identifying employees at risk for exposure to bloodborne pathogens based upon the nature of employment-specific tasks.

endogenous infections—Infections or diseases that originate within the individual's body; they are not transmitted from another infected individual.

engineering controls—Specific equipment or devices that facilitate prevention of accidental exposure.

Environmental Protection Agency (EPA)—A federal agency that regulates and registers certain products used in dental practices, including surface disinfectants; requires products to undergo and pass specific testing requirements prior to approval for registration.

ergonomics—The study of motion economy.

ethics—A moral obligation that encompasses professional conduct and judgment imposed by the members of a particular profession.

ethylene oxide sterilization—A form of gas sterilization usually reserved for hospital use because of the long cycle time.

exogenous infections—Infections or diseases that originate from a means outside of the individual's body; exogenous conditions are caused by pathogenic organisms that invade the body, radiation, chemical agents, trauma (accident or injury), electric shock, or temperature extremes (frostbite or heat exhaustion).

exposure-control plan—Identifies tasks, procedures, and job classifications where occupational exposure takes place.

exposure incident—Occurs when an individual comes into contact with a potential hazard associated with his or her employment.

F

financial responsibility form—Form required at the first appointment to establish the financially responsible party.

flash priority sterilizer—Uses steam under pressure to quickly sterilize items used in the dental office.

Food and Drug Administration (FDA)—A federal agency that regulates marketing of medical devices, including equipment and disposable items; it also reviews product labels for false or misleading information and sufficient directions for use.

H

hazard communication program—A written program outlining the methods and procedures used in the office to reduce risks to staff associated with hazardous substances, diseases, chemicals, or OPIM.

Hazard Communication Standard—The Employee Right to Know Law, which addresses the right of every employee to know the possible dangers associated with hazardous chemicals and related hazards in the place of employment; this law also requires employers to provide methods for corrective action.

holding/presoaking solution—A solution in which the dental assistant submerges soiled or contaminated instruments until such time is allowed to properly process these instruments.

I

immunity—The body's ability to resist an infectious disease and its toxins.

impairment—Any physiological disorder or condition; cosmetic disfigurement; anatomical loss; or any mental or psychological disorder, such as mental retardation, emotional or mental illness, or specific learning disabilities.

incubation stage—The interval between the exposure to a pathogenic microorganism and the first appearance of signs and symptoms of the disease.

infectious agents—Pathogenic microorganisms or pathogens, which are broken down into five classifications: viruses, bacteria, fungi, protozoa, and rickettsia; for an infection to occur, an infectious agent must be present.

informed consent form—Form granting prior consent allowing the dentist to proceed with patient examination, diagnosis, and treatment.

instrument recirculation—The steps involved in taking contaminated instruments through pre-cleaning/soaking, manual or mechanical scrubbing, packaging, and sterilization.

J

jurisprudence—Philosophy of law or a set of legal regulations set forth by each state's legislature; describes the legal limitations and regulations related to the practice of dentistry and dental hygiene.

L

latex sensitivity—Having an allergic reaction or sensitivity to products containing natural rubber latex; reaction may be immediate or delayed.

M

malpractice—Professional negligence; failure to perform one's professional duties, either by omission or commission.

marketing—Creating the need or demand for, or awareness of, a product or service the consumer may have been unaware was available, or that he may have been unaware that he desired; dental practices may ethically promote their services through a variety of internal and external marketing strategies.

Material Safety Data Sheets (MSDSs)—Written information about the content and potential hazard of specific products used in the dental office; each product that has a potential hazard must have a corresponding MSDS on file in the office.

means of transmission—How diseases are spread; most common means include direct contact, airborne transmission, bloodborne transmission, ingestion, or indirect contact.

medical/dental history form—A form that includes the patient's medical/dental history, reason for initial visit, and other pertinent information required before treating the patient.

medical waste—Liquid or semiliquid body fluid, including any items in the dental office that release bioburden when compressed; items caked with dried body fluid that have the potential to release bioburden during handling; contaminated sharps; and pathological and microbial wastes containing body fluid.

microorganisms—Living things so small that they can be seen only under a microscope (not visible to the naked eye).

N

National Association of Dental Assistants (NADA)—A national organization dedicated to promoting the profession of dental assistants.

negligent—Performing something that a reasonable professional would not do, or not doing something a reasonable professional would.

noncritical items—Those items that do not come into direct contact with body fluids; these items do not necessarily require sterilization or high-level disinfection.

nosocomial infections—Infections acquired by a patient in a hospital or long-term care facility; common examples of nosocomial infections include *Staphylococcus* and *Pseudomonas*.

O

Occupational Safety and Health Administration (OSHA)—A government agency that enforces guidelines for protection of workers; OSHA has federal, regional, and state offices.

office safety supervisor—The staff member responsible for training other employees about infectious control and hazard communication; this responsibility often falls to the dental assistant or office manager with the greatest knowledge of infectious disease containment and government regulations regarding hazard communication.

opportunistic infections—Infections that occur when the body's ability to resist disease weakens.

Organization for Safety and Asepsis Procedures (OSAP)—A national organization of teachers, practitioners, dental healthcare workers, and manufacturers/distributors of dental equipment and products; it focuses on developing and communicating standards and information on aseptic technology to dental practices and educational institutions.

other potentially infectious materials (OPIM)—Those items considered contaminated that may have the potential to transmit disease.

P

paresthesia—Loss of sensation.

pathogens—Disease-causing microorganisms that require a living cell for reproduction.

personal protective equipment (PPE)—Protective attire required by OSHA to be worn to protect the employee from the potentially hazardous contact with bloodborne pathogens associated with employment, including splash and splatter; PPE generally includes gloves, mask, eyewear, and protective attire.

portal of entry—The fifth component in the chain of infection; it allows the infectious agent to enter and potentially infect another person or a susceptible host.

portal of exit—The third component in the chain of infection; occurs when an infectious agent leaves the *reservoir* to infect another person through normally occurring body fluids such as excretions, secretions, skin cells, respiratory droplets, blood, and saliva.

process indicators—Heat-sensitive tapes or inks most often used on autoclave bags.

prodromal stage—Vague or undifferentiated set of symptoms similar to infections of any number of other diseases; the onset of a disease.

R

reservoir—The location of an infectious agent.

reverse osmosis—A purification (rather than sterilization) process that produces potable drinking water.

risk management—Strategies taken by the dentist and staff to prevent or reduce the likelihood of a patient bringing legal action.

S

semicritical items—Those items not intended to penetrate oral soft or hard tissues but that may come into contact with oral tissues. When possible, these instruments should be sterilized. If they cannot be sterilized, however, they should be *high-level disinfected using an EPA-registered product*.

sharps—Refers to all sharp, invasive objects and instruments used to directly inject or cut into soft or hard tissue of the oral cavity.

spores—Bacteria with an outer covering that protects them from many chemical disinfectants and higher levels of heat sterilization.

standard of care—Treatment guidelines that a dentist with the same knowledge, skill, and care in the same community would adhere to; there are no absolutes in standard of care.

State Dental Practice Act—A legally enforceable set of written rules and regulations set forth and enforced by the State Board of Dental Examiners.

statement stuffers—Single sheets printed with a message or promotional theme sent to patients as a form of marketing; they are so called because they are inserted along with each monthly statement sent out from the practice.

steam under pressure (autoclaving)—A process of instrument sterilization that uses time, temperature, and pressure to kill all forms of microbial life, including spores.

sterilization—The destruction of all forms of microbial life, including mycotic spores.

susceptible host—An individual who may become infected as a result of some form of disease transmission.

U–W

ultrasonic cleaner—A mechanical scrubbing device that works by *implosion* to remove debris and bioburden from hand and rotary instruments and related devices prior to sterilization.

universal precautions—An OSHA standard requiring dental staff to treat all patients as potentially infected with a communicable disease; wearing gloves, mask, eyewear, and protective outer clothing comprises the PPE required to meet universal precautions when treating patients.

unprofessional conduct—Any act or deed that fails to uphold the State Dental Practice Act.

UV radiation—A water treatment process that may not kill some organisms in drinking water, such as *Giardia* and *Cryptosporidium*.

web site—A specific form of electronic information available to computer users who log in and go online to a specific topical area; a dentist may post his or her web site on the Internet.

work practice controls—Changing the way procedures are currently performed to ensure a higher degree of safety or protection from accidental exposure.

Index